ECOLOGY WITHOUT CULTURE

Ecology without Culture

. . . .

Aesthetics for a Toxic World

Christine L. Marran

University of Minnesota Press

Minneapolis

London

The publication of this book was supported by the Imagine Fund for the arts, design, and humanities, an annual award from the University of Minnesota Provost's office.

Poetry in chapter 1 is reprinted, with permission, from Ursula K. Le Guin, "The Marrow," in *Hard Words, and Other Poems* (New York: Harper & Row, 1981; permission by Curtis Brown, Ltd.); copyright 1981 by Ursula K. Le Guin. Poetry in chapter 1 is reprinted, with permission, from Ruth Ozeki, "Thoughts in Language" (shared under a Creative Commons Attribution–NonCommercial–NoDerivatives 4.0 international license, http://www.ruthozeki.com /thoughts-in-language); and Ryoko Sekiguchi, *Heliotropes*, trans. Sarah O'Brien (Montreal: La Presse, 2008), 42. Poetry in chapter 2 is reprinted, with permission, from Kido Tamiko, "Fairyland," in *Reverberations from Fukushima: 50 Japanese Poets Speak Out*, ed. Leah Stenson and Asao Sarukawa Aroldi (Portland, Ore.: Inkwater Press, 2014), Kindle loc. 1860. Poetry in chapter 3 is reprinted, with permission, from Kusano Hisao, "Chūō wa koko," in *Mura no onna wa nemurenai: Kusano Hisao tokushū* (Tokyo: Nashinokisha, 2004; originally published 1972), 156–57; and Satō Shigeko, "Shinkirō," in *Genpatsu nanmin no shi* (Tokyo: Asahi Shinbun Publishing, 2012), 56–57. Poetry in chapter 4 is reprinted, with permission, from Kusano Hisao, "Watakushisama no sharekōbe," in *Mura no onna wa nemurenai: Kusano Hisao tokushū* (Tokyo: Nashinokisha, 2004; originally published 1972), 24–32; and Ishimure Michiko, "Mura no onna wa nemurenai," in *Hana no okudo e* (Tokyo: Fujiwara Shoten, 2014), 34–35.

Every effort was made to obtain permission to reproduce material in this book. If any proper acknowledgment has not been included here, we encourage copyright holders to notify the publisher.

Published by the University of Minnesota Press
111 Third Avenue South, Suite 290
Minneapolis, MN 55401-2520
http://www.upress.umn.edu

The University of Minnesota is an equal-opportunity educator and employer.

Library of Congress Cataloging-in-Publication Data
Names: Marran, Christine L., author.
Title: Ecology without culture : aesthetics for a toxic world / Christine L. Marran.
Description: Minneapolis : University of Minnesota Press, 2017. | Includes bibliographical references and index.
Identifiers: LCCN 2017001739 (print) | ISBN 978-1-5179-0158-5 (hb) | ISBN 978-1-5179-0159-2 (pb)
Subjects: LCSH: Ecocriticism. | Ecology in literature. | Ecology in motion pictures. | BISAC: LITERARY CRITICISM / Asian / General.
Classification: LCC PN98.E36 M37 2017 (print) | DDC 809/.9336—dc23
LC record available at https://lccn.loc.gov/2017001739

Contents

Introduction: Ecology without Culture   1

   1. Obligate Storytelling   27

   2. Slow Violence in Film   55

   3. *Res Nullius*: The Domestic Turn in Environmental Literature   91

   4. Literature without Us   117

Acknowledgments   143

Notes   147

Index   175

Ecology without Culture

We cling to images that do not correspond to changing reality.

—Cornelia Hesse-Honegger

I N WU MING-YI'S NOVEL *Man with the Compound Eyes,* mythical island boy Atile'i is banished by his village only to find himself stranded
on a strange floating island of colorful material that doesn't rot. He sur-
vives by drinking rainwater caught in plastic bags that are familiar to him
from his childhood island home and by eating the flesh of dead turtles
bloated with plastic polymers and microbeads. He builds a multiroomed
hut of the plentiful material on this floating mass and marvels at his handi-
work. He is pleased to have built such a sturdy house with these materials
that never rot and never rip "no matter how hard you yanked on it."[1] He
felt proud of the structure and "truly rich." But the island also felt haunted.
It "sometimes looked like a giant floating cage—a shadowy incantation, a
rootless place, the cemetery of all creation. Aside from a few species of sea-
bird that made nests and laid eggs on the island from time to time, nothing
else could survive there. Creatures that died from eating bits of the island
eventually became part of the island. Atile'i thought he too might end up
becoming part of the island. So this is what hell was like, he thought. So
this is the land of death."[2]

This floating island is nothing other than our own great Pacific garbage
patch of plastic particulates suspended in the upper layers of thick water
columns and double the size of the U.S. state to which all big things get
compared—Texas. Moved by the North Pacific Subtropical Gyre, the
patch travels the horse latitudes and contains within it vast swaths of small
and minute plastics that get ingested by albatrosses and other aquatic
birds, fish, and any humans who might eventually eat those fish. In the
novel, the mass of garbage bears its own history in the bold scripts of the
favorite objects of consumer culture wrapped in endless monofilament
lines, like some watery version of the Lascaux caves to be discovered by
future generations. The expansive ecological imaginary in *Man with the*

Compound Eyes is both myth and the recognizable history of our late industrial age. The floating island is humanity's grab at a more convenient life in the form of cheap plastics. Through the airy plastic bags they left, the "white man" had haunted the tropical jungles and hidden footpaths of Atile'i's island of birth, but once Atile'i rides the sea, he becomes one of those "other men who live upon the earth." He marvels at the manifold uses of plastic while simultaneously experiencing a sense of doom on this plastic island that will haunt the seas far into the future, leaving traces of a civilization about which future humans will care little.

Another island is featured in *Man with the Compound Eyes*, a bigger one that has been home to Indigenous populations, a colonial power, and a nation. At one of its beaches lives a scholar of Indigenous peoples, Alice Shih, who is on the brink of taking her own life. In one depressed reverie, she recalls her island's history as a parade of peoples. The island "had belonged to the aborigines. Then it belonged to the Japanese, the Han people, and the tourists. Who did it belong to now? Maybe to those city folks who bought homesteads, elected that slimeball of a mayor, and got the new highway approved."[3] Alice feels contempt for the "city folks," but the locals do not garner any special praise from her either: "Folks in the local cultural scene liked to gush about how Haven was the true 'pure land,' among other cheap clichés of native identity, while Alice often felt that except for some houses belonging to the aboriginal people or buildings from the Japanese era, now maintained as tourist attractions, the artificial environment had been intended to spite the natural landscape."[4] She remembers the town of Haven in better days when "the bush and the vegetation came quite close on either side as if neither the terrain nor the wild animals feared the sight of man. Now the new highway had pushed nature far away."[5] The locals to whom Alice refers are ethnically and linguistically different groups in Taiwan, like the Bunun and Pangcah (Ami), but the novel never identifies any specific, local group that will protect the land. Rather, Taiwan is depicted as a commercialized postnational space where a range of populations, ethnic and foreign, have vested interests in developing the island, though some Pangcah practices remain.

The novel's remarkable combination of myth and realism produces a climatological critique that takes no refuge in familiar human collectivities. Rather, Wu's Taiwan is a snapshot of a planet in crisis. The denizens of this postnational island of competing interests are all equally susceptible to ecological calamities. New affinities among strangers and different species arise as the novel's characters battle the elements when sea levels rise and forests catch fire. The steady gaze of Alice's adopted cat, Ohiyo, with its one brown eye and one blue, keeps her clinging to this world, compelling her to choose life, if only just barely. In this ecological imaginary, the vulnerable are a diverse population of humans and creatures enduring what writer and activist Ishimure Michiko called industrial modernity's "cannibalistic civilization" (*hitogui bunmei*), which destroys itself through its cycles of excessive production and consumption. In *Man with the Compound Eyes,* this cannibalistic civilization is witnessed by the titular hero—a formless god who watches the North Pacific Gyre spin and the eternal flood encroach upon various islands' shores through his anthropod eyes.

Wu's ecological imaginary is a touchstone for concerns addressed in the present book. In *Ecology without Culture,* I discuss texts that develop expansive ecological imaginaries that resist or explicitly dismiss exceptionalist claims made at the level of ethnicity, culture, and species in their critiques of industrial modernity. My title is a riff on Timothy Morton's study of romanticism and nature, *Ecology without Nature,* in which he argues that transcendental ideas of nature produced especially in the European romantic tradition impede ecological thinking. His solution to the problem of romanticism for environmentalist ideas is to jettison the concept of "nature": "Strange as it may sound, the idea of nature is getting in the way of properly ecological forms of culture, philosophy, politics, and art."[6] When Morton questions the epistemological stability of nature that has driven its separation from culture in modernity beginning with the romantics, he worries that the environment itself can suffer from "a reified order of nature." This reified order, unable to grapple with the ecological and cultural diversity that composes landscapes, instead fixes a landscape in order to ground an ideological or epistemological foundation. Nature is used to provide moral authority and for asserting intellectual certainty. It is also used, I would argue, to create unassailable identities. Morton's solution is to eradicate the "chief stumbling block to environmental thinking," which, for him, is the image of nature itself, described variously as fetish, stereotype, and transcendental principle: "Just when it brings us into proximity with the nonhuman 'other,' nature reestablishes a comfortable distance between 'us' and 'them.' With ecological friends like this, who needs enemies?"[7]

Morton's notion of a "properly ecological form of culture" seems a contradiction in terms. If the biological world is analyzed with a view toward culture, even a "properly ecological" one, then ecocriticism privileges the cultivation of the human world as its subject. Perhaps the chief stumbling block to ecological thinking is not the image of nature, but the image of culture. Cultural humanism, historically, has drawn on the material world for a constellation of metaphors to serve human interest and to generate processes for human groups to master themselves through self-consciousness and historical action. When human culture is the primary frame of analysis, as it has been for Enlightenment modernity, it becomes difficult to address the biological, geophysical, and atmospheric aspects of our world, which fit far less neatly into cultural humanistic analysis. Given what we continue to learn at the molecular, macrobiotic, and geophysical levels, we are increasingly confronted with agencies that are planetary, animal, and cellular. As molecular biologist Judah Rosner points out about bacteria and human cells, "there's as much of them as there is of us."[8]

The present book examines ways in which cultural claims impede ecological thinking. One example immediately comes to mind, and that is when ecocriticism's intent is to locate distinct concepts of nature in order to posit unique cultural identities. Ecocritic Timothy Clark writes that this familiar approach "usually treat[s] fiction and non-fiction in the same way, as the arena of competing cultural representations and identity claims."[9] In this case, ecocriticism functions as cultural history. The environment depicted within a text is read for the various kinds of cultural identities it presumably projects,[10] reducing environmental debate to "a function of competing identity and justice claims" of human groups, an approach that instrumentalizes the natural world toward "ideological theater."[11] Political scientist Claire Jean Kim's exceptional book *Dangerous Crossings: Race, Species, and Nature in a Multicultural Age* addresses the complex ways in which cultural claims can disregard animals or lands in crisis. Kim describes these cultural claims as "a way of seeing that foregrounds a particular form of injustice while backgrounding others," or a "single-optic vision."[12] The single-optic vision can express racial and ethnic prejudices and reveal long histories of colonialism and oppression, but these legitimate concerns share a script with dominant groups who racialize them in countercharges of ecological harm: competing single-optic visions invested in cultural claims can obscure the vulnerabilities of animal populations or lands. Kim proposes instead a "multi-optic vision" and a structure of avowal for solving injustices born of cultural claims. The point is "not to marginally broaden the category of beneficiaries of this destructiveness but rather, through a critical and transformational politics, to radically restructure our relationships with each other, animals, and the earth outside of domination" while avowing multiple concerns for ecological justice.[13] A multi-optic vision can produce an ecopolitics that addresses histories of oppression but does not frame them in purely humanistic terms.

Cultural claims can impede ecocritical thinking when we consider that the material world exceeds culture. Stacy Alaimo, a scholar of new materialist approaches to the environment, has shown in her *Bodily Natures: Science, Environment, and the Material Self* that bodies are inextricably interconnected in our physical world, particularly through the toxins of industrial modernity. Using the term "transcorporeality" to describe environments and bodies as inseparable entities, Alaimo stresses how the notion of an impervious human subject is impossible under industrial modernity. Furthermore, this transcorporeality is not limited to humans.[14] Nonhuman animal bodies similarly absorb the full array of toxins in their specific environments.

Inspired by new materialist perspectives, *Ecology without Culture* addresses the expansive ecological imaginaries that operate outside the protective enclosures of cultural identity and cultural humanism that maintain the rift between humanity and everything else.[15] The stories and films discussed in this book represent the experiences of those adversely impacted by industrial modernity's excesses. I discuss written and visual texts that address environmental health and depict affiliations among species and land. Often those affiliations are those created through the excesses of industrialism and the release of toxins by industry. These toxins impact more than the human world. Consequently, the texts demand an approach that accounts for things smaller and greater than a selective humanist "we," which is always multiple and contradictory by virtue of so many things anyway: accessibility to resources, economic disparities, gender inequalities, and so on. So, as illustrated in the last two chapters of this book, even if discourses of ecological totalities at the scale of planet purport to describe how we are all in this together, we know that we are not. We learn daily about exciting technologies that might help us and other species out of the plastic mesh we have made for ourselves, but on bad days, we hear about the most recent species on the verge of extinction, and they are only the tip of the proverbial iceberg when it comes to environmental precarity. So, it does not make sense to rehearse arguments that assert essentialist claims for humans, not only because they erase the disenfranchised in the name of asserting an undifferentiated human collectivity but also because they do not enable an expansive ecological imaginary that represents transcorporeal and trophic ties that bind. *Ecology without Culture* illustrates how ecocriticism can engage culture without making the perpetuation of *ethnos* or *anthropos* the endgame. Rather, ecocriticism will relieve the material world of having to always represent *ethnos* and cultural humanistic interests. The four chapters to come will introduce ecological imaginaries and ways of thinking ecocritically outside the protective enclosure of cultural and human exceptionalism. The present chapter addresses the problem of culture for ecocriticism.

Biotropes

In order to show how life-forms exceed what they mean for human life and politics, I first introduce the concept of the biotrope. This concept allows me to foreground the point that representations of the biological world inherently indicate both the material and the semiotic. As Serenella Iovino and Serpil Oppermann demonstrate in their collection *Material Ecocriticism,* matter is always storied,[16] and storytelling needs matter. Cultures have long defined themselves through biological elements to prove their strength and longevity, to make themselves appear as inevitable as the earth itself. This approach to the biological world in narrative fixes it, as if in amber, for the purposes of making cultural claims.[17] The agency of matter is denied in the double gesture of foregrounding the biotic world while erasing its historicity.[18] Attention to the material substratum of a biotrope allows us to animate what Donna Haraway calls "the absolute simultaneity of materiality and semiosis" and wrest the material world from always representing humanist collectivities.[19] The material substratum of the biotrope is what makes it always incommensurable with the represented object. Biotropes may be semiotically powerful in narrative because of the quality of that biological origin, even as that original scape is enfolded tightly into humanistic metaphor. America's amber waves of grain is a biotrope that the author of the hymn "America the Beautiful," Katherine Bates, wrote as she overlooked Colorado's lower hills and golden valleys from the height of Pike's Peak in 1893. Penned more than a century ago, the images of waving grain and purple mountains continue to find their way onto jumbotrons at sports stadiums or political events to represent the beauty and natural abundance of the United States. Bates's colorful bio-tropes reiterated over time have perpetuated a mythical image of America as a complacent collectivity and the paragon of a nation-state.[20]

In a more recent example, Murakami Haruki, in a speech in Catalunya in July 2011, parlayed the biotrope of the cherry blossom to claim Japan as an ethnic national collectivity that would inevitably recover from the cata-strophic experience of tsunami flooding and nuclear meltdown. Citing the common practice of viewing blossoming cherry trees in the springtime, Murakami said that, "even if humans struggle against the natural flow of things, in the end, that effort will be in vain. . . . but even in the midst of such resignation, the Japanese are able to actively discover true beauty."[21] Whether or not he had chosen to ignore the fact that the entire history of Japan has not been "going with the natural flow," but rather a dogged engineering of the archipelago for the purposes of agriculture, trade, and protection against natural calamities, Murakami's hope for recovery in the expansive disaster zone rested on a centuries-old concept of mutability as expressed in classical Japanese aesthetics.

Murakami continued in his speech to describe the concept of mutabil-ity as a transhistorical Japanese concept, as if no other world literature had wrestled with inconstancy: "*Mujō* means that there is no steady state that will continue forever in life. . . . Although *mujō* finds its roots in Buddhism, the concept of *mujō* has taken on a significance beyond its original reli-gious sense. This concept of *mujō* has been seared deeply into the Japanese spirit, forming an ethnic mindset that has continued on almost without change since ancient times."[22] It is true that, from the classical period to the present, the cherry blossom has symbolized the pathos of fleeting time and swift decay. One early poem of 905 engages the cherry blossom to re-mark that it is better to die early than linger on in this world: "It's their fall-ing without regret / I admire—/ Cherry blossoms: / a world of sadness / if they'd stayed."[23] But Murakami wrongly turned to ethnic nationalist biotropes to express the tragic outcome of the tsunami on March 11 and nuclear meltdown. In so doing, he created images of recovery that were incommensurable with the varied experiences of people and animals in the wake of nuclear contamination. Environmental issues inevitably push hard against inherited language and concepts:[24] classical poetics simply does not have within its vocabulary or mode of address any language to describe how more than 160,000 environmental refugees would survive the loss of homes, farms, and schools to radiation fallout. Murakami's

Japan is ethnically homogenous, a nation that shares an "ethnic mentality" and finds spiritual peace in the four seasons in the face of environmental calamity.[25] He further suggested that most Japanese are culpable for the release of nuclear radiation because they had ignored those "unrealistic dreamers" who had fought against nuclear power in the 1970s, a remark that Fukushima photographer Fujiwara Shin'ya called the quick and easy claim of a spectator.[26]

In an interview for the *Mainichi Newspaper* three years later, Murakami attempted to soft-pedal his Catalunya speech, but it remains that he parlayed a sentimental trope that imagined all victims of radiation fallout to be ethnic Japanese and all Japanese to have experienced the trauma of the March events by virtue of a shared cultural understanding of pathos expressed in the fragile blossom of a pale flower and joint culpability.[27] In parlaying this long-lasting, culturally sanctioned biotrope, he made the natural world a sanctuary for human and cultural drama. At the same time, the referent's geographical, genetic, and biological diversity exceeds any cultural intertextuality that Murakami's iteration relies upon. The specific experiences of environmental refugees who have since suffered the long-term consequences of nuclear contamination to their bodies and land were erased in a biotrope that performs the work of ethnic nationalism and creates the radiation crisis as a problem of the nation rather than of those specific survivors, including farmers, rural elderly, orphaned children, and ranging cattle.

In observing when *bios* is deployed to promote *ethnos*, we are not purely in the realm of the semiotic. First, we have already shown that cultural production needs the biological world. It is with this in mind that Elizabeth Grosz, in her study of time, focuses on the biodiversity of nature and argues that this biodiversity forms the deep foundation of cultural diversity: "nature prefigures and induces cultural variation and difference."[28] According to Grosz, cultural forms vary because the natural world varies: "biology impels culture to vary itself, to undergo more or less perpetual transformation."[29] Biodiversity is the condition of cultural diversity, and nature, in her reading, is "the repressed or unacknowledged condition of all cultural forms."[30] Grosz seeks to "overturn the repression of materiality in its most complex forms that has dominated the humanities and social sciences in their exclusive focus on cultural construction at the expense of natural production, and in the rigid divide that separates how we conceptualize the natural from how we conceptualize the cultural."[31] She is worried that we divide nature from culture in modernity by repressing the material world in the construction of culture and in cultural studies: "If nature is not the other, the opposite, of culture but its condition, then the relations between them are much more complicated than a binary division implies," and so we cannot understand nature as inert, but rather as "the matter of the cultural."[32] Grosz's concept of repressed materiality seems a call to be more attentive to the material world.

Still, Grosz's language of repression is potentially misleading. Her criticism of the binary of nature and culture produced in Enlightenment modernity still minimizes the way that the material world's diversity has been so explicitly deployed in producing powerful cultural ideas. The concept of biodiversity is foundational for author and occasional alpinist Shiga Shigetaka in his landmark text *On the Japanese Landscape,* which is a powerful example of how biodiversity is put toward articulating imperial interests.[33] This rich and inventive work describing the geothermal power of the Japanese archipelago provided resounding evidence for the country's manifest destiny in its nascent colonial expansionism. Shiga offers the nation's climatological diversity up and down the archipelago, its geothermally produced steam, its biodiversity of trees and plants, the sharpness and steepness of the terrain, and its volcanic activity all as proof of the uniqueness and strength of Japanese culture and the reason for Japan's power as an imperial force.[34] In order to make his point, he provides illustrations to accompany descriptions of natural features, including scientific terminology, and relies on transhistorical literary and aesthetic codes to tie the history of a people to the landscape. He quotes classical poetry to illustrate how poets were writing about the same natural world that he identified as an alpinist and scholar centuries later. This historical bridge of shared biotropes that joined classical poets with a contemporary alpinist such as Shiga himself created a sense of transhistorical continuity for his portrait of an aspiring empire that constantly cited its longevity as proof of its inevitability.

In one section, a citation of classical literary texts leads him to claim that the imperial nation's arboreal biodiversity far exceeded that of other imperial nations, particularly Britain. Comparing Fujiwara no Norikane's poetry with that of Wordsworth, Shiga considers the former to have a far more profound understanding of autumn foliage. Citing tree names in Sei Shōnagon's classical text *The Pillow Book,* Shiga insists that the Thames is sadly devoid of maple trees, suggestively comparing this with the fact that, according to Shōnagon, there are eighteen varieties of maple in Japan.[35] This insistence that the Thames lacks arboreal biodiversity in comparison with Japan's ancient capital enlists the material world to make an imperialist gesture. Grafting classical texts onto a diverse arboreal landscape produces a sense of a shared landscape that is both Japanese and diverse, a botanical twist on Benedict Anderson's well-known argument about the relationship of print media to nationalism in his classic *Imagined Communities: Reflections on the Origin and Spread of Nationalism*, which suggests that print media inspired a sense of shared space at the level of nation. In Japan, movable type newspapers in a new vernacular helped to develop a national imaginary by enabling a sense of shared time and space through the daily papers addressed to a common reader.[36] Nobuko Toyosawa describes the national imaginary in *On the Japanese Landscape* as an "aesthetic nationalism,"[37] but the detailed depiction of the landscape's biodiversity may be better interpreted as an "aesthetic imperialism." Shiga's biotropes produce an image of the empire as a diverse community with a powerful geothermal center. Just as the cataloging of landscape in Japanese classical poetry allowed for the codification of the landscape toward national interest, this popular book's biotropes enabled a geopolitical imagination for imperial subjects.

An ecocritical interpretation of this imperialist discourse reveals just how fundamental the natural world is to producing cultural and political collectivities. These modern identities do not rest on a rigid divide between human civilization and nature that denies or represses our reality. Rather, cultural humanism has founded itself assuredly and explicitly on what is a vibrant material world. There is no urge toward an epistemological distance between culture and nature in these biotropes. For Shiga, it was imperative that imperial nationalist identity and manifest destiny rest soundly upon a geophysical substratum. In Morton's terms, Shiga was engaged in a project of "ecologocentrism" for which the imaginary of nature is based on a consistent logic that excludes mutation and change, a realm of "a restricted economy in which elements of the ecosystem are fed back perfectly into it without excess."[38] In the archipelago, the extreme diversity in climate and in flora and fauna among the islands, which lie along latitudinal lines with the range of California, meant that inhabitants did not share the same landscape or weather. Far from it. Yet, Shiga created for the nascent empire a geophysical space possessing a vast inventory of shared characteristics, including a powerful geothermal aspect. Other writers would do the same with different geographies, but the point is that such ecologocentric perspectives produce biotropes whose discursive power is born of a mimetic capaciousness that comes from treating *bios* as without history and interest. Certainly, biotropes like classical Japanese literature's cherry blossom or Shiga's alps or Bates's amber waves of grain reproduce nature through a cultural logic born of nature as artlessly "there." A certain iteration of natural objects can represent the imperial "soul" of an empire, and in this way, biotropes can be potent allies in producing cultural and imperial identity because they are seemingly so benign, so neutral, so *natural*.

Global canons are veritably overflowing with depictions of the biotic world that conjure up a biological world for human culture and consumption, depictions that employ *bios* to produce *ethnos*. For example, literature of the American West founded a mythopoetic tradition of capacious landscapes of shadowy mountains and expansive rushing rivers, and these static and theatrical biotropes disappear other human and animal populations and "inhibit humans from grasping their place in an already historical nature."[39] This is to say that, when nature is recruited to serve in cultural nationalist discourse, it produces what Morton calls "nature-nations"—a constitutive exclusivity for a culture asserted through a presumed universality of the natural world. When the inscription of the biological world secures a people's link to an environment, that community becomes an inevitable, consistent entity. The natural world is made to be a catachrestic substitution for *ethnos,* and transhistorical intertextuality cannot but increase the cultural power of biotropes.

Ecocritic and classical literature scholar Haruo Shirane has called this transhistorical iteration or intertextual form of literary production "secondary nature." He emphasizes the semiotic aspect of poetry by focusing on how the landscape has been represented as perceived through human vision.[40] His definition of "nature" takes the human eye as the vantage point: nature is always already the object of human vision. While Shirane is careful to note the semiotic aspect of nature and to point out how natural elements are made to perform human value, treating the material world as "secondary nature" caught in the linguistic turn or the human gaze relieves it of doing anything but performing the interests of *ethnos* and *anthropos*.

So far, I have introduced the concept of the biotropes to navigate the broader question of how the material world has proven to be such an effective medium for representing human culture. They comprise the representational and the material, the latter of which has its own historicity. They are rhetorically powerful because they are not produced out of thin air. They have, at some point in time, been rooted in the biological and mineral worlds, and it is this materiality that gives biotropes their endurance.[41] In the case of Shiga's tropes of biodiversity, the connection between the natural space and imperial identity was strengthened all the more through the production of the citizen witness within the text. Originally, the climbing of mountains in Japan had mostly been limited to religious figures, but Shiga treated the land as newly perceivable by all citizens of the nation. Classical literature theorist Richard Okada called this new vantage point a "secularization of space." According to Okada, "Shiga Shigetaka's *On the Japanese Landscape* marked a decisive change in the representation of space from earlier formulations that had depended on received literary and aesthetic codes, or attributions of religious values, to one that regarded physical space as readily accessible to everyman."[42] The weekend alpinist inhabited previously sacred spaces that only ascetics had climbed, and this panorama-viewing subject was encouraged to go out into secularized nature and "describe what he sees from a particular, often elevated, anonymous standpoint."[43] But this led to the production of landscape in the name of an autonomous self and his empire. Just as Bates invented her biotrope of waving grain from the height of Pike's Peak, Shiga "discovered" the environment as an "anonymous" witness. The material conditions of print technology then allowed for the dissemination of this personal landscape, thereby solidifying a collective imperial imagination.

Ethnic Environmentalism

One might presume that taking seriously the "difference that nature makes" is already the task of ecocriticism. However, this is often not the case when *ethnos* is at stake, which I will endeavor to illustrate through an analysis of what I call ethnic environmentalism. Ethnic environmentalism is attentive to the material world, it has an environmentalist drive, and its ideas are rooted in science. But it works through a presumed collectivity that can be only an illusion for most industrialized capitalist nations. For example, not that long ago, Tsurumi Kazuko developed the theory of "endogenous development" to argue that the revitalization of Japan's natural resources could be realized through "native" fishing and agricultural practices. Her theory of endogenous technology suggests that, had the

Japanese stuck to native religions and technologies, many of the horrors of twentieth-century environmental problems could have been avoided. Japan would have been better off had it developed its own "modernity" through native technologies that do not simply "mimic" exogenous models of development.[44] This dichotomy of "development from within" versus "imposition from without" was the criterion for her form of ecological modernity, one that could stand only by virtue of rejecting technologies external to Japan (called "Western" by her). One of her examples is oceanic fish pasturing. Tsurumi called experiments in 1983 in Oita a "less violent technology based upon Japanese traditional views of nature":

> In the case of oceanic fish pasturing technology, its component parts (acoustic engineering, opto-electronics, measuring instruments, solar-electricity, etc.) were initially introduced from abroad and then partially improved. But the organizing principle that integrates the technological parts into a system is akin to the folk-beliefs and ethnocosmology peculiar to the fishing and farming people of Japan. Japanese used to, and still do, believe that natural objects, animate and inanimate, such as the sea, mountains, trees, birds, fish and shell-fish, are all endowed with souls just as humans are. That fish, like humans, are able to listen to and learn the sound of music was the initial idea that inspired some marine scientists to launch the oceanic fish pasturing experiments.[45]

This example of what I call ethnic environmentalism attempts to solve environmental problems through the suggestive force of ethnic belonging and ethnic histories without addressing capitalist modernity. This kind of ethnic environmentalism suggests a loss: *if only* we could return to the past; *if only* we had not forgotten communal values of the past, which are, by definition under ethnic environmentalism, sustainable. The narrative of environmental regret is complicated because it is an environmentalist articulation, which is welcome, but appears most interested in sustaining a particular ethnic nationalist collectivity.

As Naoki Sakai points out in his discussion of Takeuchi Yoshimi's version of the same binary of external imposition and internal development, this kind of narrative is built on "a *relation* of mutual self-reflectivity, or mirroring" that requires the West.[46] So, it may be that Tsurumi determined the West to be a geographic externality but, unlike Takeuchi, did not demand also an overcoming of the reactionary heritage within. Rather, all that must be resisted comes from outside. Clearly, based on this example, the environmental narrative of loss can be highly ideological. In *Contested Natures*, the editors posit that "such loss reflects a sense of threat over one's historical attachment to place, and in particular threats to the collective memories and reconstructions of place that shape one's sense of continuity with the past and with the landscape."[47] As ecologist Mark Davis describes in a different context, it is not unusual for native species to be equated with "good" and non-native species with "bad," but science does not support this kind of simplistic approach to conservation. To name just one example in my vicinity, the pine bark beetle is native to North America, but it is decimating forests while we worry in my Minneapolis neighborhood about keeping nonnative honeybee populations alive because they are good pollinators. The sort of ethnicized approach to biology that equates native species with positive attributes and vice versa has, according to Davis, dominated conservation efforts over the past few decades and is an approach that is more ideological than it is conservationist.[48] In ethnic environmentalism, broad, sweeping narratives of the loss of cultural and religious traditions are tied to hopeful environmentalist activism. But attention to cultural myths shrouds industrial technologies and aestheticizes nature to such a degree that an ethnic nationalist sublimity is all that is left.[49] Tsurumi's concept of endogenous technology, for example, distracts from the ecological fact that what has been providing fish protein for the 127 million humans on the archipelago is not music-appreciating mackerel, but bluefin tuna dangling from fluorocarbon long lines.[50] We must admit that hers is a serious underestimation of the problem.

The history of articulating *ethnos* through nature at the expense of eliding all the ways in which industrial capital has irreversibly impacted environments may be shorter than we think. While it is not within the parameters of this book to develop a history of ethnic environmentalism, I would suggest that it is especially in the hyper-industrial period that we find ethnic environmentalism deployed. Such environmentalism, particularly by highly industrialized nations, perilously leads to ambiguous claims of cultural difference that defy contemporary realities. For example, Tsurumi's ethnic environmentalism praises a specifically Japanese symbiosis of human and nature and, in so doing, ultimately denies Japan's responsibility (among other nations) for the depletion of the world's fisheries and ocean resources as a deeply wealthy corporatized nation. Instead, depletion of natural resources is framed as a problem of nineteenth- and twentieth-century Western technologies and thought. It is like saying that, if our country had not been hijacked, none of this would have happened or that, conversely, there can be a self-blame leveled at an entire cultural entity, as with Murakami, that lets the real culprits off the hook. If all Japanese are to blame for ignoring the anti-nuke unrealistic dreamers, then who is to blame for the meltdown of reactors at the Fukushima Daiichi Nuclear Power Plant? What then of the original builder of the plant, GE, or the owner of the nuclear power plant, TEPCO?

In Japan's case, ethnic environmentalism emerges as an ecocritical position that critiques Western technologies and even the nation's own historical struggle to be modern like "the West." But the impossibility of instituting such a searing difference between the two entities is difficult, likely impossible, under industrial modernity. When anthropologist Marilyn Ivy suggests the coincident modernity of Japan and the West, it is to make the point that cultural relativism can operate as a fetish in this context and that "what are imagined as the specificities of Japan or Japanese culture can never be unilaterally deployed as unexamined critical tools to undo presumed western hegemonies."[51] This point is equally true for other nations bound up in discourses of modernity, including China and India. Subaltern theorists, Ivy points out, "have provided compelling revelations of the dangers and seductions of using a nonwestern 'culture' to critique the West."[52] In ecocritical terms, those sorts of cultural-relativistic arguments get played out in a range of contexts, as illustrated by Kim in her discussion of race, culture, and animals in the United States. In Japan studies, Margaret Sleeboom has shown that ethnologist Kawai Masao insisted that "Westerners" are severed from nature and can express their closeness to nature only in terms of animal rights and welfare, whereas the "Japanese" are laterally always already connected to animals and have no use for such anthropocentric language. This kind of exceptionalism that claims one country is more sympathetic to nature uses the abstraction of the West in order to posit ethnic environmentalist ideas. One of the most extreme examples of ethnic environmentalism is Yasuda Yoshinori, who continues to argue that "a Shintoist animism renaissance" must take place to overcome the invasion and expansion of Western beliefs that have destroyed the Japanese world of animism, which is inherently ecological— and recoverable.[53]

The irony of ethnic environmentalism is that ecological claims are made by asserting constitutive exclusivity for a culture and, thus, for its attendant humanistic interests. In the case of Yasuda, for example, his call for an "animism renaissance" suggests that it is only the external forces of Western modernity that have poisoned Japan. What must be resisted, Yasuda argues, is an external threat that has mistakenly been allowed to grow as a kind of parasite on an otherwise healthy core. Notably, he is addressing only the economic growth in Japan from the 1970s that he specifically believes has caused the Japanese people to desert "the way of life which depended on the resources of the forest. The harmony between man and nature has been abandoned and people have forgotten the gods of the forest. . . . Animism, now near extinction, faces a critical turning point. Severe natural destruction started at a point parallel with that of the disappearance of Animism."[54] One can be sympathetic with the intent of the essay, which is to urge citizens to care deeply for forests, "especially Southeast Asia's forest resources which have been drained by the economic development of Japan," but it is based in a vociferous critique of an under-theorized "Western Christianity," which he calls "the civilization of deforestation." Furthermore, his claim that pre-fifteenth-century non-European societies in Asia, Africa, and South America "were golden and peaceful and based on a system of harmony between man and nature" was met with a number of critical responses: a suggestion to recognize the "stewardship" concept in Christianity; a critique of his lack of methods and systems that could realize the ethos of animism; multiple examples of environmental destruction by traditional agricultural patterns; and a questioning of his silence on ecological issues contemporary to the publication of his claim, such as Japan's use of driftnet fishing and the construction of an airport that would suffocate one of the largest blue coral reefs in the world, Ishigakijima, with runoff.[55] The insistence on a qualitatively different modernity that putatively lies just under the surface makes invisible Japan's full participation as a capitalist nation in industrial practices that have had devastating ecological consequences. Yasuda's impetus to "revivify" animistic and Buddhist ways of thinking are sympathetic in that they suggest the need to imagine agency for non-human things and to alter what it means for the human "to belong" or "to pertain" differently in the world. But that impetus is undone when it is culturalized in such a way as to treat animistic thought as a putative artifact of an idealized past.

It is also worth noting that Japanese romantics had made similar arguments for cultural exclusivity by instrumentalizing nature. Intellectual historian Julia Adeney Thomas has argued that the acculturation and sac-ramentalization of the concept of nature in Japanese modernity had blos-somed by the 1930s. It required the reinterpretation of nature as imminent rather than external, and "it had to be stripped of its universal connota-tions and made to refer to Japan in particular."[56] Thomas's most impor-tant insight with regard to ethnic environmentalism is that the acceptance of these dichotomies was meant to legitimize and naturalize power. The highly ideological nature of "nature" in this context can be seen in the mu-tually de-legitimizing claims of later Japanese romantics who continued into the 1940s to insist, on the one hand, that the Japanese were alienated from nature by Western technology and, on the other, that the Japanese were closer to nature as long as they rejected Western humanism. These conflicting views that the Japanese are both alienated from and more in sympathy with nature share the claim of cultural exclusivity for the Japanese, but one that depends on an entity called "the West."[57] Arguments of this sort, particularly by a rich nation like Japan, suggest a culture that has somehow been hypnotized by Western modernity to the point that it found itself sleepwalking through its own modern history of capitalist expansion and pollution. In short, the pursuit of ecological claims through the cherished dichotomy of the West and non-West or Christian and ani-mist is born of colonial and postcolonial claims of difference that simply do not hold under industrial modernity and corporate nationalism.

In another example of ethnic environmentalism, in 1988, Moscow tried to convince the Ukrainians of the need for a nuclear power station, and the Ukrainians mobilized and managed to stop the construction of two facili-ties. Ukrainian locals, teachers, blue-collar workers, and others gathered to counter the Soviet plans until a moratorium was reached. Yet, when the moratorium was overturned by the Ukrainian leaders, very few mo-bilized against the facility. It turns out that they had been more interested in questions of sovereignty than in those of nuclear power. In the case of Ukraine, when the political struggle waned, so did the environmentalism: "Whether or not the station actually disappeared, many people felt that their demand for the rights of self-determination had been achieved and that the struggle need go no further."[58] The Ukrainian anti-nuclear move-ment was so deeply tied to a push for national and regional sovereignty that the construction of facilities ultimately did not matter to the majority of the self-identifying group. This kind of politics does not make for good environmentalism.

Cherished Dichotomies

Despite the growing numbers of vulnerable populations under late industrial modernity, we continue to rely upon abstract human collectivities in
writing about ecological collapse for relatively familiar geopolitical reasons. Recent Anglophone ecocriticism seems to have taken up the mantle
of making cultural claims of exceptionalism in *mea-culpa*-style confessions
of how destructive Western thought has been in some form or another for
the natural world. For example, it has become a constant in ecological discourse describing the "Anthropocene" epoch (marking humanity's capacity to geophysically change the planet's earth systems) that, while the subject of such discourse is the planet, the discussion begins by bracketing off
part of the world through language that is usually unclear about whether
"Western" is being used to refer to a geographical region, an ideology ex-
ported around the world, or industrial modernity. Is the West invoked as
a specific polluter, and if so, whose emissions data will be charted? Is it
simply assumed that the West is *the* site of capitalist expansionism, and
if so, since when? Or is the assumption that the West is where modernity
and theory reside and where the dualistic episteme of nature–culture was
invented and, therefore, the logical place to start in making ecological critique? Equally problematic is the fact that the vague use of the "West" in
ecocriticism sets up a fantastical "Rest" that is undifferentiated and constituted only via the discursive construct of the "West," as illustrated by
Stuart Hall.[59] This allows some non-West polluters to essentially act as innocent bystander despite data to the contrary.

It seems that ecocriticism can suffer from the same obsession Eduardo
Viveiros de Castro identifies in anthropology, that of compulsively locat-
ing attributes that would make "them" different from "us" or "us" different
from "them." The "Rest" can deny culpability while the West can trans-
figure so-called others into fictions of the Western imagination in which
they lack a speaking part, all of which is done in the name of the West
blaming itself for environmental collapse.[60] The reason for this approach
is presumably a laudable effort to clarify the negative impact that coloniz-
ing forces, Enlightenment modernity, and migrating Europeans have had
on peoples and environment. Certainly it makes sense to account for how
some communities have not contributed to environmental crises visited
upon the planet today. Yet, when the "West" is deemed the starting point
for developing a global portrait of environmental collapse, this sets up a

temporality in which a global, environmentalist future is charted through a social imaginary of "celebrants" and "dissidents" and particularistic senses of a humanistic "we." In charting a way out of this binary born of a conflicted understanding of humanity as both shared and subject to genocidal elimination from Columbus' day ("as empires in Europe extended both their territorial claims and their exploitation of people's labor"), philosopher Sylvia Wynter posits the need for a "new world view" that "most closely reflects our actually, already existing interrelationality," a "form of connectivity to each other that has long manifested itself ecologically as well as 'sociosystemically.'"[61] Nandita Sharma describes this position as not unrelated to our planetary condition under "the global expansion of ruling relations" and the "threat of nuclear destruction hanging over all of our heads for the last sixty-odd years."[62] In short, we need not choose between "the celebrants' universality, which is little but a parochial concern of elites, [and] the alternative of dissidents that romanticizes an essentialized 'community,'" but perhaps side with those "motley crews" who engaged in action outside of sanctioned geopolitical entities. When the Grassy Narrows and Whitedog First Nations invite mercury disease specialists and victims from Minamata to test their waters in a battle against the Canadian government for water health or when activist writer Winona LaDuke describes the 300-year history of the survival and travel of a native corn seed strain throughout the northern United States, then we get a more expansive and sophisticated sense of who vulnerable groups and revolutionary collectives are.[63]

Wynter argues for a different sort of humanism that allows a more expansive sense of who dissidents are beyond predictable lines, including colonialist ones or categories that reify a particular script along the lines of "the West and the Rest." Additionally, ecological critique will include a robust critique of particular forms of humanism itself, particularly Enlightenment humanism. "Motley" collectivities may be inclusive of other species. Some new collectivities, unfortunately, have been the result of the broad reach of industrialism's toxins, consisting of thousands of environmental pollutants emitted by industrial nations since the 1950s, driving releases to never-before-seen heights. Called the "age of the great acceleration," this post–World War II era marks the stage for which "human activity, predominantly the global economic system, is now the primary driver of change in the Earth System (the sum of our planet's interacting physical, chemical, biological and human processes), according to a set of

twenty-four global indicators, or the 'planetary dashboard.'"[64] This "age of
the great acceleration" is, for some, the pivotal start of what we now call the
Anthropocene epoch. It is an age that begins with the Cold War, is ongoing,
and has produced analogous subjects across species and place by virtue of
subjecting them to toxic chemicals and radiation on a scale never before
experienced in earth history. Data measurements of toxic emissions vary
according to scale. In studies of the generation of greenhouse gasses, one
set shows that, if emissions were scaled to the size of the nation's landmass,
then emissions from 1750 onward for Western Europe, the United States,
Japan, and India have expanded immensely. Overall emissions show the
top emitters to be United States, China, Russia, Brazil, India, Germany,
and the United Kingdom. With regard to per capita emissions, rankings
change and the United States and Canada are at the top while China and
India rank much lower.[65] This kind of data shows that levels of pollution
cannot be easily determined on the basis of the "West" and the "Rest."

Yet, cherished, broad-reaching cultural dichotomies are perpetuated
within ecocriticism. For example, ecocriticism as a field has been described as overwhelmed by scholarship on the American West and one
in which intellectual questions asked stem from a bioregional bias born
of the discipline's early roots. This is likely true. Yet, the solution is not
to perpetuate a relational logic whereby ecocriticism becomes beholden
to a "spell of civilizations" argument just when climate health desperately
needs a critique of global corporate capital and anthropocentric living.[66]
The unfortunate outcome of ecocriticism articulated through national or
regional collectivities is that geopolitical regions continue as imagined
exceptions unto themselves and shared characteristics under industrial
modernity are put on the back burner.[67] For instance, as I was writing
this book, it was suggested that, if I want readers to consider these texts
outside the frame of the concerns of area studies, and more specifically,
Japan studies, then I need to include more writers and filmmakers who are
not Japanese. First, I do include writers from Taiwan, the United States,
Canada, and so on, but to pursue this strategy more directly and inten-
tionally would logically mean that I am, in the end, beholden to cultural
difference as the final word on ecocritical thought. Positivistic cultural
identification would become my primary problem to solve, and I would
have to pretend that the problem of ecocriticism being overly attentive to
the American West could and should be solved through greater peopling
of the archives of environmental literature. My collectivities would be

determined by national identity and I might have no room to consider the more-than-human world.

Poststructuralist approaches to essentialist concepts of identity have been useful for resisting national hegemonies, but as ecocritic Ursula Heise points out, "inevitably, a certain theoretical ambiguity accompanied the development of this line of argument as hybridity, diaspora, and marginality sometimes [were] turned into quasi-essentialist categories themselves, especially in some of the more emphatic validations of ethnicity, local identity, and 'situated knowledge.'"[68] Examples of this sort occur in area studies when ecopolitical problems are understood through essentializing claims of cultural practice, such as when things like fetishization of whiteness or Confucian paternalism are cited as reasons for illnesses caused by toxic industries in Japan.[69] The problem with this approach is that it suggests that we can also understand corporate Japan's meteoric rise to become a global economic power during the Cold War through cultural practice and, thus, lose an opportunity to assess the deep ecopolitical battles within local communities. We keep an imagined ethnic national identity in place even as we necessarily describe the conflicts among people and species within that place. We also may not account for corporate national and transnational interests.

While Heise acknowledges the impasse of the local and the global and embeds the problem of culture in a dialectical approach in which she combines local cultural production with global discourse of pollution and risk, comparative literature scholar Karen Thornber approaches the matter from a different perspective and attends to the problem of cultural nationalism by arguing that many texts in world literature share similar concerns: "Intercultural thematic networks are webs of creative texts from multiple cultures that focus on similar topics, whether or not the writers of these texts actively reconfigure one another's work."[70] Rather than looking at shared or repeated thematics across a transcultural, transnational or comparative landscape, I have taken the route of unpacking the problem of culture for species, lands, and seas through a new materialist approach. When *bios* is reduced to *ethnos* or *anthropos,* we severely limit our reading of texts and interpretation of the material world. It is true that my work is historically specific and informed by a knowledge of the languages and cultural histories of the texts, but I take seriously how the material world has been made handmaiden to cultural essentialism and cultural humanism. Essentially, what I am asking in these final paragraphs of this introduction is a variation of the question with which Rob Nixon opens the final chapter of his *Slow Violence: Environmentalism of the Poor*: "What would it mean to bring environmentalism into a full, productive dialogue with postcolonialism?"[71] Nixon worries that the two important theoretical fields of postcolonialism and ecocriticism have been reluctant to form a dialogue because each has an "often-activist dimension that connects their priorities to movements for social change"[72] that might conflict with the other's. The reluctance of postcolonial critics to take up ecocriticism, he suggests, is informed by a reading of ecocriticism as rooted in American studies and its early interests in nature as a sublime, transcendental imagination of nature and nationalist sensibility. This kind of ecocriticism clearly runs counter to concerns of postcolonial theorists who "have lived across national boundaries in ways that have given a personal edge to their intellectual investment in questions of dislocation, cultural syncretism, and transnationalism."[73] From this perspective, ecocriticism promotes an "exclusionary ethics-of-place" born of an American Western wilderness.

From my perspective, a critique of ecocriticism will take up, therefore, the problem of geopolitics and place and question the strict "West and the Rest" binary that founds so much discourse on ecocriticism and, now, Anthropocene discourse. Some writers are clear in addressing ecopolitics beyond the general dichotomy of West and the Rest, such as Verena Andermatt Conley's ecopolitical approach to poststructuralism, Ian Jared Miller's proof that ecological modernity's binaries of nature and culture were not a Western invention, and Fabio Rambelli's unpacking of how Buddhism has erroneously been claimed as the environmentalist antidote to Western philosophy and practices.[74] There is much room to be specific. Meanwhile, in the context of Anthropocene discourse, the engineering of our planet to the point that hardly any of us can claim not to take advantage of at least one of industrial modernity's conveniences (usually plastic) means that it is now really beside the point, not to mention anachronistic, to make industrial modernity a problem of "Western society." Such a claim unwittingly levies notions of difference that cannot hold, ecologically speaking, and continues the spell of "civilizations" that portrays the West as the behemoth that outsources ideas and knowledge. To rely on such an essentializing frame, in any case, places a human culture in a hierarchy of value with constitutive exclusivity at the level of (human) species at the core. Ecocriticism must instead find a way to engage culture without making the perpetuation of *ethnos* and *anthropos* the endgame, even the endgame of blame.

The texts chosen for this project are utterly specific, and so my criticism is contextualized. Mostly, as William Carlos Williams put it, "this is just to say" that the mere fact that I use Japanese-language texts and care deeply about the work of these Japanese authors and filmmakers does not mean that I write in order to answer any questions about "Japan" or "East Asia" or even the "non-West." As Timothy Clark provocatively asked in his discussion of how to read beyond human perception under the environmental problem of global warming, "where now is there an east to *orient* oneself to?" Systemic change to the earth systems (accelerated especially by rapid increase in production of synthetics, chemicals, fertilizers, and pesticides, the use of fossil fuels, and nuclear power) requires that we think beyond geopolitical identities. At this point in the history of global warming, from a geophysical point of view, there is no definitive "East," though there is an east as a direction on a GIS map or the Gaia app. "East" might be the direction of a radiation plume as it drifts across the Pacific. If there is no consequential question to which "the East" is the answer, it is because the toxic drift of industrial modernity either knows no such borders or is caught up in one of the swirling gyres of our anthropogenic epoch's oceans.

Affinities

As scholarship on new affinities that pertain among humans, animals, and their environments grows, claims of cultural difference cannot account for contemporary realities, especially when it comes to the environment. *Ecology without Culture* examines ecopolitical and aesthetic perspectives of artists and cultural critics whose work challenges culturalist visions of nature in the broadest sense through critiques of industrial modernity. Their work goes beyond national kinship and questions of cultural value to identify broader collectivities that emerge among organisms and beings through the material world. Their work proves the need for ecopolitical critique that more clearly accounts for the agency of the material world and nonhuman animals. The ensuing chapters discuss aesthetic perspectives for animal bodies, bodies of water, and human bodies that inhabit a toxic and beautiful world to suggest that the current environmental situation requires us to attend to environmental concerns in ways that account for the affinities produced by industrial modernity. Texts chosen for this book unravel collectivities that depend upon ethnic nationalist and cultural humanistic values. In their stories, poems, and films, affinities are depicted through biological, radiological, molecular, and climatological relationships. The texts are by activist authors and filmmakers who produced their work during the era of the "great acceleration."

Not least among the factors shared by the narratives, poems, and films discussed in this book is the fact that they were produced largely on the main island of Honshu in the geopolitical entity called Japan, originally written or filmed in the Japanese language (and translated into other languages). That said, there is no consequential question regarding their work to which "Japan" is the answer. Instead, Japan is framed through new affinities, of which "corporatio Nipponica" is one. The texts I discuss address the poisons of industrial modernity as that most significant sign of our embeddedness in the biotic world. They consider industrial modernity as having produced analogous subjects and new collectivities across species by virtue of the spread of those toxins. Even if we have not developed a clear and easy concept for collectivities that are inclusive of land, water, animals, and air despite humanity's dependence on these entities, the authors, poets, and filmmakers I discuss have artfully articulated the kinds of affinities that have emerged under industrial modernity, ones not limited to human experience.

Chapters in this book expand on how these activist writers and filmmakers conceptualize ways for making more of the biological substrata, geological time scales, and animal worlds in texts so that we might not, as readers and storytellers ourselves, miss fundamental opportunities to critique human endeavor that harms the environment. In this context, cultural humanism, defined here as the cultivation of self and humanity as the primary purpose of aesthetics, becomes an ecocritical problem to be addressed. This modern idea of culture determines that all natural phenomena must eventually refer back to the human's creation and re-creation of itself as subject. Because cultural humanism defines the material world by limiting its relevance to that which it has for humans, it presumes humanity as the relevant subject for whom we read and write and film. A critique of cultural humanism engages the very matter of the world and its living systems toward determining who we are in an ecological sense. The radical changes to the environment under industrial modernity and the contemporary science through which we increasingly understand the composition of the human body as so deeply embedded in ecological feedback loops are only the first of many compelling reasons to jettison the human as the primary organizing force for ecocritical thought.

This book returns at various junctures to the concept of scale as a method for critiquing cultural humanism. As long as culture is a primary problematic, any concept of culture necessarily assumes that the concept already makes sense. But given what we know and continue to learn about the human body at the microbiotic, molecular, and geophysical level, "culture," which works at the level of human perception, cannot begin to account for relations and affects among beings and natural or climatological phenomena. As stated earlier, the agency of things is not cultural if cultural modernity is the process of the human mastering itself and nature through self-consciousness and historical action. Encouraged by recent turns in philosophy that ask how we can theorize the agency of things by speculative realists and new materialists, I write about writers and filmmakers who reject cultural humanism. The reason to pursue this approach lies in the material world itself: the agency of toxins that ground these literary and filmic stories demands an approach that accounts for things smaller and greater than a selective humanist "we."

As it is now clear, this book eschews ecocritical encounters dependent on tired tropes that rehearse what Timothy Morton calls "nature-nations" and cultural humanism. I have chosen literary and visual texts for the ways in which they affirm life against the grain of cultural and human exceptionalism. They are mythical and metaphorical, biographical and historical. Most importantly, they are never skeptical, but rather create expansive ecological imaginaries that break the spell of civilizations.

CHAPTER 1

Obligate Storytelling

There was a word inside a stone.
I tried to pry it clear,
Mallet and chisel, pick and gad,
Until the stone was dropping blood,
But still I could not hear
The word the stone had said.

I threw it down beside the road
Among a thousand stones
And as I turned away it cried
The word aloud within my ear
And the marrow of my bones
Heard, and replied.

—Ursula K. Le Guin, "The Marrow"

Literature with Us

Storytelling needs matter. Matter is the stuff of the world—stones, ficus trees, ocean currents, bacteria. This chapter identifies a mode of storytelling that foregrounds material relations as fundamental to narrative. I call this form of expression "obligate storytelling," a kind of storytelling that emphasizes the bond, the fetter, the bowline, the *ligare,* of one being to another at the level of care and substance, of thought and matter. Obligate storytelling is important in an ecological context because it produces a deep sense of relation among its diverse subjects. As philosopher Isabelle Stengers writes, "whenever a being raises the problem of its conditions of existence, it lies within the domain of ecological approaches."[1] And so it goes with obligate storytelling, which addresses the conditions of existence for beings and matter in an aesthetic ontology that refuses humanist writing traditions, eschews authorial flourish, and rejects institutionally privileged language to attend to relations that pertain at a transcorporeal level. Fundamentally, obligate storytelling depicts relations among diverse bodies and forms without privileging humanistic endeavor.

Biology provides an interesting, if not exact, analogy for thinking about obligation. In biology, the adjective "obligate" means "by necessity": an obligate aerobe needs oxygen, and an obligate parasite exploits a suitable host. The ways in which one organism expresses an obligate relation to another are at the level of survival for the organism. In oral storytelling, the obligate relation is the interface of speaker and listener. The response of the listener influences the telling of the story when the storyteller feels obliged to listen to those for whom the story is told. This is a description of storytelling neither as plot contrived to explain a history or narrative nor as bildungsroman of a modern subject. Rather, it is storytelling as a relation. If writing is to critically address ecological problems caused by industry, then it must in some way subvert humanistic ways of writing and broaden its aesthetic ontology to include relations among different kinds of bodies. Animal bodies, animal eyes, bodies of water, and human bodies will all be material and semiotic subjects, and literary theory will account for them.

In charting this foray into obligate storytelling, we might first ask what literary studies has done with those who have not traditionally operated as agents in cultural studies. In the case of Japanese ethnic environmentalism, animals and natural objects are brought into a narrative of Japanese cultural history, but their semiotic potential has been restricted by placing them in the amber of nativism and ethnic tradition. The flourish of literary celebrity can likewise restrict semiotic potential: under the pen of so many contemporary writers, the material world need not be mentioned at all except as passive backdrop or tool to the genius of the writer. But some authors have been more keen to develop narrative and representational modes that actively deconstruct modern humanistic modes of writing. I develop here the concept of obligate storytelling to help illuminate their work and to show how particular forms of storytelling offer a way to account for human life in and through relationships with the more-than-human world. While I focus primarily on the work of Ishimure Michiko, this mode of writing is identifiable in the work of a range of authors: J. M. Coetzee, Karen Tei Yamashita, Ruth Ozeki, and Wu Ming-yi are a few authors that, to my mind, are invested in storytelling that chisels away at the hard amber of ethnic nationalism and cultural humanism.

When author Ishimure Michiko first captured in writing the curse that had been placed on the Shiranui Sea, she delivered a novel that was unexpected, incomparable, and born from no existing literary tradition save the orality of the local population about which she wrote, though even that orality had an imaginative basis. She was chosen for the Ramon Magsaysay Award for her deft expression of the raw beauty of littoral zones and long-suffering families who inhabited the shorelines and hills along the sparkling Shiranui Sea. A powerful voice for the disenfranchised, Ishimure wrote for those who had lost their livelihoods because their fishing grounds had been poisoned by methyl mercury and whose meager monthly wages were consumed by medical costs when heads of households could no longer work due to the neurological damage that unsteadied their hands and feet. She also wrote with equal passion about the cats who suffered similarly debilitating consequences of mercury poisoning as humans and the countless millions of organisms that lay suffocating or dead in the sea from the toxic uptake of organic mercury.

The national government had tried to push the local experience of that toxic curse into the past just at the point of its inception as a ecopolitical event and to treat the mercury pollution as if it had ended with the government's official recognition of the Chisso corporation's culpability in poisoning the Shiranui Sea.[2] But the publication of Ishimure's tour de force *Paradise in the Sea of Sorrow* in 1969 made it impossible for either the government or Chisso to deny the magnitude of the poisoning of the expansive fishing grounds in and beyond Minamata.[3] The novel's "bone-scraping" prose, as filmmaker Tsuchimoto Noriaki called it, led the way for all ensuing expressions of Minamata whether it be film, theater, art, music, or writing.[4] Photographers and activists flocked from Tokyo to Minamata after reading her book, and many spent years in the area, some even settling there. In the meantime, mercury poisoning incidents were occurring elsewhere around the world. In the 1960s, Grassy Narrows and Whitedog First Nations experienced their first symptoms of mercury poisoning after fishing in the rivers and lakes downstream from Dryden, Ontario, where the Dryden Chemical Company dumped fully 9,000 kilograms of mercury into the English and Wabigoon River systems from 1962 to 1970, and these First Nations peoples continue to show signs of being plagued by the aftereffects of that original dumping of toxic mercury.[5] In 1971, hundreds of Iraqi lives were lost to mercury poisoning from tainted grain shipped from Mexico and the United States.[6]

Recognizing the increasingly dangerous impacts of industrial modernity on human populations, in 1972 the United Nations held its first conference on the environment, which they called the "Conference on the Human Environment." They invited victims of mercury poisoning from Minamata to speak, and Tsuchimoto screened his award-winning film *Minamata: Victims and Their World* (1971). He made his medical films, discussed in chapter 2 of the present volume, the following year based on feedback from conference attendees. Decades later, at the United Nations in 2013, the Minamata Convention was adopted to reduce mercury use in the world. In 2015 the convention agreed to assist countries in developing a standardized inventory of mercury emissions. It is not a stretch to say that all of these events were precipitated by one book: Ishimure's *Paradise in the Sea of Sorrow.*

Ishimure's writing embodies what I am calling obligate storytelling foremost in its animation of the environmentally disenfranchised on a scale that refuses any ethnic nationalist or humanist writing tradition. Her prose thrusts aside master metaphors of an *ethnos* in order to animate the bonds that obligate one life to another beyond nation and species, bonds between the fisherman and the fish, between the mother and her unborn child, between the writer and the sea. In bearing witness to the lives of those so deeply impacted by toxic mercury, her narratives follow the twists and turns of industrial modernity's organic and synthetic agents as they unraveled within bodies of water, fish, cats, and humans, and this form of storytelling is obligate because it describes what storytelling means for its subjects. We can find an analogy in John Berger's description of the photographer, who, he argues, should be focused on the meaning of the photograph for the photographed: "For the photographer this means thinking of her or himself not so much as a reporter to the rest of the world but, rather, as a recorder for those involved in the events of the photograph. The distinction is crucial."[7] Berger's ideal photographer is concerned for the subject, not the audience, of the photograph. Similarly, philosopher Vinciane Despret wrote, regarding the ethologist, "You cannot hope to learn something about a living being unless you ask what the meaning of the experiment is for those you want to know about."[8] Ishimure was first and foremost a witness. She observed the cats of the fishing village where the ills of methyl mercury first appeared, the biological sentinels who first signaled that something was terribly wrong in Minamata. She traveled by

foot to the homes of ill fishermen and sat at the bedsides of those hospitalized with what was only known at the time as a "strange disease." But how
was she to witness in writing their physical struggles and loss of livelihood?

Since obligate storytelling is produced out of a relation, it cares little for
the conventions of an art form. In this vein, Ishimure's life-long critique
of corporate and state industry began with quitting conventional *poesis*.
Early in her career, she had grown impatient with classical literary production. Later she would articulate this impatience through a critique of
transhistorical intertextuality: how could the classical poetry form dependent on intertextual repetition of a determined canon of biotropes capture
the environmental impact of industrial modernity and the sacrifices made
under it? How could it depict the environment that supported an increasingly wealthy nation, especially those mountainsides, rice paddies, coastal
beaches, and rivers left in ruins? As she began writing more intently about
those laboring in the shadows of development, she quit the classical poetic form as insufficient for capturing material relations and a besieged
environment.

Ishimure's critique of classical poetics has much in common with
Berger's critique of painter Jean-François Millet's use of classical painting
techniques. According to Berger, Millet's paintings of peasants performing farm duties like sheep shearing, wood splitting, potato lifting, and tree
pruning were failures because the peasant's land use was incommensurable with the classical painting form that Millet utilized: "Most (not all)
European landscape painting was addressed to a visitor from the city, later
called a tourist; the landscape is his view, the splendor of it is his reward.
Its paradigm is one of those painted orientation tables which name the visible landmarks."[9] As Berger relates, Millet utilized this form of treating land
as tourist site because "there was no formula for representing the close,
harsh, patient physicality of peasant labor on, instead of in front of, the
land. And to invent one would mean destroying the traditional language
for depicting scenic landscape."[10] Berger attributes the successful unifica-
tion of the working figure in his surroundings with painterly form in Van
Gogh's paintings and the "gestures and energy of his own brush strokes."
Van Gogh succeeded at turning the artwork of his painting into an intense
gesture of empathy with the subject, but his energetic bush strokes also
turned his painting into a personal gesture: "the witness had become more
important than his testimony."[11] In the process of embedding the laboring

peasant into the landscape, Van Gogh's paintings expressed a deeply personal gesture.

In her medium of writing, Ishimure rejected classical poetics and the semiotic conventions of classical poetry with its refined biotropes of flowers, birds, wind, and moon motifs. The classical form fatally detached the subject from environment, and the realities of laboring and living under industrial modernity could not be articulated in classical poetry, which could only fail to represent the working lives of miners and fisherfolk. As Ishimure put it in conversation with sociologist Tsurumi Kazuko: "Up to a time, the lyricism of natural beauty was enough. Up to a particular century. But the poetic beauty of nature itself is now such a mess that we can't compose such lyricism. That world is dying. I anguished, wondering why no one noticed. The literati didn't address it, at least not head on. It's a dying landscape."[12] Classical biotropes froze a landscape in time so that the land and its people appeared healthy, inevitable, and everlasting. They were an incongruous response to a ruined environment and made invisible the environmental conditions that miners and fisherfolk confronted under industrialism.[13] As described by literary scholar Kitagawa Fukiko, amateur poets of the generation preceding Ishimure who had left the countryside to rush to Tokyo as it burgeoned into a modern industrial capital, in fact, depended upon that function of the classical biotrope to freeze a place in time when they accommodated their hometown landscapes to the classical form. Engaging in "beautiful writing" (bibun), the newly arrived poets composed euphoric poems about their home towns written in the classical 5/7 rhythm. These poems performed the authors' cosmopolitan success by freezing their rural past in a nostalgic picture born of classical biotropes, but Ishimure rejected this aestheticism of the rural scape.[14]

Curiously, Empress Michiko, long-time friend to Ishimure, seems to have understood the problem of using classical biotropes in the expression of environmental damage. In describing the experience of the 400,000 people initially displaced by the tsunami and nuclear meltdown in March 2011 on Japan's northeastern seaboard, the empress composed an ironic poem in classical verse on the impossibility of expressing the tragedy through a transhistorical, intertextual tropes: "Waiting to return home / Without seasons or time / The poetry glossaries [saijiki] do not contain / the word 'shore.'"[15] In citing a lacuna within the intertextual tradition of citation (honkadori) and its inability to speak to the new landscape of the northeastern seaboard, this poem suggests a situation in which the landscape cannot be perceived through the overdetermined classical form of *waka*. By acknowledging this lacuna, Empress Michiko references the toxic condition of the land and the plight of its refugees, for whom normative time frames could be but a dream as they attempted to rebuild their lives in temporary shelters. This surprising poem expresses how the catastrophic ruin of land and air exceeds the capacity of classical tropes to represent it. By introducing more contemporary language and irony, it interrupts the modern link between classical biotropes and ethnic nationalism evident in Murakami Haruki's use of the cherry blossom biotrope in the aftermath of the events of that March, although the empress, by virtue of her political position, is hard-pressed to escape the ecologocentrism of her chosen form of expression.[16]

Obligate storytelling refuses literary forms that turn a vibrant and living environment to amber. Ishimure rejected biotropes of the classical tradition because they could not capture how people and organisms struggle to survive under industrial modernity and its landscapes. French anthropologist Philippe Descola's point that culture's nature keeps those sacrificed for capital in the shadows implies that cultures produce symbolic devices that "encode a uniform nature" distinct from culture. This uniform encoding distorts certain properties of reality by positing a divide between nature and culture, which he ascribes to Euro-American ethnocentricity.[17] By illustrating how it was that nature and culture, or the nonhuman world of nature and the cultural world of humans, came to be divided, Descola asks that anthropology remove the divide: "[The division] does not lie in things themselves; it is constructed by an arrangement that makes it possible to discriminate between them."[18]

Descola creates four ontologies using non-Euro-American examples (Amazon, Australia, and Mexico) of collectivities that emerge if our thinking is not burdened by the provincialism of treating nature as a domain "subject to autonomous laws that formed a background against which the arbitrariness of human activities could exert its many-faceted fascination."[19] His ontologies structure human experience beyond a nature–culture divide. Animism, naturalism, totemism, and analogism are ontological categories for expressing collectivities anew. His revision of traditional anthropological ontologies pushes against cultural humanistic ideas: interiority need not belong only to the human species; human intentionality is provincialized; and so on. Obligate storytelling similarly makes this kind of effort to introduce greater ontological complexity into the realm of aesthetics. In other words, the creation of an aesthetic ontology that rejects the nature–culture divide is the work of obligate storytelling.

Linguistic Mutiny

As described above, obligate storyteller Ishimure was deeply skeptical of aesthetic traditions for the way that they turned living nature to amber. In the late 1950s, she quit contributing to the journal in which her poems had been published previously because she was disgruntled with the form and method of publication. The local poetry journal, she felt, had turned poetry into performance and churned out "new stars" with no criteria for what constitutes relevant poetry, no internal criticism, and especially no "problem consciousness" (*mondai ishiki*): "Poetry is not cheap property but occurs in the endless destruction by a critical eye."[20] She also quit her membership in Circle Village, which was a community of activist artists and intellectuals established on the outskirts of Fukuoka during the strikes at the Miike and Chikuho coal mines, because she could not imagine how material produced in a writing salon could capture the experiences of wives whose husbands and sons were devoured by the mining industry. According to Ishimure, the social atmosphere of a weekly writing salon for which widows thickly applied perfume to cover the smell of soil could not rise to the critical occasion confronting them at the mines with its back-breaking labor, forced division of families, and poor pay.[21] Perhaps it comes as no surprise that she also refused the Japanese Communist Party's invitation to write for them, stating that she was "repelled by the party's twisted logic that even nuclear weapons are justified if they are in the hands of one's allies."[22]

Ishimure's iconoclastic approach to writing emerges out of a series of rejections of classical and modern uses of the Japanese language. Her contemporary Morisaki Kazue, who helped found the Circle Village, also experimented with Japanese to find a literary voice expressive of the labor performed by miners on the island of Kyushu. Morisaki's search for a language that interrupted the standard Japanese associated with ethnic national identity took her to the villages of fishermen and coal miners, where she found a different language in the same tongue. She called it the language of "underground culture" (of the mines), versus the language of the "above ground" culture of Japan's ethnic national, imperial, and agrarian society. The language of underground culture was of the miner, and the language of those above ground was of the state. Not unlike Gilles Deleuze and Félix Guattari's concept of "minor literature," Morisaki developed a political concept of language created within the dominant language to account for a minor collectivity. Ecocritic Masami Yuki describes Morisaki's development of a minor language as a refusal of the institutional in her work, an institutionalism that the use of standard Japanese would invite.[23] It was also a personal gesture—an effort to express herself as a second-generation colonial in Korea who grew up indebted to Korean women around her.

Ishimure's critique of the corporatized state was also expressed through language use. Her rejection of transhistorical poetic expression and medical jargon was, overall, a rejection of institutionalized language and, ultimately, a rejection of state authority, but not in favor of personal expression or flourish. Instead, we can find in her writing an effort to express layers of meaning that get erased in the presumed transparency of institutional language. In 1971, in conversation with mine laborer and journalist Ueno Eishin, Ishimure recalled the last testaments left by miners who suffocated to death from a cave-in while working for the largest extraction company in Japan in the 1960s, in the Miike mine in Kyushu. The miners, having no other means of expression, scratched their final testimony on shovels, battery backs, and cave walls with nails and stones. Seeing these last testaments to a life in a photograph in Ueno's book, Ishimure told Ueno that she was "dumbfounded, as if having witnessed the trampling of raw entrails":

> With the onset of the cave-in, miners on the verge of death, closed in and trapped in complete darkness used pieces of stone or nails to write in katakana their last testament on shovels and walls before dying. I understood then what modern industrial history is. Those dying words of the trapped miners' were my first encounter with language.[24]

The final words that the miners etched were simple things like: "make sure that hitoshi and miyako get along," or "yoshiko take care of dad sayonara," or "we're suffocating everyone blown up watch over mom dad kids take care sayonara."[25]

When Ishimure describes these steely hard notes as her first encounter with language, this language had traversed multiple mediums. The original etches of stone on metal had been photographed, then quoted in Ueno's book, and finally referenced by Ishimure to create a testimonial palimpsest. Obligate storytelling records this palimpsest through the voices and materials involved in the story. This form of storytelling does not thrive on the personal gesture or charisma of the storyteller. Ishimure put this point in even greater relief when she wrote: "Living is embarrassing. Your face is visible. Your feet and hands are visible, your laughing face is visible, your odd voice can be heard by other people. I couldn't bear it. So gradually I eliminated them. My face disappeared and my form disappeared to become only voice. But that voice too was different from the one I imagined as mine, so I kept only song."[26] While Van Gogh or Morisaki refused conventional expressive forms, they still produced highly personal works. In contrast, Ishimure's obligate storytelling does not thrive on the personal gesture, but instead speaks of the impossible desire to erase it. She seeks to disappear the storyteller through a figurative escape hatch of metamorphosis.[27] Through self-erasure, the shape-shifting narrator can assume other subjectivities in writing, just as Ruth Ozeki's narrator expresses in "Thoughts in Language": "If language / is the line / dividing us / from them, / then words fail me, / and I grow / molluscan, or / bang my brain / against its limbic / limits, or ape / and parody / poetry even / as I fail / to articulate / this one sigh / to you."[28]

Because the task of environmental writing is so often an act of witnessing ecological problems, it matters to track what kind of witnessing that is. For the obligate storyteller, as we have discussed so far, witnessing means to refuse conventional habits in writing: to refuse self-flourish, to give up mimesis and documentation, and to track palimpsests of expression. It may even be the wish to express silence, as when Ishimure wrote: "The history of the Minamata disease patients and their relatives—this wandering tribe of exhausted, half-dead outcasts carrying their ghosts like clay dolls with big holes instead of eyes, noses and mouth—is about to be shown and trumpeted everywhere. Their curse is gradually becoming audible. I won't rest content until my creation, my own dolls made of the stuff of words, speak, or rather, keep silent like these people."[29] The obligate storyteller aspires to write the experience of her subjects even if it means aspiring to an impossible silence.

The obligate storyteller often describes voices in conflict. In describing the fisherman pitted against the suits of Chisso corporation, Ishimure wrote of those who spoke in a poetic idiom versus those who could not

understand it, of those who spoke only of wishing to fish and pull sea let-
tuce from the ocean floor versus those who took great pride in their life
as a corporate laborer, of those who stumbled over the officious language
of the state versus those factory workers who spoke the militaristic ban-
ter of war returnees and "lived in the fast lane" (*wasamono*). All of these
voices represent the human divisions that ruined the bay for decades.[30]
This conflict under industrial modernity was expressed first in Ishimure's
Paradise in the Sea of Sorrow, which is a critique of the absolutist narrative
that treated the lives of the diseased purely as a record for the courts, the
state, and medical programs at universities.

"The brutality of jargon" (*yōgo no zangyakusei*) was Ishimure's term
for the way that medical language used by researchers and physicians
could turn a living body into an empty vessel of symptoms. Institutional
language's stripping of liveliness and personality of victims was put in
stark relief by the placement of bed charts and official reports as counterpoint to poetic idiom in her novel. For example, when Ishimure quotes
Dr. Tokuomi Haruhiko's medical chart of a patient suffering from "acute
fulminate form" of Minamata disease in *Paradise in the Sea of Sorrow,* it appears as no more than a sum of symptoms:

> Apathetic facial expression. Forced laughing and crying.
> Choreoathetotic movements. Inability to understand articulate
> speech. Pulse was at 83. No conspicuous changes in the heart, lungs
> and the abdominal region. Rigidity of the neck. Kernig's sign. Eye
> movement normal, no blepharoptisis. Pupils were isocoric and re-
> acted to light rather slowly. Eye fundi normal. Measurement of the
> visual field impossible (visual field constriction was detected later).
> Muscular rigidity. Tendon reflex was exaggerated. No pathologic
> reflexes present. Waddling ataxic gait . . .[31]

The impersonal medical language used to describe the symptoms of the
disease makes the patient and physician (the writer in this case), replace-
able by another.[32] It is a perspective by no-one-in-particular for no-one-
in-particular. It is a perspective that allows the physician to write off the
child as a "vegetable existence" or "the living dead," as some physicians
referred to some of the most severely affected patients.[33] This is the prose
of the unobliged observer who may speak the evasive language of ne-
gotiators, like the one from the Chisso corporation who said in response

to Ishimure's call for justice, "Ms. Ishimure, these are negotiations, and there's no place here for the literary."[34]

In contrast, when the *Asahi Journal* asked Ishimure for stories about children with what was now called Minamata disease, Ishimure began with quotes of children's voices. Each line is meant to be an utterance by a victim of mercury poisoning. Each utterance but the last repeats a first-person pronoun "I" inflected differently for gender and formality, nuances impossible to represent in English translation:

"Boku wa, boku wa, boku wa boku wa boku wa . . ."
"Oraa, oraa, oraa, oraa, oraa, oraa, oraa"
"Watashi, watashi, watashi, watashi, watashi, watashi, watashi"
"Uchi yo, uchi yo, uchi yo . . . uchi, uchi, uchi, uchi, uchi . . . u."
"Koraa, koraa, kora-, koraa-, koraa- koraaa- koraaa, aaa, a."[35]

After depicting children exploring their shaky voices in strings of first-person pronouns, Ishimure concluded, "When I witnessed a single tear stream down the cheek of a weeping child who they say is leading a vegetable life, I can't help but think that there are countless words existing in this universe just as there are countless existences, measureless in all directions."[36] Deeply critical of the medical institution that would treat these children as human vegetables, she describes the words of these intrepid souls who struggle heroically to express themselves through a deeply debilitating neurological disease as part of a vast planetary vocabulary only just being accessed.

This form of obligate storytelling, as I define it through attention to Ishimure's prose and politics, refuses language that enjoys institutional privilege. Expression that purports to instruct, the language of the public institution, is one such privileged language.[37] In *Paradise in the Sea of Sorrow,* the standard inflection of hospital and court reports stands in stark contrast to an idiosyncratic poetic idiom invented by Ishimure. Comparative literature scholar Livia Monnet, who translated *Paradise in the Sea of Sorrow* and other of Ishimure's works, describes this idiosyncratic voice as a combination of two dialects altered by Ishimure's poetic invention,[38] and literary critic Kawamura Minato called this juxtaposition of standard inflected language of the state and creative poetic idiom in her work "linguistic mutiny."[39] The poetic idiom appears especially fresh and vibrant, while the data gathered by medical and academic communities and painstakingly reproduced turns the debilitating and deathly mercury disease into something stark and uncannily lacking a sense of reality. Obligate storytelling in Ishimure's work here brings attention to the agency of the diseased through the active disenchantment of institutional, especially medical, discourse. This comparative iteration of personal voice with the language of science functions as a critique of Enlightenment science in its disenchanting repetition. Hers is the kind of politicization of science that Stengers argues, in a different context, is needed so that science is not seamlessly allied with public order and health, and "this means learning how to address scientists, how to activate their disentanglement from the role of guardians of rationality that has captivated them and put them at the service of power, both state and capitalist power."[40]

So far, obligate storytelling has been discussed in terms of its investment in a particular kind of voice that quits conventions in art, draws attention to the ways that language is made transparent in institutional forms complicit with industrial modernity, and refuses the personal flourish. It also reshapes imagination through a greatly expanded range of expression that has the interests of the vulnerable at its core. In obligate storytelling, the vulnerable are more than cultural humanism can account for. The final sections of the present chapter illustrate the most fundamental aspect of obligate storytelling: its investment in depicting relations among organisms and matter for an aesthetic ontology that expands the range of voices for storytelling.

Stone Stories

In Ishimure's literary worlds, things tell stories and this storytelling takes various forms. For instance, it may take the form of a stone's sweat, as in an essay called "Thoughts of a Stone," in which the narrator describes the stones she found on a slag heap in the Chikuho mining area. The stones had been separated out from the coal that had been mined and left in large piles as unusable waste. Some had been brought up with ore dug months earlier, but others had been there far longer. The stones contained within them fossils of the plants, animals, and shellfish of the Carboniferous era. The stone is described as having a deep history embedded within it:

> It holds the leaves of sweet flag and flowers, carved and held by stone, buried for some hundred millions of years. Exposed to the

surface of the earth, the shape of the stone remains, but it weathers, and as it weathers it sweats, or in scientific terms "releases moisture." Seeing the heavy sweat it emitted, it seemed to me that while the stone couldn't speak, it contained within it a long and distant memory, thoughts of hundreds of millions of years ago. We also have human history alongside that, but it's the stone that has deep thought next to our half-baked language. The unspoken thought of the stone contains the essence of expression, condensed expression.

Compared to thoughts of a stone, the words we spew in a generation or two are no more than foam or phantom.[41]

In this essay, the stone's sweat is a language that tells a history of more than human language can ever account for. The sea, too, is an expressive body in Ishimure's larger oeuvre, in which she articulates its destruction by mercury poisoning: "And that fate is the anguish of an epic poem spoken by the dying Shiranui Sea."[42]

In obligate storytelling, there is no epistemological question of how we can know whether a stone or an ocean speaks. Rather, it expresses an invitation to hear other histories—those before humanity's birth and after the delivery of industrial modernity. She has written in a number of essays that the writer's job is not to function as an arm of justice, but rather to give voice to the invisible spaces between the mountains and between minds.[43] These spaces between mountains and minds are akin to "that cleavage between this word and that word, between this action and that action. You know that something is there but you can't see it, you can't give it a name. You want to express it, and while you are writing the sprite, the 'sekontaama,' passes!"[44]

The obligate storyteller grants birds and animals the capacity to express. For example, poet Ryoko Sekiguchi's long poem *Heliotropes*, originally written in French, describes the different ways that plants are identified in an arboretum. Signs in Latin provide the words for the classification of plants in the urban green house, but the poem quickly outgrows the Latin terms. The birds, it turns out, have their own names for those same plants. One passage reads: "On this clearly / bounded earth, / only birds call / plants by their / own names."[45] To describe the language of birds, Sekiguchi incorporates the language of Dari so that both Latin and Dari are used to write the language of the natural world. Latin represents institutional expression: "The Latin names / of plants, however / long they take to / say, all have exactly / the same weight." If a flower doesn't bloom, the plant is transformed or hard to identify: "we can't name it so we leave / it there, a bare noun."[46] In other cases, we name "out of fear of leaving it unidentified."[47]

Birds in the arboretum have multiple capacities for expression: "Once done phonating, / they have no reason to / stay up so high; they / dive, revealing the / symmetry of their flight / feathers."[48] And when a human whistler imitates the bird, he cannot understand the bird's reply:

> The sound of the call reaches the birds,
> And the whistler faithfully imitates the
> beak's cadences without understanding
> the language he's speaking; from the
> foliage, another voice calls back; the
> bird's response is not always understood,
> consonants uttered to follow vowels, and
> vowels follow other vowels, making the
> center of life out of something like a flood
> or circuit—no one doubted it at the time.[49]

Bird language includes the sound that can be represented only by introducing another human language that is visually contrastive: ﻓ. Birds have a tongue that speaks the truth, and only *they* "call plants by their real names."[50] Their language must never be considered the language of instinct: "This irregular chirping / isn't meant to claim / territory, or signal food, / or attract a mate—it's / meant to keep this rare / sound in the throat."[51] Any Cartesian notion that birds function as machines would be greatly in error. They are tremendous readers of signs because they are the ones who know the truths about plants; it is the human reader who cannot read some of the plant signs, at least not any longer: "This stoma / takes a form / we can no / longer read."[52]

Obligate storytelling is invested in nonhuman forms of expression. The stone's sweat, the expressive space between the mountains, the bird's call, the tiny gaping hole of the stoma—they all express something we humans have no idea about. So, how is literary theory to account for this kind of expressive ontology? New materialism provides a narrow path in. Political theorist Jane Bennett has written extensively on taking seriously the "call" from things or objects "as more than a figure of speech, more than a pro-jection of voice onto some inanimate stuff, more than an instance of the pathetic fallacy."[53] She asks, "What if we admitted that things really do or can hail us, can participate in transmissions across bodies . . . and offer us a glimpse into a world of swarming, lively materials that are neither quite subjects nor objects?"[54] Bennett's use of the terms "call" and "hail" recalls Louis Althusser's scene of interpellation in which one turns at the sound of a police officer shouting "Hey! You there!" At the moment of the turn, one is hailed by the apparatus of the law. Judith Butler's critique of Althusser is to say that, to be interpellable, one has to be already inside the structure of interpellation. Bennett reasons that we are hailed not just by institu-tional apparati and discourses, but by things in the world. In her examples, the range of who can hail is quite vast: it might be an ape or it might be a spoon. Her point is that all matter and things in the world have some kind of capacity to affect another. That vitality can be revealed through careful anthropomorphization, but it also resists full translation. Bennett's passion to articulate a "vibrancy" for matter is rooted in an ethical concern to enliven human interest in all things and direct it toward a more sustain-able planet. For her, the profound inability to imagine agency for beings and things beyond the human subject drives a lack of care. Consequently she makes a case for recognizing the affectivity of all things, lest we be left with the false notion that "a world without us, a world from which our own values have been subtracted, is therefore a world devoid of values altogether."[55] Bennett's work, like that of other new materialists, offers "a challenge to some of the most basic assumptions that have underpinned the modern world, including its normative sense of the human and its beliefs about human agency."[56] As Steven Shaviro writes, "In fact, there is good scientific evidence that all living organisms, including such brainless ones as plants, slime molds, and bacteria, exhibit at least a certain degree of sentience, cognition, decision making and will."[57]

In expanding what counts as affective or agential, a critique of Enlightenment humanism is raised. With so much productive theoretical work being done in the name of critiquing Enlightenment humanism's di-chotomy of mind and matter, it may be unfair to put it so prosaically, but when it comes to industrial toxins, there are those for whom the macabre consequences of the "vitality" of matter have been readily apparent for some time. In the context of environmental health, on the most basic level, industrial pollution has made it impossible to imagine life and the health of air and water as anything but relational. In the 1950s, in Minamata bay, after the release of toxic mercury into the Shiranui Sea unbeknownst to almost anyone at the time, bowlines were no longer simple tools for tying up one's boat. They were an irrefutable metaphor for the obligate relations among beings and environment, relations that had become more visible than ever with the daily death of fish, birds, cats, and humans from mercury poisoning. This obligate relation was expressed in the simple act of fishing and the consumption of fish. Something was moving through all organisms of the sea. When the young housewife began to spend her days at the bedsides of the growing number of ill and dying fisherfolk, the reason why so many were dying was not yet known, though at least one researcher in the Chisso factory had his suspicions. He had run multiple experiments on both domestic and feral cats who had been witnessed rushing headlong into the sea and performing a kind of perverse "dance" with their hind legs in the air as early as 1956. Humans who ate fish and shellfish experienced numbing of the extremities, limited eyesight, and an inability to control their hands and feet. Birds lay dead on the shores. Fishermen returned from their daily catch and told of the whitening of the sea with the underbellies of fish floating breathless on its surface.

We now know that the toxic methyl mercury had moved up the trophic tiers in processes of bioaccumulation and biomagnification, important concepts for understanding the risks of consuming fish that contain mercury.[58] It was at Minamata that these principles were first identified for science—a historical fact long forgotten. Further research at the site of Minamata's growing population of ill and dying would reveal even more startling truths of the impact of methyl mercury. It was discovered that the placenta did not act as a barrier to protect fetuses. Rather, it retained toxins, filtering them from the mother, and this caused increased damage to the fetus. Mercury was transported into the fetal blood through transporters that normally bring in neutral amino acids that are important for fetal growth and development. Research has shown that this system caused the fetal blood to have a higher concentration of mercury than the maternal blood. Once in the fetal blood, the mercury passed through the blood–brain barrier, exposing the developing fetal nervous system to the neurotoxic metal. Called "fetal methylmercury intoxication," the symptoms are different from those in adults who get the disease, which also vary from person to person (as discussed in the following chapter).

Ishimure's writing shows mercury poisoning to be one of the most profoundly debilitating of industrial diseases. The new materialist perspective offered by ecocritic Stacy Alaimo is essential in understanding the tragic agency of mercury. Her concept of "trans-corporeality" offers a corrective to the more materially benign concept of "vibrant matter" by acknowledging "the often unpredictable and unwanted actions of human bodies, nonhuman creatures, ecological systems, chemical agents, and other actors."[59] As a concept, it emphasizes that agents and their environments can cause negative and even insidious effects on other bodies, and this concept operates as a corrective to benign conceptualizations of matter's agencies that address only what Alfred North Whitehead called the "creativity" of things. A new materialist approach to things is an ecocritical corrective to human exceptionalism because it allows for a recognition of the agency of the nonhuman world, but this embrace of the "creativity" of things seems valueless without acknowledging the unpredictability of matter, which may pass through us like a benign sprite or settle within us as a haunting toxin.

Metamorphosis

Metamorphosis is one way that Ishimure's prose accounts for the living spirit beyond the transcorporeal impact of mercury. One passage in *Paradise in the Sea of Sorrow* describes how mercury disease victim Yuri is referred to as "Patient #41" at the hospital: to the medical community, she is nothing more than a "human vegetable." This medical terminology is countered with an association of Yuri with lively beings in the world rendered through the voice of Yuri's mother: "If Yuri is no longer a human being but a tree or weed, I am a tree or weed. If Yuri is a lizard, I am a lizard's mother. If she is a bird, I am the bird's mother. If she is an earthworm, I am the earthworm's mother."[60] Through an imagined metamorphosis that links her with other lively entities, Yuri is unloosed from the medical terminology that would deny her a sense of movement and vitality.

Another passage depicts a similar imagination of metamorphosis. Yuki, a mercury-poisoned patient, has been hospitalized and her fetus aborted, presumably to save her own health. When served fish for her evening meal, she hallucinates that the fish on her plate is her aborted fetus, and as the fish is knocked from her plate to the floor by her mercury-induced spasms, she cries out, "Come here darling. Don't run away from your own mama."[61] There is a real biological basis for this connection of fetus to fish: the fetus in the womb, like the fish, lives in water and is even more susceptible to toxins through the processes of bioaccumulation in the amniotic fluid. But it is not just fetus and fish that are haunted by the toxins. When the mother on whom the abortion has just been forced, Yuki, strives to put the fish-fetus out of its misery by eating it, she brings herself into the trophic tier all over again, that biological connection that had caused her illness in the first place. The physiological impact of bioaccumulation finds its way into the narrative through an imagination of metamorphosis. In environmental history, this scene has been read as testimony and treated as the pure experience of victims of methyl mercury, but it is by no means a transparent reporting of the victim's voice. To interpret it as another "heart-wrenching" story of a methyl mercury victim would be to ignore Ishimure's form of obligate storytelling, which avoids the transparent language of mimeticism and simple testimony. Figures of metamorphosis disrupt the perception that mimetic representation of the illness is possible or even desirable. They create a multifigured palimpsest of expression that frees the ill body from the stark depictions perpetrated by the medical community.

Ishimure's later novel *Lake of Heaven* (1997) uses simile to describe the ways that industrial modernity impacts the vulnerable. The novel depicts the construction of a dam that will flood an old village. In one scene, denizens of a village are silently aghast at the creation of a lake where they had once lived, and as the water pours into the valley, the insects seem to scream:

> What surprised everyone most of all was seeing the amazing variety of insects—beings that normally went unnoticed—floating about in a mass, covering the surface of the water. All sorts of creatures were drifting about—numerous kinds of ants, both large and small, along with fantastic-looking tiny light green butterflies in the process of breaking out of their cocoons, with their thinner-than-paper wings torn apart. Okera bugs and salamanders were swimming about. Even tiny baby birds that looked like they'd just been hatched were floating in the water in their nests. . . . They watched their fields, paddies, pathways and houses all being taken under by the water, right before their eyes. Yet all they could do was stare vacantly in a daze. . . .
>
> Along with the insects, who seemed to be crying out from hell, they felt as if they too were being exterminated, even before they knew what was happening.[62]

Humans, insects, and birds share the experience of the flooding of the valley, but while the humans stand silently in a daze, the insects appear to cry out at the moment of their death and the villagers can hear them. This village that is being submerged has always been inclusive, and a gravestone now memorializes this inclusivity: "Now enveloped in water, it had been chiseled with the words 'Memorial for the souls of the ten thousand beings.' And when it said it was for the souls of 'beings,' that didn't mean just humans. That stone marker on the hill as dedicated to the souls of all beings—and not just the birds and insects either; it was also for the souls of the things we can't see with our eyes."[63]

The narrative is thick with simile: village dweller Ohina's speech was like a bird, and when the cherry tree was cut down to fill in the valley with water, all of its broken remains were stained as if with blood.[64] In this aesthetic ontology, the insect who can be heard crying out from hell and the human who speaks as if she is a bird form a dreamscape through which obligate relations are expressed. Bodies get mapped through their shared voices and through the expression of likenesses among beings. This may sound not unlike Deleuze and Guattari's concept of animal becoming, which has provided some posthumanist philosophers a concept for critiquing Enlightenment humanism's seemingly impassable division between humans and animals. "Becoming-animal" is not a fantasy of becoming anything in particular, but rather entering into an alliance with another entity, and these "becomings" are fueled by a desire for proximity and sharing.[65] Humans, in becoming "animal," are freed from dichotomous relationships in which the human dominates. The world is no longer reduced to dualisms such as the "human" and the "animal," "culture" and "nature," and so on. The concept of "becoming-animal" embodies a commitment to let go of standard power relations. Socially and symbolically sanctioned modes of being are no longer desirable.[66] Rather, there is a readiness to be guided toward a different mode of being.

But, as Lori Brown suggests, becoming-animal has very little to do with animals: "For one who desires a process of becoming for the sake of exploring relational and ethical possibilities with other animals, Deleuze and Guattari offer a rather sparse account of these possibilities."[67] For the purposes of describing obligate storytelling, in becoming-animal, the writer or the artist is the "sorcerer" and the point is to undo human identity, especially the identity of the putative singular, well-formed, and individuated subject. Animal becoming is accompanied in their work by a sense of violence and bewilderment that attaches to the self who is thrown into "upheaval" and "reels" ("qui soulève et fait vaciller le moi"): "Who has not known the violence of these animal sequences, which uproot one from humanity, if only for an instant, making one scrape at one's bread like a rodent or giving one the yellow eyes of a feline? A fearsome involution calling us toward unheard-of becomings."[68] Becoming-animal seems to be the fierce task by the artist, for the artist.[69]

In contrast, in Ishimure's writing, the use of simile creates a metamorphic imagination that is less a violent reaction of self-metamorphosis than an organic process of being supplemented by other bodies or supplementing other bodies. A youth, Masahiko, who comes to visit his grandfather's grave, gradually learns to hear the natural world around him and has a flight of imaginative transformation: "If I were to look upward from the pathways along the edges of the fields that now lie at the bottom of the lake, the fish would be swimming up in the sky along with the dragonflies. I'd be like a sea ray, swimming along the mountainside."[70] As a relative from Tokyo visiting the village, he feels like climbing into a cocoon or becoming a ray but also recognizes this impossibility. Old woman Ohina may feel as if her body is composed of animals, but she does not dissolve into the newt. Villagers feel as if they hear the insects scream. The Tokyo grandson is beckoned and invited to relinquish his deadened imagination of coastal cement tetrapods and drifting mercury to listen for the seas and mountains.

As mentioned above, space that is opened up through simile is one that might be described as "oneiric," a dreamscape that depends on an imagination of metamorphosis. This space of metamorphosis unravels normative anthropocentric habits in writing. The emphasis in not on a delimited object or "I" who acts, but on minds and ideas "whose boundaries no longer coincide with skins of individuals."[71] This mutual mapping of humans and nonhumans, as Ishimure has alluded elsewhere, might be something akin to one Minamata fisherman's claim that he has dual citizenship—as both a Japanese and a fish of the Shiranui Sea.[72] Scholar Iwaoka Nakamasa sees in Ishimure's work a return to community (*kyōdōsei*), but her ecological vision must be understood as more than a return to such a humanist model.[73] At the very least, Ishimure's narratives do not conceal her skepticism that the Japanese liberal humanist state and corporate modernity have any capacity to revitalize what it means to be human. The monkey, the cocoon, and the ray enrich human life more than any state system, even if the reverse is not the case.

Obligate storytelling not only admits the affectivity of other organisms but also seeks ways to illustrate that affectivity. Ishimure's aesthetic ontology, driven by an imagined metamorphosis of its literary subjects, breaks the seemingly impassable division between humans and animals on which so many humanist practices and philosophies are based. Ishimure, in fact, spoke of her struggle to express the agencies of matter and beings. In one example, she takes advantage of the three writing systems in Japanese to denaturalize human existence. She wrote, "In the universe is the womb and it is not only the life of those we call 'people' [ヒトという生命] who feel this."[74] In this short phrase, two things happen: the nonhuman is characterized as like a perceiver of the human, and the human is written out of the national imaginary by using the syllabary for foreign words in Japanese, which is also, visually, the simplest writing system, *katakana*. She puts "people" at double remove through the combined use of *katakana* and the modifying phrase *to iu* for a statement something like "those we refer to as 'people.'" The human, in a sense, is subordinated to other lives by using the more complex *mora* for "life." This is only one example of how her writing, in its form, subordinates human to environment.

Ishimure's imagination of metamorphosis, use of simile, and reflective approach to writing rejects the petrified language of human culture and human subjectivity. In some critical discourse, such nonhuman voices get interpreted by way of animism, especially those depicted in non-Western narrative, but such an interpretation confines narrative to humanist interest, particularly when animism is cited to produce a cultural world. Philippe Descola defines animism as:

> [the] attribution by humans to nonhumans of an interiority identical to their own. This attribution humanizes plants and, above all, animals, since the soul with which it endows them allows them not only to behave in conformity with the social norms and ethic precepts of humans but also to establish communicative relations both with humans and among themselves. This similarity of interiorities justifies extending a state of "culture" to nonhumans, together with all the attributes that this implies. . . . All the same, this humanization is not complete, since in animist systems these, as it were, humans in disguise (i.e. plants and animals) are distinct from humans precisely by reason of their outward apparel of feathers, fur, scales, or bark—in other words, their physicality.[75]

Animism proposes to recognize the vibrancy of things yet maps humanist culture onto other bodies. Contrastingly, Ishimure's obligate storytelling is not invested in pressing human culture upon the insect or newt. There is little investment in producing for them a mirroring interiority. They need not be gods; they need not be human; they need not have culture.

The aesthetics that emerge out of obligate storytelling rescue us from the task of attributing human culture to things. Timothy Morton's concept of "aesthetics as causality" is another approach to reading for vibrancy in objects. In describing how attention to objects helps us read poetry, Morton takes up the pleasing Aeolian harp and the ringing reverberation that it makes when a breeze passes through it. When placed on a windowsill, the harp vibrates to air currents, and it is for him a "beautifully elegant" example of "aesthetics as causality" because we never hear the wind itself yet the harp vibrates with music. This aesthetics as causality describes a relation of two vital musical entities, neither of which is a musician. When the wind passes through a treetop, it "translates" the wind. The chalk translates the mountain. The nail is an anthropomorphic form of iron. A vibrancy of things is expressed when two entities react to each other without an explicit human interlocutor. This approach to aesthetics felicitously removes the vibrancy of things from the grasp of human culture and animism.

Lake of Heaven translates the experience of an old woman through other kinds of interlocutors. When old woman Ohina frequents the lake that has tragically buried their original village of houses and trees and a cemetery on a hill, she peers through the dark water to catch a glimpse of the remnants of roofs and treetops. Joyous memories of dancing there as a young girl are mediated through the gaze of playful monkeys who look into her eyes:

> Gazing into the depths of the water, she saw a mound of earth
> from the mountains gathering up and spreading out, supporting a
> thicket of wild grapes. Visions of piles of rotting leaves with white
> fungus glared out at her like successive images cast upon a screen
> in the back of her eyelids. The smells of mushrooms filled her nose.
> Wild young monkeys pranced about on piles of decaying leaves
> and dirt. Without a sound, they danced nimbly about the saseppo
> and tabi trees and bit into the small fruit from the trees, staring into
> Ohina's eyes from time to time.

Their eyes looked innocent to Ohina, as if they were drunk on liquor. How lovely. She realized she was being revived, little by little. From deep in her heart a sinking voice called out. . . . Years ago when I was young there was a night I danced with a hat like this covering my face. It was in a garden.[76]

Ohina recalls being hailed by the monkeys and passes into a reverie. She imagines her hat strap, reflected in the lake, to be a red newt floating under her chin. As she washed rice in the water or combed her hair, "a newt was always there, showing its red belly, crawling slowly along the wall and walking through the water. . . . For a moment Ohina felt as if she were crawling toward the bottom of the water where Amazoko lay. The vision of the red newt was already leading Ohina on."[77]

One of the most famous scenes of looking at oneself in a pool of water is the story of Narcissus. There are many versions of the story, but generally, when Narcissus sees himself reflected in the water, he sees only himself reflected back and no one else. Bob Dylan expressed it thus it in the song "License to Kill": "Now he worships at an altar of a stagnant pool / And when he sees his reflection, he's fulfilled." When Ohina looks into the pool, the past merges into the present. The body reflected to Ohina is both less than human and more than human as she sees herself and remembers that the newt had always been there. When a visitor from Tokyo first approaches Ohina, she looks to him like a bird: "Wearing a white robe and a hat, she was standing at the water's edge, staring downward. At first, seen from a distance, it had looked as if she might be a water bird, a part of the landscape, with the pale green lake silently reflecting the shadows of the surrounding mountains."[78] Ohina's body is mapped through animals and she finds refuge in being with monkeys and newts.

If Narcissus quenched his desire by gazing at his own reflection, Masahiko found his desire through listening. He can hear more in this quiet village than in Tokyo and begins to feel as if he is about to climb into a cocoon. He has become like an insect, "wrapped inside the thin covering of a semi-transparent cocoon, groping its way toward a corner of the heavens."[79] His metamorphosis into a new self is described as emerging from a carapace. This radical approach to the human figure becomes Ishimure's own articulation of a minor literary approach. Unlike the retrieved voice in Morisaki's work, which is the voice of the humans "underground," Ishimure's narrative is invested in the recognition of the self through the eyes of the monkey or a self that is inhabited by a newt. This aesthetic ontology consistently expresses relations through figures as ephemeral as the spatial cleavage between mountains (*yama to yama no aiwa*).

An old woman staring into a dammed up river who sees a newt crawling at her chin is this poet's way of "subjectifying" the universe, a notion that comes from writer Ursula K. Le Guin, who remarked that poetry in particular has a capacity to "subjectify the universe rather than objectify it."[80] Le Guin's is a pithy remark, but it suggests the power of aesthetics to enable a subjectivity for those things beyond human subjectivity.[81] Subjectifying the universe requires poetry. That is, it requires figure and metamorphosis. Poetry scholar Mary Jacobus wrote about the way that poetry can articulate the voice of the more-than-human world: "The regulated speech of poetry may be as close as we can get to such things, to the stilled voice of the inanimate object or the insentient standing of trees."[82] She continues, "Things look back at us. They may even seem to talk back."[83]

In Ishimure's world, things do talk back. The earth speaks. To return to the scene that opens the introduction of the present volume, after the tsunami and nuclear meltdowns on the northeastern seaboard of Honshu, many writers weighed in, and Ishimure was among them. March 11, 2011, was her eighty-fourth birthday. That afternoon, nurses delivered simple field flowers in a handmade vase to the author suffering from Parkinson's, knowing that she preferred the spindly, bright faces of field flowers to nursery-grown blooms. Curious as to what the day might bring, Ishimure turned on the television to find that there had been an earthquake and tsunami along the nuclear plant corridor known as the nuclear Ginza, named for the tremendous amount of energy the northeastern seaboard sent to Tokyo to light up its sparkling shopping districts, including the famed Ginza. For the ensuing tense hours, like so many of us, she tracked the futile attempts of self-sacrificing laborers to avoid reactor meltdown and eventually weighed in with this solemn remark: "The suffocating earth took a deep breath and exhaled. It killed innocent people who had to die. We've entered a major turning point for civilization."[84] Murakami's and Ishimure's initial responses to the tsunami contrasted sharply: the former invoked the cherry blossom, while the latter invoked plate tectonics; the former spoke of nature as static and stage-like, the other of a heaving earth; the former spoke of the power of ethnic resilience and stoicism in the face of natural disaster, and the other spoke of environmental challenges faced by human civilization.[85] Ishimure listens for the rumble of a shifting sea floor and wonders how to calm a wounded earth.

The attribution of affectivity to nonhuman agencies is a way out of

ethnic and humanist culture and enables the physical and biological lega-
cies borne by the land and by the sea and its inhabitants to be accounted for
in ways that go beyond the specter of cultural practice. In *Lake of Heaven,*
after the village head collaborates with developers to build a dam, his home
is burned to the ground, but the story does not focus on the human drama
of the arson or solve the mystery of who lit the match. Rather, the flames
are featured as a fiery embodiment of resistance to the dam. Ecological
critique works in this novel through figurative aspects that are not forc-
ibly solved or explained through an unpacking of human relationships.[86]
Ecological critique as expressed in *Lake of Heaven* and other works is that
of a "decolonial imagination," as is demonstrated by Monnet. Ishimure's
experimental project *Villages of the Gods* (1970–2004), for example, creates "another world in this world" (Ishimure's term) for a radical perspective on modern industrial history through a "delinking or disconnecting
[of] itself from modernity's hegemonic epistemic paradigm" of industrial
capitalism, and her narratives even transcend "the frame of environmental
literature and environmental activism," instead decolonizing knowledge
and being and making no attempt to inscribe "the same culture."[87] In the
context of thinking about ecology without culture, Ishimure's decolonial
imagination rejects the claims of the self-indulgent national collectivity
that silences critical voices within that presumed collectivity.

As Donna Haraway stated in a lecture on the new geologic epoch of the
Anthropocene, it takes "serious denormalization to destabilize worlds of
thinking. It matters to be less parochial."[88] Classical Japanese poetry, with
its conventional biotropes, reduces the landscape of the archipelago to a
pathos-driven beauty and a sincere human emotion. The imagination of
culture can make it hard to critique common practices that are bad for the
environment, and geopolitical and cultural exceptionalism may lurch us
toward environmental collapse. The importance of Ishimure's form of obligate storytelling lies in the frame it chooses for ecological critique. Her
attention to the affectivity of things rectifies the long-dominant tradition
of humanism that often denies the obligation of humanity to the rest of
the living world. As the concept that we are living in a new geologic epoch
continues to gain momentum, the deep concern to explain the ecological
and social consequences of industrial capitalism with recourse to unten-
able cultural and national identities may finally fall away, as illustrated in
chapter 4 of the present volume.

Cultural coherence produced by established paradigms of expression is challenged only if criticism refuses the antiquated practice of reading literature as cultural instruction.[89] Novelist and performance artist Tawada Yōko, who writes regularly in three languages, once stated that, when one language gets loosened through an encounter with other languages, it is freed to produce something like "a web that catches floating plankton."[90] The encounter of languages produces something sticky and organic, something beyond cherished dichotomies produced out of ethnic understanding. The emphasis is not on a delimited object or "I" who acts but, rather, on language and ideas whose boundaries no longer coincide with skins of individuals who speak a particular, ethnic language. The mutual mapping of the human and nonhuman is a refusal to repress or to submit to a socialized, ethnicized imagination of being and language.

The apex of obligate storytelling is to listen for the water traveling under the earth's surface and furtively bear witness to the stray cat. Wu concluded his story of the Pacific trash vortex when Alice's cat Ohiyo hears Alice call out and "raises her amazing little head, opens her eyes one blue and the other brown, and responding to Alice's call, looks right back at her."[91] This scene recalls Jacques Derrida's essay of being naked before his cat and feeling as if this encounter helped him confront humanism's shallow sense of animal being.[92] He wrote about the experience as if it had been an encounter, but it is mostly a quizzical first-person narrative deeply invested in the author's own mind. Ishimure writes differently: she writes not about her own embarrassment, but about the embarrassment that might be expressed by a flower or a cat. She wrote recently, "The phrase 'the flower, too, blushes' applies not just to humans but when life meets life [*seimei*]."[93] Nearly half a century after the demonstration, Ishimure recalled sleeping in front of the Chisso office in Marunouchi neighborhood of Tokyo, where Minamata activists were staging a sit-in to protest the mercury that had been dumped in their fishing grounds by the corporation. At dawn, she heard a scratching sound, "kari-kari-kari-kari," and lifted her head to see a kitten scratching at the concrete with its nails, trying to bury its business. For her to witness the cat and pretend not to see is for the human to understand. This is the gift of the obligate storyteller.[94]

CHAPTER 2

Slow Violence in Film

The Good Shot

Fukushima author Kido Tamiko wrote the following stanza of a poem called "Fairyland" after the nuclear reactor meltdowns on the northeastern seaboard of Honshu:

> The sea where I was born no longer exists.
> Waves shine, pungent with the smell of the ocean.
> Silver fish jump and flash in this calm and deep place.
> Fine sand touches my toes.
> The sea is still there, however.[1]

In a biotrope of the shining surface of an ocean, Kido treats the sea as both utterly the same and utterly different after radioactive fallout in Fukushima. On the one hand, it is the sea of the speaker's childhood: it sparkles, it has an odor, and the sand of its beach where the waves stop is still soft between the toes. At the same time, though, it is utterly changed, as intimated in the first line: "The sea where I was born no longer exists." This first-person narrator alludes to the active ocean currents that flowed past as TEPCO reactors released trillions of becquerels of radiation into the Pacific and continue to do so as contaminated water is released from spent fuel pools on a daily basis. The poem references the problem of the invisibility of radiation: the sparkling waves and jumping fish give no evidence of contamination, but the radiation is there. The fishing industry of the area is decimated.

The paradigmatic toxins of modernity are those that escape visual perception. Veteran cameraman Ōtsu Kōshirō worked with Tsuchimoto Noriaki on many of his films on mercury poisoning. On the first day of filming *Minamata: Victims and Their World* (1971), Ōtsu could have taken a picture postcard shot of the Shiranui Sea. The sea sparkled in the sun and the fish jumped.[2] The familiar sound of fishing boats putt-putting across the bay might as well have been a scene from an Ozu film. But, instead, he and Tsuchimoto eschewed the picturesque or what Martin Lefebvre called an "intentional cinematic landscape" in which landscape arises as object of contemplation.[3] As Lefebvre argues, landscape in cinema has been treated either as ambient background or as a site through which the cinematic apparatus gets featured by way of the gorgeous landscape on the screen. Either way, the landscape offers itself up for contemplation and, according to Lefebvre, "has come to signify a view of nature emancipated from the presence of human figures and offering itself for contemplation."[4] Film scholar Adrian Ivakhiv, in his discussion of cinematic landscapes, is more literal, asserting that there is a background or landscape that preexists new moving images of the earth. Even within "geomorphing," elements are mobilized "against a background of landscapes that remain relatively stable and unchanging" in the cinematic endeavor, according to Ivakhiv.[5] In either context, landscape is the subject of what Gilberto Perez called "the outlook of a confident humanism" where a "commanding view of the scene" by the individual human gaze enables a sense of it being "relatively stable."[6] It makes nature ambient while humans and the objects they take up are the source action and life, a landscape that Lefebvre has called not only an "intentional landscape" but a "spectator's landscape." The tension that film theory is particularly poised to resolve from an ecocritical perspective is articulated by Lefebvre: "Is landscape the world we are living *in,* or a scene we are looking *at,* from afar?"[7] How can we theorize landscape as part of an ontology for film that better accounts for the agency of things as they may exist beyond the human gaze?

The idea of landscape as either ambient or a stable space in which we dwell is precisely what a critique of industrial modernity refuses. An ecocritical approach to landscape for moving images will ask how film theory can account for the mutual constitution of self and the world within the film frame. How can film theory interpret interconnection in the world, which Timothy Morton calls "the mesh" and new materialists have called "distributed agency," without treating landscape as ahistorical ambient space. We need a concept of the mise-en-scène that is more attentive to the vibrant materiality that has been rendered moribund through film theory's historically humanistic approach to landscape in particular and mise-en-scène more generally.

Tsuchimoto, who dedicated most of his life to documenting fisher folk living in and around the Shiranui Sea, did not interpret landscape as aesthetic object or ambient background.[8] The good shot was not the one committed to landscape; it was the one committed to ecological systems. Even if the gorgeous Shiranui Sea could easily play the role of the dystopic sublime just like long shots of empty farms and overgrown gardens in documentarian Fujiwara Toshi's filmic record of lands contaminated with radiation in *No Man's Zone* (2012), that kind of landscape shot is absent in Tsuchimoto's Minamata films. Rather, the landscape is a place to fish, to bob on the waves, to wonder at the crabs crawling under the stones, or to discuss symptomology of mercury poisoning from the deck of a boat. Or it might be the object of the mercury disease victim's lively gaze, a penetrating gaze that made it impossible to treat the sea as ambient scape.

Filming Slow Violence

Six years before returning to Minamata to film *Minamata: Victims and Their World,* Tsuchimoto had endured scorn from locals for his filming of a 1965 television documentary on mercury disease victims. He was accused by one mother of treating her child as a performer in a freak show (*misemono*) and other criticisms followed. Award-winning poet and Minamata denizen Sakamoto Naomitsu remembers this incident and recorded it in his poem "Requiem for a Documentary Filmmaker":

> That life
> at the heart of Minamata
> unapologetically lays words flat
> and levels the proud claim "I am Chisso"
> and refuses any easy expression.
> He was
> sent back.[9]

The "he" of this poem is Tsuchimoto, who had yet to realize that there were no easy claims to be made about the victims of the disease. He returned to Tokyo until he read Ishimure Michiko's masterpiece of environmental literature, *Paradise in the Sea of Sorrow.* Deeply moved by the work, he determined to record the fisherfolk's ongoing struggle for justice and ended up spending the next thirty years of his life filming the Shiranui Sea and its people, experimenting with how to make visible the disastrous impacts of industrial modernity. As the failure of Tsuchimoto's first television documentary illustrates, the mode of treating the devastating environmental pollution in Minamata as part of a news cycle was not at all ideal for representing the various impacts of environmental pollution by industry.

Postcolonial ecocritic Rob Nixon makes this point in his *Slow Violence: Environmentalism for the Poor.* "Slow violence" is a term he uses to describe the violence done to humans, animals, and the environment over time, a violence that is often invisible because it is difficult to represent pollution events like radioactivity, eutrophication, mercury poisoning, and so on: "Slowly unfolding environmental catastrophes present formidable representational obstacles that can hinder our efforts to mobilize and act decisively. . . . Violence is customarily conceived as an event or action that is immediate in time, explosive and spectacular in space, and as erupting into instant sensational visibility. We need, I believe, to engage a different kind of violence, a violence that is neither spectacular nor instantaneous, but rather incremental and accretive, its calamitous repercussions playing out across a range of temporal scales."[10] Nixon offers the useful concept of "slow violence" to describe the long-term effects of polluting industries, toxic technologies of war, and environmental problems associated with global warming. He asks how we might "convert into image and narrative the disasters that are slow-moving and long in the making, disasters that are anonymous and that star nobody, disasters that are attritional and of indifferent interest to the sensation-driven technologies of our image-world?"[11] In his view, semiotic conventions for representing violence in media contribute to a lack of attention to slow violence: "In an age that venerates instant spectacle, slow violence is deficient in the recognizable special effects that fill movie theaters and boost ratings on TV. Chemical and radiological violence, for example, is driven inward, somatized into cellular dramas of mutation that—particularly in the bodies of the poor—remain largely *unobserved,* undiagnosed, and untreated. From a narrative perspective, such invisible, mutagenic theater is slow paced and open ended, eluding the tidy closure, the containment, imposed by the visual orthodoxies of victory and defeat."[12]

Slow violence poses representational obstacles because it unfolds over a length of time utterly out of pace with our spectacle-driven media. More interested in producing "disaster porn," media news cycles are not interested in slow violence and the habits of viewers eschew all but the spectacular in their daily rush through digital media. Filmmaker Fujiwara

Toshi's voice-over to his long shots of post-tsunami debris left in the "no-go" zone of radiated land makes precisely this point. Disaster images "become stimulants, often consumed as drugs. Today, perhaps, we have become simply addicted to all images of destruction."[13] Nevertheless, his films feature countless images of eerie expansive shots absent of humans portraying the rubble of the earthquake and long shots of overgrown farms and schools in radiated territories in Fukushima that feel prurient and voyeuristic.

Nixon suggests that moving images essentially cannot capture slow violence and that the only "good" use to which media images of environmental violence might be put is in using "the emotional jolt" of shocking images to achieve environmental justice.[14] Instead, Nixon privileges various forms of writing, including fiction, memoir, and essay, as most capable of representing slow violence because they are not beholden to visual media's thirst for spectacle: "Writing can challenge perceptual habits that downplay the damage slow violence inflicts and bring into imaginative focus apprehensions that elude sensory corroboration. The narrative imaginings of writer-activists may thus offer us a different kind of witnessing: of sights unseen."[15] The writing of atomic bomb victim Hayashi Kyōko is a good example. Her short stories constitute a textual rejection of the bomb's spectacularity in media as most evidenced in the widely circulating image of the mushroom cloud since 1945. Her prose is deeply conversational. Even descriptive passages about radiation are embedded in multiple frames of dialogue, letter, and first-person narrative. In her early work, Hayashi focused on the effects of radiation on the bodies of women, but decades later, she expanded her range of victims of atomic bombs to include all kinds of bodies, including those who endured nuclear tests in the United States. In a deeply moving epistolary collage of dialogue and storytelling in "From Trinity to Trinity" (2000), the iconic victim of nuclear war is the nameless snake that slithers in the grasses of New Mexico: "From the bottom of the earth, from the distant mountain range exposing its red surface, and from the brown wilderness, soundless waves pressed toward me. I squeezed myself. How hot it must have been. Until I stood on Trinity Site, I had thought that the first victims of nuclear damage on earth were us humans. I was wrong. There were elderly victims here. They were here, without being able to weep or cry out."[16] Hayashi came to write short stories that portrayed the slow violence of radiation in bodies of shy snakes and desert plants as counterpoint to the state-sanctioned ressentiment that gets folded into dramatic Japanese nationalist discourse as the neoliberal government attempts to reconstitute a standing military.

Still, as literary critic Njabulo Ndeble points out, the written word is not immune to spectacularity. Literary forms can also produce a predictable drama of "ruthless oppressors and pitiful victims that calcifies the imaginative range of explorable experience," reproducing the seductive hegemony of spectacle.[17] Writing that calcifies the binary of oppressor and victim appears in predictable places, like apocalyptic fiction. For example, Frederick Buell finds 1970s American literature (contemporaneous to Tsuchimoto's films) as appropriately spectacular in its portrayal of environmental pollution. His example is Philip Wylie's 1972 novel *The End of a Dream*, in which the real-life event of the 1969 burning of the Cuyahoga River in Cleveland, Ohio, is transformed into an "explosion so cataclysmic it was attributed to an atomic bomb . . . registering a force at ground zero of 21 kilotons."[18] The elevated language of author Thomas Disch, who prefaced his collection of short stories with the following, is written in the vein of immediate crisis that Buell associates with Rachel Carson: "In effect the bombs are already dropping—as more carbon monoxide pollutes the air of Roseville, as mercury poisons our waters, our fish, and ourselves, and as one by one our technology extinguishes the forms of life upon which our own life on this planet depends. These are not catastrophes of the imagination—these are what's happening."[19] Disch resorts to violent visual metaphors of bombs in order to garner interest in the problems of carbon monoxide and other kinds of invisible toxins. So, while it can interrupt the sense of virtual immediacy that visual media produce in instantly showing violence as spectacle, literary narrative can offer the very same type of spectacle.

Conversely, visual media can represent slow violence without resort to spectacle. Films like Todd Haynes's *Safe* (1995), Kamanaka Hitomi's *Hibakusha: At the End of the World* (2003), and Jeff Orlowski's *Chasing Ice* (2012) portray ecological issues of multiple chemical sensitivity, radiation, and global warming without giving themselves over to Hollywood-style battle scenes and charged melodrama. *Chasing Ice* utilizes data visualization and time-lapse photography of melting glaciers to make global warming visible (though this film does have a masculinist, warrior-style narrative), while *Safe* effectively creates haunting mise-en-scène featuring long shots of the protagonist in her suburban dwelling with eerie gray and green hues to depict her slow physical and mental deterioration.[20]

Hibakusha: At the End of the World depicts the effects of radiation poisoning on humans through comparative examination of the impacts of depleted uranium leakage on communities in three countries: Iraqi victims of depleted uranium, particularly children; nuclear bomb victims in Japan; and American women living downwind of the Hanford Nuclear Site in Washington State. She could have included so many more groups like indigenous populations subjected to depleted uranium in the American Southwest, but Kamanaka's merging of three distinct sites of radiation nevertheless trumps the geopolitics of "America versus Japan" that often frame nuclear issues. As scholar and antinuclear activist Norma Field put it, Kamanaka's films do not reduce the problem of nuclear to perpetrators and victims: "Kamanaka's films are consistently sensitive to the economic needs behind communities' acceptance of nuclear reactors: there are no simple enemies. At the same time, they urge us—urban beneficiaries of the conveniences dependent upon electricity generated in modest rural communities—to become aware of our own complicity in the structure of risk."[21] All are examples of different film techniques that visualize slow violence and anthropogenic damage to the planet.

Filmmakers not satisfied to ignore the complexities of living in an industrial age engage various strategies for making slow violence visible in order to illustrate what Linda Nash has called the most basic and primary discoveries of the twentieth century: that people are inescapably part of a larger ecosystem and the extent to which human life is vulnerable to environment is heightened under industrial modernity.[22] Ecocritic Harold Fromm put it in strikingly visual terms: "The 'environment,' as we now apprehend it, runs right through us in endless waves, and if we were to watch ourselves via some ideal microscopic time lapse video, we would see water, air, food, microbes, toxins entering our bodies as we shed, excrete, and exhale our processed materials back out."[23] Film is particularly suited to capture the environment because it can capture the environment at different scales, from the microscopic to the macroscopic.

The rest of this chapter will examine the ways in which Tsuchimoto has depicted slow violence in cinema. His films' treatment of bodies and mise-en-scène will be discussed as formal, theoretical, and social modes for depicting industrial toxins. The broader point is to illustrate how the specter of slow violence was visualized in his moving images. The filmic elements discussed in this chapter include: Tsuchimoto's avoidance of landscape shots that make the land and sea ambient; his refusal of montage and spectacle; his analytical rather than presentational approach to the body as revealed through an optics of ambulation; the lively ontology of his mise-en-scène; and the reconceptualization of the body in motion within the context of cinema history.

Optics of Ambulation

Cats were the beloved pets of Shiranui Sea denizens, as cats killed the rats who chewed holes in fishing nets. When fishing boats returned from the morning's catch, cats, along with dogs and even foxes, recognized the slow chug, chug, chug of the engines returning to port and sauntered down to the docks for fish scraps. But in the late 1950s, the cats began to die, and as the cats began to die, the rats grew in number and damaged the fishing nets. More cats were brought in to protect the nets, and they died too. As researchers tried to get a handle on why the cats were dying, they experimented on hundreds of domestic and feral cats and filmed their experiments. Donning white coats, researchers gathered at the shore to collect small clams, extracted the flesh from the shells, and placed the clam flesh in large bowlfuls in front of cats, who relished the meals but then exhibited profoundly disturbing behaviors within weeks of eating the shellfish. The toxin that polluted an entire sea and its denizens was eventually discovered through these countless experiments on cats.

Tsuchimoto uses original film footage from lab experiments on cats in his three medical documentaries (*Minamata Medical Film: A Trilogy*, 1974). Each is subtitled according to its focus: *Documents and Testimony*, *Pathology and Symptoms*, and *Clinical Practice and Epidemiology*. Scholar of Japanese media and activism Justin Jesty provides a clear analysis of the primary thrust of each of these sophisticated medical films, which use data visualization, dialogue with physicians in voice-overs, original medical film footage, and other strategies for depicting the long and arduous road to understanding the disease that afflicted particularly fish, cats, birds, and humans.[24] The first film combines the screening of original lab films of diseased cats with the filmmaker in dialogue with the physicians who filmed them. Some were of pets who had gotten the disease through their daily habit of scrounging for food and others were of subjects fed a rich shellfish diet by lab technicians in order to prove that the food source from the sea was toxic. With the eventual onset of the disease, which took hold of their bodies after a few weeks, the cats struggled to control their back legs.

They flung themselves into walls, ran willy-nilly at high gear into the ocean water, and appeared to walk on their front paws only. In one shot, the film uses entirely original film footage of a solemn looking cat lying on a red blanket hissing at a rat that had been placed between its paws. It strains to bite the rat's hairless pink tail, but its body has become a useless rag (Figures 1 and 2).

This and the original medical film of cat #400, which appear in the medical film trilogy and in Tsuchimoto's *Minatama: Victims and Their World*, are bleak shadows of the very first films of animal locomotion in early moving image technologies. Named for the "zoe" of the animal world, Eadweard James Muybridge's "zoopraxiscope" projected still images of animal locomotion from a spinning disc to create the illusion of motion. The visual magnificence of the zoopraxiscope and other early technologies was touted through images of lively animals. It was animals in cinematic motion that lead us from nature to technology, according to theorist Akira Mizuta Lippit: "Animals were particularly useful in the development of technical media because they seemed to figure a pace of communication that was both more rapid and more efficient than that of language."[25]

In early cinema, the running animal celebrated both the spectacle and the apparatus of cinema in a single, long, and unbroken motion. Muybridge's *Animals in Motion* and *The Human Figure in Motion* "display the fascination with which animals and animal movement captured the photographic imagination":

> What is remarkable in Muybridge's work, what immediately
> seizes the viewer's attention, is the relentless and obsessive man-
> ner in which the themes of animal and motion are brought into
> contact—as if the figure of the animal had always been destined
> to serve as a symbol of movement itself. The movement of
> Muybridge's animals, at first across the frames and then eventually
> the screens of a new industrial landscape . . . aided the advent of a
> new mode of representation—cinema.[26]

As analyzed by John Ott, in addition to offering a new example of the communicative possibilities of moving images in cinematic history, animal locomotion on the screen was handmaiden to industrial modernity. Ott claims that Leland Stanford and his colleagues, advocates of the animal

Figure 1. Mercury-poisoned cat and chicken (Tsuchimoto, Minamata Medical Film: Documents and Testimony, *1974).*

Figure 2. Mercury-poisoned cat and rat (Tsuchimoto, Minamata Medical Film: Documents and Testimony, *1974).*

images of Muybridge, "publicly staged and disseminated these photographs in order to consolidate, promote, and naturalise the developments
of industrial capitalism," and he continues: "At every stage of the images'
production, Stanford and his carefully chosen representatives framed,
staged, and promoted these experiments as the product of a rational, posi-
tivist science. . . . The very set-up of the camera shed and complex recording instruments recall the forum of a research laboratory, a milieu that
grew to maturity in the industrial sector in the 1870s and 1880s."[27] At the
time, Muybridge's ability to capture movement in still frames and replay
them for motion was featured in science and nature journals. He filmed
birds and animals of all kinds in motion and these became the first examples of photography and moving images to give birth to what Ott calls
an "industrial gaze." This industrial gaze observes the body as kinetic energy that could be understood through motion photography. Muybridge's
horses proved the dynamism of locomotion that was being invented in
the locomotive. The industrialized eye saw within both kinds of bodies—
horse and locomotive, animal and machine—a kineticism that would be
foundational to the new industrial order.

The Muybridge photos encouraged viewers to imagine the horse
and, by extension, all of nature as another kind of machine. The horse is
a cog in the burgeoning industrial economy for the way that the photographs show the horse in motion: "Thus these experiments did not just
prove that horses acted like bundles of gears, levers, and engines; rather,
for Stanford and his backers, they epitomised the necessity and inevitability of a new corporate industrial order buttressed by scientific authority, managerial supervision, and complex, capital-intense technologies."[28]
The industrial gaze was produced in the mechanical treatment of the body
in image. Cameras were counted and placed, and time was measured, all
to reveal the mechanism of the body through stop-motion photography
that would habituate the naked eye to new industrial optics. This, Ott argues, is the logic of the industrial gaze: the Muybridge photographs "stan-
dardised a sort of a physiological time, so to speak, by which the actions
of animals and humans could be clocked and against which they could be
measured."[29]

Early trends in cinema unanimously identified the camera as uniquely
able to capture and reveal physical reality because photography could
reproduce nature with fidelity and precision. The visual attention to the
photographs, data imagery, and microscopic image could appear as an

affirmation of positivism—an intellectual attitude that Siegfried Kracauer coincidentally described as "in perfect keeping with the ongoing processes of industrialization."[30] Scholar of early cinema Alan Williams, in an analysis of scientific records of living motion as illustrated in Mayer, Muybridge, and August Lumière, argues that living motion pieces were done not for the sake of their subjects, but rather to illustrate "the work of the apparatus itself." But the body and the apparatus were linked. The body filmed for medical studies and scientific techniques of motion recording produced a model of the body as a dynamic system. As Lisa Cartwright explains, "The film body of the motion study thus is a symptomatic site, a region invested with fantasies about what constituted 'life' for scientists and the lay public in the early twentieth century."[31] At its inception, cinema as a technology was deeply anticipated for its ability to record and reproduce a particular mechanistic form of bodily movement.

Tsuchimoto was not unfamiliar with the visual goals of contemporary industrial cinema, with its positive images of mechanization. Before his sojourn to Minamata, he made films for industrial corporations and state-funded projects as a public relations filmmaker for Iwanami Productions, filming for companies like Yawata Steel and Nissan. By the time Tsuchimoto returned to Minamata after reading *Paradise in the Sea of Sorrow,* hundreds people had been subjected to mercury poisoning. The symptoms included numbness in the extremities, narrowing of vision, and loss of control, especially in the hands and feet, and many had died. While it had been clear since 1961 that mercury was accumulating in bodies up the food chain in a process later called "bioaccumulation," the Chisso factory continued to dump effluent into the bay so that the methyl mercury was carried throughout the Shiranui Sea, poisoning various forms of life in the littoral zones and inland sea for over seventeen years. It was learned only in 1998, from the deathbed of a witness who worked at Chisso, that a 1953 change in the oxidizer used (from manganese oxide to nitric acid) had increased the amount of organic mercury emitted per year by the Chisso Corporation by tenfold to 100 kg per year. Despite decades of complaints from the fishing union, the Chisso factory had continued dumping effluent into the sea until they were forced to stop by the government in 1968. It was in this context that Tsuchimoto made his three sophisticated medical films, which explicate the complicated biology of mercury disease, used an analytic rather than presentational approach in the mise-en-scène, and developed what I call his optics of ambulation, all toward the primary point that makes these films so important for environmental justice and reparations: no body experiences the cumulative effects of mercury poisoning in the same way.

The herky-jerky movements of cats in the medical films that were edited into Tsuchimoto's own medical trilogy compare solemnly with the fluid movement of animal locomotion in early cinema. The locomotion of Minamata cats looks so unnatural that physicians watch their films over and over again for clues as to why the cats exhibit such strange movement. Tsuchimoto hardly ever uses slow motion in his films, but he occasionally slows down the original medical footage to better illustrate how impaired the village cats are. Industrial film history takes on a different cast in these moving images of the biological sentinels of industrial modernity's excesses. Animal movement, which had been so important for presenting moving image technologies as synonymous with the promises of industrial modernity can no longer do that symbolic work for the apparatus.

In addressing cinema history's fantasy of bodily movement, Georgio Agamben describes Gilles de la Tourette's 1886 studies of the human step using footprint reproductions from feet inked with iron sesquioxide powder, which stained the sole of the foot of subjects suffering from disease:

> If we observe the footprint reproductions published by Gilles de la Tourette, it is impossible not to think about the series of snapshots that Muybridge was producing in those same years at the University of Pennsylvania using a battery of twenty-four photographic lenses. "Man walking at normal speed," "running man with shotgun," "walking woman picking up a jug," "walking woman sending a kiss": these are the happy and visible twins of the unknown and suffering creatures that had left those traces.[32]

Thus, he contrasts dynamic images of Muybridge's optics of ambulation and running with images of ambulation that track a different movement. Tsuchimoto's optics of ambulation in his broad oeuvre, unlike early cinema's films of locomotion, are for the sake of the subjects represented and future victims of industrial pollution. This is particularly true of his medical films, which were disseminated to communities and universities around the world to provide visual examples of the newly revealed impact of organic mercury on bodies.

What is especially remarkable about these films, as the director of

Cinema Is about Documenting Lives: The Works and Times of Noriaki Tsuchimoto points out, is that they show that the impact of mercury was different for each body and explicitly illustrate the impossibility of treating the body as a predictable entity, particularly under industrial modernity. Tsuchimoto carefully lays out this point in the third medical film, which had tremendous implications for victims seeking compensation in order to pay for medical care. In certification exams, people were asked to perform the impossible: to behave with a kind of consistency that no body ill with mercury disease could be expected to produce. Despite the impossibility, compensation boards became increasingly rigid in certifying patients, requiring them to show five of the primary symptoms of mercury disease all at once during the certification exam, regardless of the day or time of the exam. The medical films demonstrate that such a standardizing approach was unrealistic, as no two bodies react exactly alike to mercury poisoning.[33]

Tsuchimoto's persistent attention to the difficulties patients had in being certified rested on the scientific evidence that chemical toxins react differently in every body, and he makes this point most powerfully with images of ambulating bodies that actively embed the human subject in environment. In one poignant long take in the second of the three medical films, Tsuchimoto walks with a victim of mercury disease and asks him how difficult it is to walk and to describe those difficulties to him (Figures 3, 4, and 5). This is the medical documentary loosed from its origins: a man in pain ambles along as the filmmaker asks questions and bears witness. The frustrated attempts of an afflicted man to walk are captured in a voice-over conversation between the two men as they cross a muddied field ruined by Chisso's holding ponds. A brief close-up follows the interviewee's quiet voice describing how his bodily movements are not predictable even to himself, especially when he tries to move quickly. His unsure footing, he says, leads to embarrassment. The third medical film, contains a further dialogue between Tsuchimoto and a physician who reveals, as Dr. Tokuomi does in the first film, that there is no rehabilitation. Once a cell is damaged it only deteriorates further.

Another powerful sequence in Tsuchimoto's medical film depicts footage from 1956 of a man walking through his orchard and then of the same man walking through the streets of the city of Kagoshima with a cane, having developed a way of moving relatively swiftly through the world despite the challenges of walking after having been poisoned with methyl mercury

(Figure 6). The camera follows him through a shopping arcade filmed in black and white, and then the film cuts to a shot that zooms out to a bird's-eye view of a man standing with megaphone in hand, and finally to a bird's-eye view of the expansive campus of Chisso corporation with its smoke stacks belching fire in the distance. The three connected shots are accompanied by a man's booming voice-over:

> Look at my body. When I was nineteen years old, I was afflicted with this industrial pollution disease [*kōgai byōki*]. Daily I endure the agonizing struggle with this disease and today I have come to Kagoshima on this fundraising campaign. Should we let this happen to each and every citizen, year after year? We want to show all of you directly, so that you can know of the horrors of industrial pollution and not just Minamata Disease, but the horrors of industrial pollution itself. That's why I am here.

Figure 3. Optics of ambulation: walking with mercury disease (Tsuchimoto, Minamata Medical Film: Pathology and Symptoms, *1974).*

Figure 4. Optics of ambulation: walking with mercury disease (Tsuchimoto, Minamata Medical Film: Pathology and Symptoms, 1974).

Figure 5. Optics of ambulation: walking with mercury disease (Tsuchimoto, Minamata Medical Film: Pathology and Symptoms, 1974).

Tsuchimoto's images of ambulating fishermen in pain could not be more unlike those early films so invested in marking predictable lines of movement. Visualization of life was seductive on the screen at the birth of cinematic technology, but when that life meets dangerous chemical compounds, Tsuchimoto's cinema gives us disrupted gait as the appropriate subject of the frame.

In Tsuchimoto's films, the optics of ambulation—a long take of a teen watching TV who drags his body across the tatami mat to answer the ringing phone, or a tracking shot of a young woman bustling home with the familiar jaunt of the afflicted with shopping bags in arm, or the slow water ballet of an octopus hunter filmed in underwater shots of his toes finding sturdy footing among the rocks in the shallows of the Shiranui Sea—are fundamental to his depiction of the slow violence of methyl mercury.[34] These shots of how the afflicted move as they work and pursue daily activities give expression to the toxic load that Minamata victims have been forced to bear.[35] Locomotion is not the mechanistic or reflexive movement

Figure 6. Optics of ambulation: walking with mercury disease (Tsuchimoto, Minamata Medical Film: Clinical Practice and Epidemiology, *1974).*

of early cinema, but the singular and deliberate movement of victims who bear corporate industrialism's excesses.

The Medical Gaze

Tsuchimoto expressed in large calligraphic text now hanging in the Minamata Disease Research Center that: "People cannot just live with disappointment. Minamata taught me that." Tsuchimoto's portraits of daily life create an optics of ambulation for which physical movement is unique to each body. Attending to normal patterns of daily life was essential because to speak only of tragedy, danger, and illness is to engage in what Hidaka Rokurō called, in 1975, "pollution sadism" (*kōgai sadizumu*), which determines that the greater the increase in people who suffer from pollution, or the greater the suffering, the easier the political movement to end it. This, Hidaka says, is a perverse logic that reduces life to a pessimistic apocalyptic vision or misplaced optimistic hope for rebirth.[36]

Tsuchimoto's approach in these films is to edit and include the bounty of over four hundred 8 mm and 16 mm medical films (*igaku eiga* and *igaku kiroku*) and to interview the recorders, who were often physicians, as they watched the films together.[37] Itō Hasuo from the Kumamoto Hygiene department and Dr. Harada Masazumi, a researcher at Kumamoto University who spent decades working with Minamata patients, are animated in their descriptions of the patients they filmed. While Tsuchimoto is often included within the frame engaging them in conversation, the camera zooms in and out of the original medical film as they are screened on the physician's wall. Other times, the camera is focused on a physician who is barely visible in the dark of the screening room. The projector hums in the background, but the camera does not return to the screen of the medical film.

As Tsuchimoto witnesses the physician/researcher watch his original medical films, the close relationship of the researcher to his patient is evident. The medical films seem almost a kind of home movie for these physicians. Itō is initially quiet until the patients begin to appear and then he begins calling out their names and talking about them fondly: "Oh that's the child of Matsuda. Oh, that's Mayumi-chan! She . . ."; or "Oh there's Tanaka-san. He . . ." Tsuchimoto learns about the patients from these early researchers who worked particularly hard to create a record of the circumstances, symptoms, and patient narratives in order to solve the riddle that mercury poisoning originally was. Harada was particularly active in his efforts to listen to the victims in solving what came to be revealed as a Chisso cover-up.

Tsuchimoto made his medical films to provide an explanation of the ecological and physiological pathways that caused mercury disease for both the victims of mercury poisoning themselves and specialists. The rash of requests for the medical films from various universities in Japan and around the world after the screening of *Minamata: Victims and Their World* at the United Nations in 1972 proved the films were a valuable resource as medical documents. But the three films are not without "excess" in the sense that they include shots of patients in their daily life, in intimate interviews, and in scenes of political action, such as a contentious meeting with the certification committee that would vote on whether a petitioning disease victim would be confirmed as an official victim of mercury poisoning.

The soundtrack of sympathetic physicians and researchers explaining the original medical footage in conversation with Tsuchimoto is a significant reworking of those original films because it shows the deep concern on the part of the medical community to discover the root of the illness, the politics of compensation, and the struggle for just recognition of Chisso's culpability. While the original films appear to insensitively objectify the earliest victims of mercury poisoning, they were made to discover the symptoms of an unknown disease. Nevertheless, the embedding of the original medical films into a larger narrative fruitfully compromises them. In the intermedial space of Tsuchimoto's medical films, there is no objective perspective on the illness. His films provide supplementary discourses that personalize the visual intensity of the original films of the earliest deeply ill patients who could hardly control their hands and bodies, supplementing them with an explicit interpretation through conversations with patients and physicians.

And, as stated earlier, Tsuchimoto sometimes does not even bother to show the original footage, keeping the camera trained instead on the physician's or researcher's face in the dark of the screening room. The original medical footage is no longer the sole object in the frame and this interrupts the medical gaze. The introduction of multiple speakers within the film space of original medical film footage diminishes the sense of intrusion that the original medical films inevitably create with such long takes of the uncontrollable seizures of victims of mercury disease in the final weeks or even days before death. In this way, Tsuchimoto's medical films involve a complicated character proxemics that cites medical footage not as unassailable data, but as contextualized medical gaze. The framing of original medical film recordings through a focus on the humans viewing those films affirms cinema as a site of active analysis rather than the presentation of scientific fact and observation found in conventional medical films. This revision and historicization of the medical gaze is another aspect through which Tsuchimoto films slow violence.

Social Ecology

Tsuchimoto's long-term travel through the bays and hamlets of the sparkling Shiranui Sea anchors his visual capture of slow violence. Each film is dedicated to a different aspect of the long history of discovering and then living with a terribly debilitating disease: the efforts of fishermen to earn a living on a toxic sea; the daily struggles of victims of mercury poisoning to claim compensation; the activism of those seeking justice; the artwork to which the travesty gave rise. As a whole, the seventeen films he made over the course of over thirty years exhibit a rare commitment to an ecological problem that is continual, everchanging, and varied in its presentation of mercury's effects on a wide range of bodies in terms of size, age, species, and location. This commitment was not lost on the people of Minamata. At his eulogy, marking fifty-three years since his first trip to Minamata, they sprinkled his ashes in the Shiranui Sea. Fisherman Ogata Masato recalled that Tsuchimoto had a penetrating gaze, not only into the eyes the people but also toward the sea. By taking such a long-term view of mercury poisoning, Tsuchimoto relieved himself of the need as a filmmaker to drive his story toward an artificial conclusion that could never exist for the victims anyway.

Tsuchimoto's long-term dedication to the problem of industrial pollution is one straightforward way that he attended to slow violence in cinema: he simply filmed the environmental disaster for decades. But there are other ways that we can consider his filmmaking to have addressed slow violence, ways that are more broadly relevant to film theory and the problem of environmental pollution. As Ivakhiv explains it, there are two angles from which we can consider ecological issues in film. One primarily addresses how the health of an environment is depicted in cinema in "shopworn clichés that populate the modern environmental imaginary . . . [and] typically counterposes a positive or ecotopian imaginary to a neg-

ative, dystopian and apocalyptic one. The former inspires, while the latter enjoins us to action or to despair."[38] These are the kinds of images that
Nixon appears to critique when he says that the media cannot capture the
slow violence to land and sea. They are the kinds of images that reduce
complex ecological problems to emotion and spectacle. An examination of
an "ecology of images," on the other hand, includes "much broader kinds
of relations—social, economic, political, ethical, and technological—
surrounding the production, circulation, and consumption of images."[39]
Following Félix Guattari's notion of "three ecologies," Ivakhiv divides the
broad category of "ecology of images" into three smaller categories: the
material, social, and mental (or perceptual).[40] "Material ecologies" concern the raw materials and physical objects that are used in the production
of the object seen by movie viewers, "which span the entire production
cycle from the ecosystems and factories where minerals, plastics, silicon
chips, and other resources are extracted, processed, and manufactured, to
the locations and sets where narrative ideas and shooting scripts are shot
and crafted into cinematic works, which are then distributed and viewed,
with waste products emerging at each stop of the way."[41] The "social ecology" includes how people are brought together through film "for commer-
cially or artistically productive work or for recreation, social mobilization,
and other purposes."[42] I might also call this a political ecology for the way
that the communities created around the film are also political in how they
"raise questions about differential access to production, consumption, interpretation, and control."[43]

From my perspective, the material and social are deeply linked, but in
order to bridge a perceptual gap that might be produced in positing the
first two categories of the material (biophysical world) and social (culture), Ivakhiv follows Guattari in introducing the third ecology: the "mental" or "perceptual." The mental or perceptual ecology is introduced to
suggest an "intermediary register." It is "the interactive dimension through
which a world comes into being for world-bearing beings."[44] This perceptual dimension is meant to intervene so that how the film shapes the world
cannot be explained solely through perspectives produced out of the circulation of "image-commodities." In a short critique of Jonathan Beller's
The Cinematic Mode of Production, Ivakhiv writes:

> Beller's analysis [of cinema as an "attention economy" that man-
> ages its viewers], like other Marxist analyses, posits such an
> overwhelming level of coordination between the parts—the

material-economic, the social, and the perceptual—that little room
is left for understanding how change occurs or how people, indi-
vidually or in groups, can act to ameliorate the world from within
the conditions that determine them. Furthermore, these analyses
do not sufficiently discriminate between the studio-centred "classical Hollywood mode of production" and the more hybrid modes.[45]

The ecocritical angle that Ivakhiv intends to pursue through his use of the
conceptual ecology of images is to introduce a more material dimension
into film criticism and to do so in a way that can account for the ecocritical
import of what filmmakers do.[46]

Ivakhiv's concept of the social ecology of film suggests that examining
how Tsuchimoto's films traveled constitutes an important aspect of his
professional response to slow violence. *Minamata: Victims and Their World*
(shortened from 167 minutes to 120 minutes for international release)
was shown at Stockholm's first United Nations Human Environment
Convention in June of 1972 and took Tsuchimoto, Minamata disease victims Hamamoto Tsuginori, Sakamoto Fujie, and Sakamoto Shinobu, and
Dr. Harada to Europe. In the ensuing months, Tsuchimoto was asked to
screen the film in China, North Korea, Paris, London, Rome, Hamburg,
Moscow, and elsewhere. He visited more than ten countries and held 163
screenings in less than two years. Today, the initial environmental conference at the UN is considered to have been the start of a global environmental movement and to have had a tremendous impact on future environmental protection policies.[47] Harking back to this legacy of mercury
toxicity, 140 nations, again at Stockholm on January 19, 2013, agreed to a
range of limitations on mercury use in products and in gold-mining, to developing appropriate waste facilities for disposing of the toxic substances,
and to ending the export for profit of mercury waste. This agreement has
been named the "Minamata Convention on Mercury" (which is not un-
controversial, since many in Minamata prefer to build a new legacy for
Minamata as a green city).

Tsuchimoto made his medical films after the UN trip to provide further detail about the disease. Upon completion, they were sent to hundreds of medical institutions around the world that had requested them
and functioned as resources for understanding the etiology of mercury
disease, its personal and social impacts on victims, and the difficulties en-
countered in certification tests. However, while in conversation with an

old widower on one of the Shiranui Sea's more distant islands, Tsuchimoto found that his most important audience—the potentially afflicted—had not seen the films. As he tells the story in the film *Record at the Heart of Adversity,* Tsuchimoto met a man in Goshonoura whose wife's hair had shown 920 parts-per-million (50 was the level at which Minamata disease was determined to have officially set in, although many victims showed symptoms at a lower ppm rate). She had had no contact with physicians or authorities concerned for her and other fishing families' welfare. Her husband, then an old man who had watched her die, said to Tsuchimoto: "Minamata disease? Who knew about Minamata disease? I'd never heard of it. I didn't know if it was a cold or what. After I saw it on TV I thought— What?! That's the same thing my wife had!" Tsuchimoto recalled, "I was stabbed in the chest by his remarks."[48]

In response, Tsuchimoto put together a staff of five and developed a map for screening his films for locals. He traced a circle in the bay with a radius of thirty kilometers and determined his screening sites to be as frequent as a single bus stop away so that anyone could attend: those who could not walk could get there by a short bus ride. The screening tour's name was a homonym for "religious pilgrimage" but used the Sino-Japanese characters meaning, instead, "sea pilgrimage."[49] Tsuchimoto planned to take his films to what he called the coastal and island "nether regions" (*ankokubu*) of Minamata's polluted areas. In calling these areas "nether regions" he was being neither derogatory nor assuming that these were unenlightened areas. Rather, he pointed to the fact that scientific discourse of Minamata disease had not yet arrived in these places, to the detriment of fishing families.[50]

The months-long film tour screened medical films to those who most needed to see them. These areas were inhabited by people who exhibited some of the highest levels of toxicity ever witnessed because, as Tsuchimoto illustrates in his medical film trilogy, they had been living off of the Shiranui Sea's bounty throughout the decades of its highest levels of toxicity. Even if they had known the high levels of toxicity of Shiranui's waters, these fishing folk living on small islands had little land for farming. As two older women in one medical documentary put it: "There's nothing else to eat. The sea's all we've got." While the Chisso corporation would have an investment in keeping victim numbers lower, and while many residents did not want to face the discrimination of being a Minamata disease victim, Tsuchimoto wanted to avoid even one case of unrecognized toxicity by arming potential victims with knowledge of the disease. Therefore, he created a perceptual field for invisible toxicity through various techniques, including early forms of data visualization, film footage of certification tests, and so on. The importance of visual evidence for diagnosing the disease is depicted in one dramatic scene in which Tsuchimoto presses an island physician on how he could properly diagnose a person if he had never made an effort to see a case of Minamata disease on the mainland. These films were intended to help locals identify disease for health care and compensation because, from 1956 to 1977, physicians, especially epidemiologists, had taken samples only from specific points in the region.[51] Furthermore, even after hidden data of hair mercury levels had been released and the hygiene ministry estimated that between 10,000 and 15,000 people were affected by organic mercury, no active measures had been taken.[52]

By traveling to one hundred venues, Tsuchimoto created the conditions for people to identify themselves as a community of people who were all potentially afflicted. This is another social ecological aspect of his filmmaking. He also discovered in his film-screening tour of the islands (begun on August 1, 1977, in famed people's historian Irokawa Daikichi's Volkswagon van) people who felt they had been discriminated against in their lack of information about the disease and lack of official recognition as victims of the disease because they lived so far from Minamata: "It's like racial prejudice," they said in a filmed interview.[53] By expanding his audience to include the local population, it became clear the degree to which mercury disease affected so many more fishing families beyond the villages near the Chisso factory, including those living on the islands ringing the far corners of Shiranui Sea. This is the mental ecology produced by the pilgrimage. His medical trilogy gave witness to the psychology and position of victims long after Chisso's culpability had been established. This is also what makes Tsuchimoto's medical documentaries such a clear example of the visual witnessing of slow violence: they document the symptoms and history of a toxic event that had already lasted more than two decades and would continue to impact fishing families. The sheer detail and information included in them required a Herculean effort of organization and persistent checks on the narrating physicians to keep them from introducing mind-numbing jargon so that the films could fulfill their function as educational films.

The film tour addresses slow violence by meticulously tracking the pollution throughout the region in film and literally carrying the films to those places. The screening tour's expressed material and social ecologies put pressure on a familiar pattern that was emerging: the marginalization of certain types of victims. Those with "lighter symptoms" or those newly recognized as sufferers, or those who did not live in Minamata city, or those who lived in Kagoshima prefecture, or those who lived in Amakusa and outlying islands, or those whose disease was discovered outside of the original region where Minamata disease was first discovered, or those who did not exhibit all five symptoms of the disease—all of these people were acknowledged far less frequently by the medical community. In traveling to outlying areas, the "nether regions," Tsuchimoto reported that the outlying islanders had experienced some of the highest rates of mercury poisoning (based on hair analysis) because they had never refrained from eating fish. Tsuchimoto surmised that it took ten years for knowledge of the disease to reach ten kilometers from what he called "Minamata ground zero." It took twenty years for word of the disease to travel twenty kilometers from ground zero. This is why the hair samples of fisherfolk furthest out from Minamata showed the highest levels of mercury toxicity. Tsuchimoto called this "criminal negligence" toward fishermen at the margins (*shūhen gyomin*).

The medical films served as a record of violence by government and corporations. Victims armed with knowledge gleaned from watching Tsuchimoto's medical films, even in the face of a denial for compensation (which became increasingly common), would have the confidence and courage to go back for more testing time and again to eventually get certified. Tsuchimoto's efforts to create his medical films as reliable historical resources rather than films woven together by an "image author" (*eizō sakka*) meant avoiding montage. Shots are sutured through simple, predictable cuts.

While the medical films use data visualization rather sparingly, charts are employed in the third film to plot the dip in the number of patients certified with the disease. This kind of data visualization is a clear strategy to make visible, as a cinema of slow violence will, the culprits who perpetuate environmental injustices. At a public screening of his medical documentaries, Tsuchimoto revealed that at least one medical personnel stated in 1960 that Minamata disease was over. For eight years, only congenital cases were admitted. At one point, Dr. Harada resigned from the certification process in protest because the board was not certifying those with compromised health.

To keep these gatekeepers honest, as described in the medical documentaries themselves, Tsuchimoto made and screened these medical films using archival footage from the 1950s–60s and new footage he created himself between the 1960s and the 1970s to provide a record that would disprove any claim by specialists that new cases had not emerged since the 1960s. What one chart shows is that, by 1972, sixteen years after the first recorded case of mercury poisoning and after the culprit Chisso Corporation was finally indicted and a compensation system set up for victims, the number of those certified decreased! Since 1953, physicians had become the ones to distribute compensation money through the certification committee, and at some point, the committee became quite stingy with their results. As one victim put it in the third medical film, "It became harder to pass a certification exam than to pass a college entrance exam to Tokyo University" (and only about one high school student went to Tokyo University every twenty years according to Ishimure). One patient depicted in Tsuchimoto's third medical documentary had given up on going to the board, and he was not alone: many went back three or four times before being confirmed, if at all. The third film documents the various tests of vision, hearing, and sensitivity in the extremities (Figure 7).

Tsuchimoto's medical films document physicians and researchers before and after they had been co-opted by the registration and certification system so that his footage could remind the physicians of their roots. The second medical film is dedicated in part to the work of this same Dr. Takeuchi Tadao, who had taken a wide perspective on who qualified as a victim of mercury poisoning, naming thousands on the shores of Shiranui Sea as victims. He was the chair of the board of petition claims but was eventually ousted from the certification board, after which the criteria for qualifying for compensation became much more rigid. Dr. Takeuchi had researched the pathology of Minamata disease for seventeen years and used microphotography to convey his results in medical footage. In the third film in particular, the increased difficulty in being certified as a victim of Minamata disease is depicted through interviews with multiple victims. Voice-over narration explains how one of the physicians most dedicated to getting certification for victims was ousted.

Tsuchimoto's early philosophy of filmmaking as expressed in his

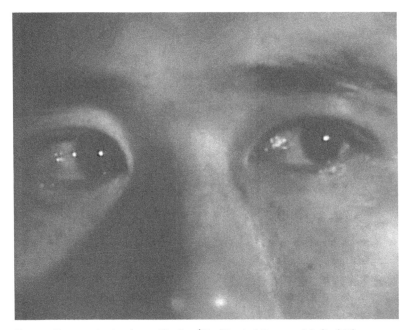

Figure 7. Eye examination for certification (Tsuchimoto, Minamata Medical Film: Clinical Practice and Epidemiology, *1974).*

"What Should Film Do?" argues that film will never relieve anyone's pain. Therefore, empathy is not truth. The most affective visual and narrative modes by which he effectively gets at what he called "the real image" are, to my mind, the ways in which he films the slow violence of mercury poisoning through an optics of ambulation, through an embedded medical gaze, and attention to the social ecology of his films.

Mushroom Clouds on Paper

Tsuchimoto's film on nuclear technology takes a different tack from the medical films in representing slow violence, perhaps because the media context for representing radiation was so different. Radiation had long been linked to the sensational image of the mushroom cloud, which came to be one of the most ubiquitous icons of violence and power in film history. It is an icon of U.S. military power and the ressentiment of a once occupied nation. It is the icon of a cold war–era struggle for global domination and the destruction of South Pacific islands. In apocalyptic cinema, it also serves as an ominous symbol of our capacity as humans to annihilate everything we have known, including ourselves.[54] But the bomb's iconic capacity to depict total annihilation when actually deployed in war overshadows the kinds of slow violence that occur as a result of this technology in other arenas, including bomb testing. Plants, animals, soldiers, and countless communities and environments in the South Pacific have been subjected to radiation from over one thousand U.S. bomb tests in the atmosphere, on the earth's surface, on boats and barges, and underwater. Ever since the first bomb test on July 16, 1945, on the Alamogordo Air Force Base in New Mexico, indigenous communities and environments have suffered from radiation exposure. Yet these communities have featured little in moving images. Nixon asks a fair question in his *Slow Violence*: how often have the Marshall islanders, who have borne the impact of sixty-seven atmospheric nuclear tests, been represented in film? How often does film depict jellyfish babies who live for only a few hours after their birth because of the severe defects suffered as a result of radiation?[55] Meanwhile, the repetitive use of the iconic mushroom cloud in the visual arts has diluted it of semantic power. Artist Kyo Maclear writes: "Hiroshima's Mushroom Cloud, while periodically stamped with fierce meaning, has also inspired as much trite imagery as any other twentieth-century phenomenon.... The collective shiver once induced by this image has passed into a pervasive sense of ennui."[56]

Tsuchimoto's *Nuclear Scrapbook* (1982) is an astute representation of the slow violence of radiation, for its utter lack of action and stifling of movement. A forty-six-minute film presenting articles about nuclear bomb tests and the dumping of nuclear waste, it simply presents shot after shot of thirty-seven years' worth of newspaper articles about radiation-related events around the world. Occasionally, a hand holding a pair of scissors cuts out an article or words are highlighted on the screen, but otherwise, the film is composed entirely of words on the newspaper page, stories chosen from over 10,000 articles collected by Tsuchimoto and his crew. The repetitive shots of the yellowing pages of newspaper articles about nuclear bombs, bomb testing, nuclear power, and nuclear waste from 1945 to 1982 make the point that nuclear bombs and nuclear power are "the same thing" (*onaji shitsu*). The two bombs dropped on Japan by the United States are featured only briefly. Rather, articles presented on screen feature bomb tests in the Marshall Islands, the dumping of nuclear waste off the Tsugaru peninsula, Three-Mile Island leakage, the exposure of Americans to bomb tests at the Nevada Yucca Flats test site, nuclear test sites in Asia, Japan's attempt to export nuclear power into Asia, Japanese and U.S. government plans to dump radioactive waste in the islands of the South Pacific, and the planned construction of dozens of reactors in Japan.

Time is compressed in shot after shot of newspaper print, itself a medium that explicitly indexes time and depends on the passage of time as a medium. In the pamphlet for this film, Tsuchimoto addressed the problem of time, saying that Pacific islanders and American soldiers who had been exposed in the south Pacific "had within their bodies a scary ticking time bomb."[57] The time gap between the onset of symptoms and death was long for some. A Canadian nuclear gypsy with cancer is depicted in the film as the first human facing death by a nuclear power industry that calls itself "safe." That 1961 article is sutured to other articles about those ill or dead from leukemia caused by Bikini Island bomb tests. These shots of newspaper articles are not invested in depicting the original site of nuclear exposure or a mimetic representation of that moment. Rather, they produce the passage of time through the filmed textuality of the newspaper page. The two-dimensionality of the newspaper interrupts the indexicality of the filmic image.[58]

An occasional zoom-out captures a half page of the newspaper in a single shot. A zoom-in allows for the reading of nine or so lines. The newspaper articles, sometimes yellow with age, are accompanied by a voice-over narration by Ozawa Shōichi, who provides a stream of details on nuclear bombs, power, and waste, such as the facts that, from 1976 to the present, 300,000 drums of radioactive waste have been piled in Shimatsu and that 1700 drums of radioactive waste were dumped in the Sagami and Suruga bays between 1955 and 1970. The article headlines appear in various areas of the screen and multiply as the shots pile one upon another. They read: "Cobalt 60 / Cesium 137: Fears that Seafood is Affected,"; "Concentrations 32 Times Normal"; "Radioactive Waste"; "Seafloor Pollution"; "Oil Drum Leaks?: Detected in Suruga Bay"; and so on. This multifaceted perspective greatly expands the sense of who is a perpetrator when it comes to the release of radiation. The Japanese nation-state is no victim in this stream of articles about various forms of nuclear technology.

The panoply of stories about all things nuclear is sutured together through two words: "radioactivity" and "radiation."[59] Radioactivity, that invisible thing, takes shape over and over again through textual image.

Tsuchimoto called the newspaper page presented on screen a "picture" (*e*).[60] The articles are visually sutured by a series of loose match cuts on the word "radiation" in newspaper print such that the word on the page becomes the synecdoche for a web of toxic communities and many sovereign powers not linked by a single event but by the slow spread of a deadly technology turned into a toxic drift. The film also shows that some victims of nuclear bombs have become supporters of nuclear power.

Stylistically, the film could not be less spectacular. The politics of Tsuchimoto's visually unremarkable film of newspaper clippings lie precisely in the film's strict refusal of visual spectacle. (Figures 8 and 9). The iconic mushroom cloud, when it does appear, is a blurry faded photograph among a sea of newspaper lines. The slow violence of radiation is instead depicted in a multiplicity of shots of newspaper articles about a range of victims from various nations and climates. Both the United States and Japan are shown to be complicit in spreading nuclear contamination and ill health at multiple international sites. If one shot lingers on the newspaper photo of an American military soldier with a hand swollen beyond the size of a football from radiation poisoning who is traveling to Japan for aid, the next features a story about the fact that half the film crew for the American film *The Conquerer,* shot near the Yucca Flats test site (with Genghis Khan played by John Wayne), have died from cancer. The shutdown of the Three Mile Island to fix a coolant leak is depicted freshly through its connection to an earlier shot of Bikini Island victims of bomb testing.

The drama of the film, such as it is, rests in the highlighting of words and phrases on screen, the theatrical voice-over of Ozawa, and the hard plucked strings of a guitar. In their visual repetition, the articles of the daily press levy proof that the proliferation of nuclear power plants has not been the result of an off-screen movement or a secret development. It has been a public project all along, a "project of mimesis" in the public arena. As nuclear literature scholar John Treat points out, "The rationale for their proliferation is not governed by the logic of market economics, nor is it mere proof of technological prowess; rather it has to do with Japan's assignment within the post-1945 American world order to redouble the pace of its modernization as a project of mimesis."[61] In this context, the project of mimesis is the scourge of construction of nuclear power plants, which constitute yet another example of the built scapes of agricultural, industrial, and energy technologies that get mimetically multiplied in global modernity.[62]

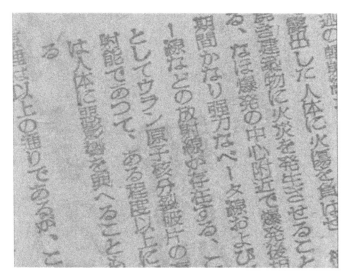

Figure 8. One of tens of shots of newspaper articles in postwar Japanese newspapers featuring the term "radiation." This one refers to the first atomic bomb dropped in Hiroshima. (Tsuchimoto, Nuclear Scrapbook, *1982).*

Figure 9. One of tens of shots of newspaper articles in postwar Japanese newspapers featuring the term "radiation." This one refers to radiation exposure at Three Mile Island and bottlenecked traffic as evacuees fled the area. (Tsuchimoto, Nuclear Scrapbook, *1982).*

The film's patient and meticulous history of the introduction of a new public vocabulary for the burgeoning nuclear industry clearly reveals how complicit the media was in the the Japanese state's determination to be the leader in nuclear sales in East Asia through a new kind of so-called "co-prosperity" sphere. Without making too powerful a suggestion of continuity, the film begins with descriptions of the Hiroshima bomb and concludes with Japan's postwar colonialist endeavor whereby it sells nuclear plant parts and technology to its Asian neighbors. One shot cuts to a newspaper photograph of Indigenous children and adults on a Pacific beach while Ozawa's voice-over narration explains the resistance to Japan's dumping of radioactive waste by people in southern islands, especially Guam and the Marianas. Ozawa's narration also treats the sea as victim: "The victim of this dumping is the Pacific. The arrogance of the Japanese state that tried to force a dangerous load onto the weak met with resistance and criticism from the Pacific islanders."

The political and technological mimesis of the cold war that deeply impacted "ecosystem people" who subsist on land and water are all "indexed" through the word "radiation."[63] In other words, *Nuclear Scrapbook* makes no attempt to visually reproduce the pain and damage of radiation on bodies and the oceans in a mimetic sense. The impossibility of such a project lies first in the problem of measuring internal radiation and the delay of symptoms from the contaminant. Given the impossibility of mimetic representation, the newspaper page and the textual image of "radiation" and "radioactivity" served to represent the slow violence of radiation on bodies.

On Mise-en-scène

In this last section of my discussion of Tsuchimoto's filmic approaches to slow violence, I address the lively ontology presented in the mise-en-scène of another film that features a two-dimensional medium. His 1981 film *Minamata Mural* documents the creation of a very sizable new work by two artists, Maruki Iri and Maruki Toshi, both nominated for the Nobel Peace Prize in 1995, who had been painting giant murals of wartime atrocities in human history, including the aftermath of the bomb dropped on Hiroshima, the Rape of Nanjing, and death camps at Auschwitz. In *Minamata Mural*, the Marukis turn to a different kind of atrocity. The film begins with artist Iri describing his efforts to paint watercolors of the

Shiranui Sea. As he looks out at the Shiranui Sea with a slim paint brush held loosely in his hand, Iri explains that his experience in Minamata fundamentally changed his approach to painting. He admits that he was wrong when he thought he could paint Minamata through its landscape (*fūkei*). He could not. His wife, Toshi, was even more stymied at the prospect of representing Minamata in painting and describes her dilemma as an artist in the language of "slow violence." Reflecting on the other murals she and Iri painted of violent events in human history, she says that what made Minamata different was not the violence of the crime, but that it played out over such a long swath of time: "Minamata is Hiroshima in slow motion . . . Hiroshima was awful, Nanjing was awful, and Auschwitz was awful. Then I went to Minamata where slowly, slowly [*yukkuri, yukkuri*], terrible things occurred. Hiroshima was a nuclear bomb. The form [that violence] takes in Minamata is not a bomb that blows up in an instant [*shunkan*]. The same victims emerge, but they emerge over a long period of time." Toshi explains that conventional affective modes for depicting violence could not work for Minamata: "I traveled around to victims' houses and I met them and watched them closely. They were really innocent. What do they see, where we see nothing? When they didn't know what expression to make, it seemed they had a deep melancholy about them. They laughed, but they didn't just laugh. It seemed they had a lot going on in their heads."

In this film, Tsuchimoto witnesses the efforts of these two artists to portray the poisoning of a sea and its denizens over decades of history. As the camera passes over the mural, a long, original poem is narrated by Ishimure.[64] The camera focuses steadily on Toshi's brush, which moves in deliberate motions, creating clean, slightly uneven black lines, and her skill as a painter of figures is captured in close-ups of inky black birds and crabs on their backs. The film revels in close-ups. One giant close-up of a cat's white eye that is missing a pupil is viewed so closely as to reveal the tiny holes of the Japanese paper on which the mural is painted, giving the impression of a translucent, milky eye. The white eyes of humans, also without pupils, stare out of the mural as Ishimure's voice-over recites a poem of living things who want to live but are shut tight in a sarcophagus of death. This is a reference to the huge reclamation project by Chisso that trapped millions of organisms and their habitats in the most toxic parts of the bay in large drums. The poem describes the living creatures as buried alive and their torment as a restless sleep of the dead. Crooked fingers and bent bodies and saliva dripping from the mouths of babes, drawn in charcoal black, are also depicted in extreme close-ups. Countless octopuses float in the air in an inversion of sea and sky that represents the topsy-turvy world perpetrated by Chisso. Each body part, each animal, and each eye will be impossible to see up close like this once the enormous mural is hung.

The film's critique of slow violence lies in this intimate mise-en-scène that records in the simple materials of ink and water the people, organisms, and sea in a consistently inclusive frame. The two-dimensionality of the mural helps draw attention to the trophic connection from water to algae to fish to human. In this two-dimensional medium depicted in black and white, landscape cannot be ambient. The film, therefore, contains no "good shot" of an aestheticized landscape. One of Tsuchimoto's oft quoted points is that "film is a work of living things." As Jesty describes in his discussion of Minamata disease, in Tsuchimoto's cinema, this reference to living things is a way of approaching film production as a product of relationships: "Rather than in the authorial/technical procedures of cutting and splicing, films work took place in the specific relationships and interactions among living things."[65] One of his cohort called Tsuchimoto's filmmaking "symbiotic" in the sense that he and the subject of the frame worked organically to produce shots. But this interpretation of his relationship as a documentarian to his subject still depends on a dichotomy of the subject of human gaze and the person or object on which the gaze lands. I would suggest that Tsuchimoto's comment that film is a work of living things is better read through the rich life depicted in his mise-en-scène. The "world" of his first film's title, *Minamata: Victims and Their World,* suggests that all of the elements of the mise-en-scène are integral to each other from an ontological point of view. In *Minamata Mural,* Toshi's carefully drawn figures of humans and animals, fish and cats, are on the same plane. The film captures her exquisite detailed drawings, which are then covered by a dark wash spread over the line drawing by Iri. Nearly every figure is caught up in his wash, and it suddenly appears to be a metaphor for the shared experience of the denizens of the Shiranui Sea who have been subjected to the same toxic drift, though Iri used this method in earlier murals.

This dark wash that captures every creature and entity within it denies the ability for landscape to function as ambient space. The mise-en-scène here becomes an ontologically rich site in which fish, animals, and humans float together on a two-dimensional plane. In such an approach to mise-en-scène, landscape is not imagined as fundamentally stable for human culture to draw upon for its actions. The slowly moving camera is not put in service to any particular *ethnos* or *anthropos*, but rather expresses the affinities among the range of bodies on the mural, which becomes the film screen. Each mise-en-scène, each shot of the mural, contains a diverse ontology that includes sea and sky, organisms and toxins. The memorable two-dimensional mesh of the mural so emphasized in close-ups reduces syntagmatic approaches to film like the constructing of atomistic character, humanistic meaning, humanistic gaze, and a suturing of image to human gaze. A critique of slow violence, in this film, takes form in the close-ups of human and nonhuman figures on the mural and on the screen representing the intimate trophic connections of fish, cats, and people.

CHAPTER 3

Res Nullius

The Domestic Turn in Environmental Literature

Don't call Tokyo the center . . .

That's right . . . The village is our capital.
For starters, if Tokyo is the center
What center is that?
Whose center is that?
The plot they've hatched there
Makes it increasingly hard for us to survive . . .

Why do you revere that Tokyo?
Why do you set out for that Tokyo? . . .
Spit on the phantasm of the center
Live in the original capital
In the hollow of the bellflower
The allusive feeling of this season
The quiet morning
Entrust your body to that quiet sunset . . .

—Kusano Hisao, "The Center Is Here"

O N MARCH 23, 2015, seventy-two-year-old Endō Shōei did what many environmental refugees of Fukushima do nowadays: he looked at his old home from Google's street view. After the meltdown of the Fukushima Daiichi reactors, his home in Futaba was designated an "area to which it is difficult to return" for the high levels of radiation fallout.[1] The vague appellation makes it hard for the displaced to sue for damages to their land and homes though hundreds have already begun the process. Endō built his family home in 1983 by financing it with wages earned working on engineering projects for the newly resident Tokyo Electric Power Company (TEPCO). The family gave up farming when TEPCO purchased the family farm in 1964. As Endō put it, "Once construction starts, there's no need to work away from home, so everyone happily sold their land."[2] The nuclear power plants offered a chance to avoid seasonal labor and maintain healthy populations in the village towns rather than lose young workers to the siren call of the nation's capital. Now, years later, Endō and his wife have evacuated 1,200 kilometers from their home and moved four times in as many years.

Driven by economic hardship in depopulated communities, farmers and rural dwellers around the globe have accepted toxic industries in their communities. Recently in New York state, fracking has become an example of a controversial energy industry whose local backers show their support by critiquing urban elites. When New York governor Andrew Cuomo banned fracking in the state early in 2015, fifteen New York towns threatened to secede from the state and join neighboring Pennsylvania where, they argued, fracking has turned fiscally ailing small towns into thriving communities. The threat of secession from the keystone state was far-fetched, but they levied it against those they referred to as "New York City environmentalists" out of a sense of economic crisis.[3] It is one of countless stories in which the economic health of rural communities is framed through a dialectical relation with the urban.[4]

This chapter examines how spatial relations in environmental writing change the sense of who is vulnerable to environmental toxins. The first spatial relation considered here is the dialectic of the rural and the urban, familiar in the work of such writers as Raymond Williams, Wendell Berry, and Vandana Shiva. The other spatial imagination discussed is that which potentially collapses the rural/urban dialectic, that of domestic space, as expressed in Ariyoshi Sawako's 1975 novel *Cumulative Pollution*. Through an analysis of spaciality in *Cumulative Pollution,* I illustrate how the domestic use of industrial and agricultural chemicals in industrial modernity essentially dissolves the rural and urban dialectic that is such an essential aspect of postwar ecocriticism.

"The Village Women Can't Sleep"

In the wake of nuclear meltdown, Kainuma Hiroshi, sociologist and Fukushima resident, published his controversial study *On "Fukushima":*

The Birth of a Nuclear Village, which explains his view for why rural areas took on the risk of nuclear power. Kainuma argues that one of the reasons for accepting the risk of nuclear meltdown was to create the rural town or village in the image of the metropole in a process of "self-colonization."[5] Nuclear power plants and other industrial sites built in northeastern Japan are, according to Kainuma (himself from a so-called nuclear village), symbolic of an internal transformation and subjugation.[6] The success of this self-colonization is realized when the act of working with metropole authorities is considered a success for the locals. To avoid deep poverty and out of a desire for parity with urban dwellers, nuclear villages accepted the burden of producing energy for metropoles and national economies. It is not an unfamiliar scenario. Ishimure Michiko addressed this dynamic when she described the fishermen's embrace of the Chisso factory: "Though few of them had any desire to work at the Chisso plant, they felt that even living on the city's periphery like oysters and barnacles clinging to rocks in the sea would make them part of a cosmopolitan scene. And although they themselves did not work for Chisso, they took pride in the plant as it grew larger and more imposing. They would gaze at it proudly from their boats when they were out fishing."[7] The factory song that Ishimure sang as a child in the 1930s of a smoky sky that melted into the dream of a small village treated the new industry as a chance to enjoy "the capital" in their own backyard. She recalls, "The deep-grassy village heart, like that of a virgin girl, mistook the figure of modern industrial capital as clouds or mist and even sang of it in a children's whimsical song."[8] With alarming consistency, rural communities beyond the archipelago, eager to lift themselves out of poverty and keep youth home rather than send them off to the metropole for education and employment, build their own capital by inviting industry in.

Labor scholar and antinuclear activist Norma Field refers to the problem driving acceptance of long-term environmental exposures to toxins in order to be financially solvent as a case of "disassociation of life from livelihood." Her example is nuclear villages in Japan where "radiation exposure to their long-term health (life) is taken on in order to gain sustenance (livelihood) for today and tomorrow." As Field notes, it is "disgracefully pervasive" even in the twenty-first century, and "in its starkest forms it is not typically a choice faced by those in economically privileged positions."[9] One of her primary points in her critique of nuclear power is that the risk taken on by nuclear villages must implicate those living in the metropole. Remarking on the films of Kamanaka Hitomi, she writes, "Kamanaka's films are consistently sensitive to the economic needs behind communities' acceptance of nuclear reactors: there are no simple enemies. At the same time, they urge us—urban beneficiaries of the conveniences relying on electricity generated in modest rural communities—to become aware of our own complicity in the structure of risk."[10] Kamanaka explains that rural areas invited nuclear power onto their lands in order to keep the family together: "Fathers would go to the city in the winter as seasonal workers because they couldn't make enough money with just fishing or farming. When that happens, it's the mother who raises the children and keeps the home together. Fatherless families emerge and family life falls apart. The father is in Tokyo working as hard as he can for his family, but the family's love for the father gradually weakens.[11]

Kusano Hisao's 1972 poem "The Village Women Can't Sleep" details the emotional trauma a family endures when the head of household is forced into seasonal work for lack of a living wage:

> Women rest their arm on their husband and sleep
> Women put their bosom up against their husband, and sleep
> Women's backs are embraced by their husbands, and they sleep
> Women feel secure next to their husband, and they sleep
>
> When they can't rest their arm on their husband, women cannot sleep
> When they can't entrust their bosom to their husbands, women
>   cannot sleep
> When their backs can't be rubbed by their husbands, women cannot
>   sleep
> When they are not enveloped in their husband's warmth, women
>   cannot sleep . . .
>
> Women's husbands   Come home
> Leave your bunkhouses behind   Return so that your sleepless wives
>   can sleep
> Blow your snot at your insolent bosses and announce to them that
>   you're done with seasonal labor and come home
> A man's most important work is not to send money home
> A man whose wife cannot sleep is worth nothing

Come home husbands of women
Come home every one of you
Come home to consider the core reason why women can't sleep
Come home to understand the high economic growth structure for
    women who can't sleep

Come home   Come home so that you too can sleep
Come home even with the tax dues, the farm machinery receipts, the
shuttered storehouse, the empty stomach, to sleep.
Come home to fill your bowels with rage
Come home to extinguish all those hateful thoughts that burn in your
    sleepless woman's heart
Come home to bring back the days when you and your woman were
    fulfilled and could sleep
Come home to fight

Come home   Come home

The village women can't sleep
The women whose men are in faraway bunkhouses can't sleep
I object to an age in which women can't sleep
I object even more to the degenerate souls who allow this
    objectionable age.[12]

"The Village Women Can't Sleep" is a denunciation of the economic structure that provides so little compensation to those of rural areas for their
labor that they must leave home to pursue day labor in the metropole. The
haunting refrain of "come home" intones a wretched sense of displace-
ment. It is a mournful rendering of the circumstances under which nuclear
power plants were accepted into rural towns and under which U.S. farmers
allow fracking sites on their land. It is an old story of rural families trying to maintain financial solvency in an economy that devalues their labor
even as metropolises are dependent upon it.

 Risky power technologies are accepted for the financial stability that
the income from them can potentially provide. Nuclear fallout refugee
Satō Shigeko, at age eighty-four, wrote about that dynamic in her first poetry collection: "We'll create jobs / We'll bring you wealth / Encouraged

by honeyed words / to shovel our own grave holes / Deliriously we've
worked / Making the nuclear our business." In this poem called "Mirage,"
Satō juxtaposes "compensation" with "radiation":

> . . . That light
> blesses the city folk with riches
> through power lines
> We grew affluent
> The country prospered . . .
> Now, there's nothing more dangerous than all that we've achieved
> "compensation"
> With our own hands
> We rend our own gut
> and scatter hell's ash
> spitting up the poison called
> "radiation"
> the two guardian kings stand.[13]

These poems by award-winning poet Kusano and amateur poet Satō both
engage the dialectic of the country and the city as the spatial relation that
dictates the health of their community.[14]

When Raymond Williams surveyed literary passages of the country
and the city in English literature in his eponymous book, he found that
literary production contributed to a dialectical imagination of space under
industrial modernity as if the country and the city were actually completely different spaces.[15] Within that dialectic, the rural could represent
a range of ideas, but particularly dominant was the idea that an innocent
realm of authentic experience was being spoiled. This imagination of the
countryside did not capture the realities of rural life, but at the same time,
there was certainly a material basis for this image of the despoiling of rural
lands in the 1960s and 1970s. When Rachel Carson depended on the pastoral in introducing her landmark critique of the insecticide DDT, she invoked the biotrope of a silent spring that had befallen a rural farm. In her
fable, no birds had survived the farmland of America. It had been saturated
with pesticides: "The town lay in the midst of a checkerboard of prosper-
ous farms, with fields of grain and hillsides of orchards where, in spring,
white clouds of bloom drifted above the green fields. In autumn, oak and

maple and birch set up a blaze of color that flamed and flickered across a backdrop of pines."[16] This "every town" that changed its seasonal colors every few months underwent a mysterious transformation. Feeding stations were suddenly empty, and those birds who had not yet succumbed were on the brink, trembling feebly: "It was a spring without voices. On the mornings that had once throbbed with the dawn chorus of robins, catbirds, doves, jays, wrens, and scores of other bird voices there was now no sound; only silence lay over the fields and woods and marsh."[17] Carson's biotropic imagination calls the way of environmental pollution "a super highway" of careless living, and she much prefers the "less traveled" rural road. This rural road is a prominent feature in Ishimure's writing as well. It is a white, dusty road and a little girl, Micchan, travels it with her grandmother in nostalgic prose depicting rural living.

The dialectic of the village and urban life under industrial modernity is described in a vivid shot from Tsuchimoto's documentary *Minamata: Victims and Their World,* in an anonymous voice-over criticism of city dwellers as unaware of the impact their consumption has on rural areas and their lack of awareness of the toxic burden of industry that drives profits for those in the capital but leaves villages in ruins:

Have you heard of the children born with Minamata disease? Heads that loll? Eyes that can't see? Ears that can't hear? Mouths that can't speak or taste? Hands that can't grasp? Legs that won't walk. *You* make people bear such babies. *You* make the sea unfit for bacteria and you talk of rapid economic growth. *You* boast of Expo '70. What is poverty to us, huh? Try to remember. Tell those who don't know how we survived on potato leaves. Remember! If *you* are human rise and fight! Fight the war against pollution.

In this example, the use of second-person address indicts the urbanite as the primary reason that risk has been assumed by rural folk. Here, the split use of the pronouns "us" or "we" and "you" levies the same charge as Field when she says that urbanites must account for their own culpability in the burden of risk taken on by those in the rural areas. But, as the construction of an expensive new Olympic stadium continues in Tokyo for 2020 while thousands of environmental refugees remain in cramped "temporary" housing six or more years after nuclear fallout on Japan's northeastern seaboard, it seems that the concerns of the metropole and the rural have been neatly folded into national interest.

The Domestic Turn

This chapter discusses a novel that rejects the dialectical imagination of space in favor of an emphasis on shared vulnerability in an era in which chemical use has risen astronomically. The biotrope that titles Ariyoshi's novel *Cumulative Pollution* is the compounded toxic effect featured in Carson's *Silent Spring* twelve years earlier. The chemical event of cumulative pollution refers to how chemicals interact within a body to cause an increase in their toxic load. The pairing or combination of particular chemicals can increase or potentiate the toxicity of a chemical:

> The full scope of the dangerous interaction of chemicals is as yet little known, but disturbing findings now come regularly from scientific laboratories. Among these is the discovery that the toxicity of an organic phosphate can be increased by a second agent that is not necessarily an insecticide. . . . What of other chemicals in the normal human environment? What, in particular, of drugs? A bare beginning has been made on this subject, but already it is known that some organic phosphates (parathion and malathion) increase the toxicity of some drugs used as muscle relaxants, and that several others (again including malathion) markedly increase the sleeping time of barbiturates.[18]

Carson describes the difficulties of proving the long-term, cumulative effects of chemical toxins: "Like the constant dripping of water that in turn wears away the hardest stone, this birth-to-birth contact with dangerous chemicals may in the end prove disastrous. Each of these current exposures, no matter how slight, contributes to the progressive buildup of chemicals in our bodies and so to cumulative poisoning,"[19] though "it is admittedly difficult . . . to 'prove' that cause A produces effect B."[20] The curious biotrope of water dripping on a stone depicts cumulative pollution as a slow wearing down of the body.

For her part, Ariyoshi defined "cumulative pollution" in this way:

Cumulative pollution is a technical term. It refers to pollution caused by two or more toxic elements or to the activation of two or more elements' synergistic reactions. Put simply, if you breathe air polluted with exhaust fumes, then eat food polluted with pesticides and wheat that probably was grown with pesticides except that it is imported so you don't know what kind of pesticides they have used, and then you use miso made with imported soy beans and preservatives to make miso soup, and then eat foodstuffs boiled in that, then eat vegetables grown with yet again different pesticides, drink Japanese tea with color enhancers grown with insecticides; then, in this way, on a daily basis, you inject chemical substances into your body. The number of chemical substances we take in only through our nose and mouth, just limiting it to foodstuffs and additives, is over 80 (and if we add pesticides and air pollution that number goes into the hundreds).[21]

Ariyoshi brought cumulative pollution to bear on urban domiciles in examples that collapsed the space between the urban and the periphery. Her conclusion in 1974 that it would take fifty years for the impact of various kinds of cumulative pollution to be measured was, in hindsight, optimistic. Chemicals are irreducibly woven into everyday life, with numerous new chemicals produced every day, and their effects on different bodies are nearly impossible to track, much less prosecute. Cumulative pollution as a biotrope, therefore, invites a different kind of narrative than one about trophic relations created through the passing of a single toxic chemical (such as methyl mercury) from a distinct source to an organism. It cannot focus on a specific incident of industrial pollution, since it features the invisible accumulation of chemicals whose reactions to each other are as yet unpredictable.

Consequently, in Ariyoshi's ecocritical writing, the afflicted are not identifiable victims of a singular toxic event, but rather anyone living in the industrial world of chemical compounds. Chemical and radioisotopic pollutants have no boundaries. Ariyoshi's novel therefore does not treat industrial pollution as a problem of peripheries and metropoles. Instead, it describes a toxic environment in terms of everyday life and in the most banal terms in her long discussions of laundry detergents, fertilizers in foodstuffs, and toilet cleaners.

Despite her use of the pastoral in the opening to *Silent Spring*, Carson had similarly framed cumulative pollution as a problem for all consumers. Of chemical pollution, she wrote, "For the first time in the history of the world, every human being is now subjected to contact with dangerous chemicals, from the moment of conception until death."[22] She wrote of the "sinister effects" of DDT and related chemicals that, like organic mercury, move "from one organism to another through all the links of the food chains," with organisms higher up the food chain experiencing greater toxic loads in the process of bioaccumulation.[23] In the age of acceleration, new chemical substances and agricultural fertilizers are discovered approximately every nine seconds and new compounds are introduced into global commerce at about three per day. If PCBs (polychlorinated biphenyls), DDT, and dioxins are present in daily foods and more than 120 chemicals in the environment are reported to have reproductive or endocrine-disrupting effects, then most denizens on the planet are vulnerable to immunosuppression and other effects of cumulative toxins.[24] Carson writes: "In the less than two decades of their use, the synthetic pesticides have been so thoroughly distributed throughout the animate and inanimate world that they occur virtually everywhere. They have been recovered from most of the major river systems and even from streams of groundwater flowing unseen through the earth."[25] The pastoral with which *Silent Spring* began collapses and is replaced with an ecological imaginary that ironically renders cumulative pollution as the tie that binds. Even Vandana Shiva, who writes about food security for female farmers in rural areas, describes their plight at a global scale as one of "world wide destruction of the feminine knowledge of agriculture evolved over four to five thousand years by a handful of white male scientists in less than two decades."[26] Philosopher Michael Marder and artist Anaïs Tondeur write that "the impression that one can flee from the calamity that is our civilization is no less immature than the sunny ideology of progress itself."[27]

But, unlike Carson, who kept her most memorable biotropes to those of pastoral flora and fauna, Ariyoshi focuses on the daily objects at hand to describe the decay of land and bodies by chemical contaminants. She used the form of things, the consumer's plate, the air one breathes in, the things one touches, to represent our world.[28] This use of everyday objects and spaces for describing environmental contamination is indicative of what I am calling a "domestic turn" in some ecocritical writing. In *Cumulative Pollution*, the kitchen becomes the privileged place for understanding the modern human's undeniable link to the biotic world. It is a turn toward seeing humans as closest to nature when they open the refrigerator door and take an egg out of a carton to fry or spread cheese on a cracker, or when tangerines huddled in a bowl on the kitchen counter are no longer sweet, or when tomatoes taste like candy, or when the faded color of seaweed sheets lined in quiet rows in an aluminum tin betrays the eutrophication of Japan's aquacultural bays caused by agricultural runoff of heavily fertilized lands. In her work, the household is a microcosm of ecological affiliations that have come to link humans to their environment in industrial modernity. This domestic, transcorporeal angle offers a different conception of what a toxic event is. It refuses the dialectical imagination of space that treats industrial and agricultural pollution as an event determined by place of production. Rather, a toxic event is no event at all, but rather a systemic inundation of food, air, and water identified at the site of use.

In writing about her choice of language to describe cumulative pollution, Ariyoshi stated that she specifically avoided any term usually associated with industrial pollution events. The term *kōgai,* for example, had been used for its conventional association with the pollution of a specific place of industry,[29] and that standard use has a long history. From the 1880s, it was commonly applied to specific pollution disasters in outlying mining and agricultural areas, as well as industrial towns. It is common to see analyses of pollution on the archipelago focusing on Japan's "four major industrial pollution events."[30] This attention to "sacrificial zones" funnels the problem of toxins through the dialectic of the rural and the urban once again. Much of earlier environmental history speaks of industrial modernity in terms of *kōgai* and pollution events, and these toxic events are often known for the place in which they occur: Bhopal, Minamata, Kamioka, Fukushima, Hiroshima, Three-Mile Island, Chernobyl, and so on. This environmental historical approach might be described as "event-driven" for its focus on a specific toxic event at a specific site by a specific culprit. *Cumulative Pollution* is oppositional in its approach. It illustrates through a loose story how chemical compounds have become such a part of quotidian life under industrial modernity, whether they entered that life through farmers' subsidized soil-nitrogen-enrichment programs or through the nostrils of housewives cleaning their floors and eradicating kitchen pests.

Despite the firestorm that *Cumulative Pollution* ignited, literary critics with a penchant for highbrow fiction dismissed it as yet another prosaic social-problem novel by Ariyoshi, who had recently gained notoriety for her bestseller about the struggles of a working wife caring for her aging, incontinent father-in-law while holding down a job and raising a child. *The Twilight Years* (1972) drew back the curtain on the lack of decent health care and support for the aged to reveal the shadow labor and sacrifice this failing system required of women. As her follow-up work, *Cumulative Pollution* scrutinized another problem of modernity: chemical pollution. But in this case, she wrote not of a cultural problem, but rather of what she considered to be an international issue after having traveled to multiple countries, including China, to warn of the dangers of cumulative pollution. This new work tracked the ways in which chemical fertilizers, pesticides, food preservatives, PCBs, and 20,000 other chemicals had soundlessly deluged the islands and exposed people in both rural and metropolitan areas to lethal chemical substances. These new chemical products took environmental pollution to a heightened level precisely by their mass use.

Agricultural activist Okada Yoneo had written about how the association of pollution with a specific place made it far less relevant to him when he observed in 1971, "Industrial pollution [*kōgai*] felt like it didn't have anything to do with me, and that if I wanted to flee it, I could. I came to realize, however, that my body was destroyed along with the environment that was supposedly outside of myself—that not only could my body not be separated from the environment, but that it *was* the environment."[31] Okada continues, "The problems visited upon the livelihoods of farmers and fishermen are also those visited upon the lives [*seimei*] of consumers."[32] Instead of writing about pollution as a discrete and confined event, Ariyoshi insistently attended to the systemic circulation of chemical toxins through modern agricultural, industrial, and consumer structures. Pollution events are not the mode through which she makes sense of toxins.

The novel, first published as a serial in the major liberal newspaper the *Asahi*, took the reading public by storm.[33] The serial instantly became a lightning rod for debates about toxins in the environment, such as the growing reliance on pesticides and herbicides in agricultural production, the prevalent use of synthetic detergents, and the ubiquity of chemical food preservatives. It so captured the imagination of newspaper readers that, every month during its publication, at least two hundred letters poured in to the *Asahi* editors, and the author's residence was inundated with epistolary responses.[34] Inspired by its broad readership, the *Asahi* published more than sixty articles about *Cumulative Pollution* during its eleven-month serialization, including direct replies to the serial and separate articles on environmental topics such as agriculture and environmental health. When the controversial work was expeditiously published as a two-volume, 500-page novel, the first volume sold 680,000 copies and the second retained most of its readers, with 540,000 copies sold. Ariyoshi published an additional book of conversations with scholars and writers[35] as a further response to a rebuttal that had followed shortly after the publication of the novel called *Against Cumulative Pollution,* which published the comments of seven critics, ranging from scientists to journalists, who took issue with Ariyoshi's science.[36] She had clearly struck a nerve.

Based on Ariyoshi herself, the protagonist of *Cumulative Pollution* first learns of chemical compound contaminants while traveling with a female political candidate, Ichikawa Fusae. When a supporter of the candidate describes, in a stump speech, the alarming number of children experiencing ill health as a result of the rampant use of chemicals in Japan,[37] Ariyoshi's first-person narrator exhibits an awakening similar to that described by Lawrence Buell as a common narrative pattern in toxic discourse. As she travels with Ishikawa, she becomes increasingly appalled at the indiscriminate use of chemicals and the population's ecological illiteracy.[38] A review of the book in the popular women's journal *Fujin Kōron* described the protagonist's chemical compound muckraking as "heroic indignation" toward unregulated producers and ignorant consumers who pay so little attention to what they use and consume.[39] At a rally, Ariyoshi's protagonist describes her interest in cumulative pollution through the specter of "ill health":

> I hesitate to bring up my novel, but a few years ago in *The Twilight Years* I wrote that among problems considered having to do with "life" or "death" are unavoidable problems specifically associated with the "aged."
>
> We've always judged the physical fortune of a human life through the binary of health and sickness, but what I'm trying to write about is the swath of ill-health lying between those two. In this highly advanced material world, we—that is, *all* Japanese—are bound by this swath. What kind of future do we face?[40]

In terms of her own writing, Ariyoshi figured her work to be a logical follow-up to *The Twilight Years,* for its protests against health-related systems and policies. However, she also linked it to a broader canon of other contemporary ecocritical texts, specifically Ishimure's *Paradise in the Sea of Sorrow* and Carson's *Silent Spring*.

In 1975, Ariyoshi wrote that Ishimure's tour de force on mercury poisoning convinced her that pollution could not be captured in conventional fiction. As discussed earlier (chapter 1), Ishimure herself has insisted on the need to jettison nature writing and conventional poetic metaphors, given that the environment is in tatters.[41] In dialogue with scholar and cultural critic Tsurumi Kazuko, she complained that Meiji-era literati had not bothered to pick up a pen to describe contamination events such as the turn-of-the-century Ashio copper-mine disaster because they primarily lived in Tokyo and had no interest.[42] Ariyoshi has made strikingly similar claims about the need for a new prose to describe the battered environment in terms other than those that treat space dialectically. In the afterword to *Cumulative Pollution*, she wrote, "When the traditional subject of classical Japanese literature—"landscape"—is in crisis, is there any reason a novelist should not have done this kind of work?"[43] The main character of the novel also stated that her experience reading *Paradise in the Sea of Sorrow* was critical to understanding that pollution could not be captured in conventional fiction: "When Ishimure Michiko's *Paradise in the Sea of Sorrow* came out, I realized that you can't grasp pollution through purely novelistic fiction. The weight of the facts is just too great."[44] At the same time, because cumulative pollution is so difficult to track, novelists can address invisible toxins in ways that scientific discourse cannot.[45]

In the same afterword, Ariyoshi also mentions Carson's *Silent Spring* among nine others as a founding text for understanding toxins.[46] Carson's 1962 masterpiece chronicles the contamination of the environment through detailed descriptions of the ecological impacts of radiation, arsenic, strontium, DDT, chlordane and other chlorinated hydrocarbons, and organic phosphates, including parathion. The aural biotrope to which Carson returns again and again, which also furnishes its memorable title, is the quiet of a spring morning after all the birds have died after unwittingly ingesting the organic phosphates and chlorinated hydrocarbons in the water they drink, the seeds they eat, and the soft flesh of worms they peck at. But, unlike Carson and Ishimure, Ariyoshi develops her toxicity narrative through the household experiences of the urban population. Her first-person narrative provides no telos, but instead continually refigures ecological systems through the specter of chemical chains that may afflict those at a particular toxin's place of origin but also affect those in *any* developed place. When a farmer mentions the term "death agriculture" (*shi no nōhō*), the protagonist asks him to define it, and he replies: "It's modern agriculture. It's agriculture that uses fertilizer and pesticides. The land dies. The farmers die. And those who kindly purchase [the food from those crops] become ill when they eat it and they die too, right?"[47]

Cumulative Pollution as Biotrope

This domestic turn in ecocritical fiction emerges out of the biotrope of cumulative pollution. While bioregional ecocritical writing usually treats a singular toxic event or toxin as its subject, writing of the domestic turn features the unremarkable world of any home to convey a deep sense of the susceptibility of humans, plants, and animals to the kind of contamination that is hard to trace. For example, one passage of Ariyoshi's novel depicts her returning home from a political rally wondering why her rice bin contained none of the usual weevils gorging on grains: "Was it because of residual contamination from DDT, BHC and other hydrin-based pesticides, or was it from the low-level insecticides used after those pesticides were banned, or was it because of mercury-based pesticide used to purify the rice seed? Or did atmospheric PCBs and other materials penetrate the soil with the rain and pollute the rice? Was it from cadmium or piperonyl butoxide?"[48] Through internal monologue and dialogue among characters, food items embody the toxic. Large, unblemished apples and straight cucumbers are also biotropes that signify chemical contaminants that enter the bloodstream.

The pesticides and insecticides that Ariyoshi tracks throughout *Cumulative Pollution* are delineated equally clearly in books like Ruth Ozeki's *All Over Creation* (2004) and *My Year of Meats* (1998) and Sandra Steingraber's autobiographical *Living Downstream* (1997), *Having Faith* (2001), and *Raising Elijah* (2010). Such texts exemplify this domestic turn in ecocritical writing by tracking chemical toxins consumed in our daily lives.[49] This domestic turn in writing should, in many respects, be considered "ecocosmopolitan," a term coined by comparative literature scholar Ursula Heise. The texts depict "the abstract and highly mediated kinds of knowledge and experience that lend equal or greater support to a grasp of biospheric connectedness."[50] Bioregional writing depicts a particular place, a particular ecology, and a particular ecological dynamic, whereas cosmopolitan writing in environmental literature, or ecocosmopolitan writing, depicts ecologies that are transportable, transnational, and consequently more broadly germane. The ecopolitics that depend on attachments to the nation or are legitimated through geopolitical exclusivism are not relevant to this ecocosmopolitan imagination. Nevertheless, Heise shows how the natural world is made to produce culture, especially at the level of nation, even by theorists of cosmopolitanism who

> share the assumption that there is nothing natural or self-evident
> about attachments to the nation, which are on the contrary estab-
> lished, legitimized, and maintained by complex cultural practices
> and institutions. But rather than seek the grounds of resistance
> to nationalisms or nation-based entities in local communities or
> groups whose mobility places them at the borders of national
> identity, these theorists strive to model forms of cultural imagina-
> tion and understanding that reach beyond the nation and around
> the globe.[51]

Heise suggests that new conceptions of culture emerge in response to increased global interconnectedness and planetary consciousness.

In terms of ecology, biotropes can also be bioregional or cosmopolitan depending on the frame of the biological or chemical entanglement that has given rise to it. Still, identifying a domestic turn in contamination discourse is different from forwarding a theory of ecocosmopolitanism because the former emphasizes the body in space and the personal, shared vulnerabilities under industrial systems we engage with daily. Even if a toxic substance has a global reach, substances are not presented as such in the domestic turn, particularly when it comes to household substances. For example, as Stacy Alaimo shows, chemicals, solvents or pesticides will not be mentioned with regard to their use elsewhere or connection with toxic sites (like Minamata). Even warning literature meant to save lives—pregnancy handbooks, March of Dimes literature and so on—does not mention the global reach of particular toxins. In this form of what Alaimo calls "manufactured ignorance," a toxin is still couched in terms that downplay its environmental impacts more broadly.[52]

Steingraber has written three compelling books on toxins from a first-person perspective, but her work may contribute to a sense that vulnerabilities to toxins are never cosmopolitan. This is the double-edged sword of the domestic turn. Yet, while Steingraber's central conceit is to focus on domestic space, the habitat of her own body and home, Alaimo argues that her personal and scientific exploration is explicitly shown as coextensive with broader biological and chemical systems.[53] Ariyoshi's narrator also achieves this universal applicability, and she differs from Steingraber in that, rather than coextension of personal experience with broader systems of contamination, she instead uses an explicitly journalistic style and a second-person mode of address that demands that the reader too think about his or her own domestic space and recognize his or her own complicity as a consumer: "For those of you kindly reading this book, I'd like to ask each of you, are the hands with which you hold this book polluting the water? Do you have synthetic detergents in your kitchen? Do you know that synthetic detergents are deadly toxins? Are you washing with synthetic detergents in your home? Do you know that synthetic detergent is equally as toxic as fertilizers?"[54] And in the first person, Ariyoshi's narrator says, while on the political trail: "Cars emit noxious gases as they travel. And my car is no different. Am I a victim or a perpetrator? The answer is simple. I am a victim and a perpetrator. I know that exhaust fumes are bad, but those who know the convenience of cars can't imagine a world without them. The difficulty of solving pollution problems is that it's a two-sided coin, of convenience and toxins."[55]

Ariyoshi consciously endeavors to prove the vulnerabilities that swaths of people share in detailed histories of the international political and technological decisions that led to the production of chemical compounds. In writing about PCBs, for example, she begins with their use in the United States, goes back in time to their invention in Germany in 1881, and traces how they came to be imported into Japan as part of the "civilization and enlightenment" movement in the modern imperial era of Meiji, during which Japan desperately sought to overcome colonial vulnerabilities created through its unequal treaty status. The importation of industrial science to drive national economic growth and imperial military expansionism was implemented through the creation of chemical compounds. By tracking the transnational histories of such environmental contaminants, Ariyoshi explicitly makes the point that toxic events in the twenty-first century need not be associated with a specific place and that, in fact, the most insidious aspect of national progressivism has been a reliance on lethal food production and transportation systems that have come to dominate international economies, including but not limited to Japan. No specific place of industrial aggression is needed to perform this metonymic task: no Minamata bay, no Bhopal, no Fukushima, no Flint.

While so many studies and novels of industrial pollution focus on sites of specific pollution events, Ariyoshi's thrust is how toxins travel and eventually arrive in our domestic spaces. When philosopher Takahashi Tetsuya says, "Residents of the Tokyo metropolitan region have benefited from imposing the risks of nuclear power plants on Fukushima, but they are also clearly victims insofar as they themselves face the threat of radioactive contamination," he is referring to the cosmopolitan nature of the contamination. He continues: "As I have said, there was actually a worst-case scenario in which 35 million people of the Tokyo metropolitan area could have become nuclear power plant refugees. It seems that within me there exists a child of Fukushima and a resident of the Tokyo metropolitan area, victim and perpetrator, complexly intertwined."[56] While Takahashi still depends on the dialectic of the rural and the urban, his overall depiction of radiation is as a toxin that knows only the wind. In this depiction, toxins interacting with geophysical forces have a heartlessly consistent agency.

Ariyoshi was writing at a time in which high growth policies were deployed in an ideological and economic struggle to be "number one." Bureaucrats and academics relied on the fruits of development to assert Japan's transnational power, this time through economic rather than military might. The environmental strains of these high growth policies may not have yet been striking in the early 1960s, but by the end of the decade, a monumental change had taken place in the health of both urban and rural environments. Ariyoshi was critical of industrial capital's effects on bodies and addressed it not via the state but rather through the specificity of gender and the "unsophisticated" site of the household.

All three texts mentioned thus far—Carson's *Silent Spring*, Ishimure's *Paradise in the Sea of Sorrow,* and Ariyoshi's *Cumulative Pollution*—fuse literary image with biological mechanism. Carson's primary biological mechanisms in *Silent Spring* are those of bioaccumulation and biomagnification, which are also the fundamental mechanisms driving descriptions of biological affinities and connections in *Paradise in the Sea of Sorrow.* Bioaccumulation, as discussed in chapters 1 and 2 of the present volume, occurs when an organism accumulates a substance in the body through consumption. When a toxin is introduced in an environment, it can travel through the trophic tiers when one organism consumes another. Through the process of biomagnification, toxins can became increasingly noxious to specific organisms up the trophic layers. As *Paradise in the Sea of Sorrow* illustrates, the ability for organic mercury to travel through the trophic tiers at ever-increasing toxic levels meant that the mercury released by the

Chisso corporation poisoned the fish and snails in the water where it was released and grew increasingly toxic as it reached the bodies of cats, birds, and humans further up the trophic levels. Ishimure's narrative creates a literary cosmology in which living entities linked through this chemical connection are consequently accorded narrative value. Carson's memorable biotrope of a "silent spring" also invokes trophic connections in its expression of the dead bird who has eaten the poisoned seed or lethal worm. She refers to DDT, which Hara Tsuyoshi called "white snow" in comparing it to the "death ash" of the atomic bomb.[57] Both were lethal over time. The death ash was the result of a powerful and dramatic moment that lasted only a few seconds in the air but a lifetime in its victims' bodies. White snow had similarly long-term effects. Japanese under U.S. occupation would randomly be pulled off the street and their heads sprayed with DDT as part of a hygiene campaign, and the use of DDT on so many Japanese and Koreans began what Carson calls the era of insect resistance, during which lice and houseflies developed resistance to DDT. By the start of the 1950s, it had been documented that 100 types of insects had developed a resistance to DDT, and by the end of the 1950s, that number had reached 540, in Israel, Italy, France, the United States, and Japan.[58] The spatiality proffered for imagining the range and ubiquity of cumulative pollution was not as something "out there" in sacrificial zones of industrial modernity such as nuclear reactor sites or mines. Rather, the domestic turn for environmental literature occurred in the domestic space of rural, suburban, and urban households where the newspaper was read, which is where *Cumulative Pollution* was serialized for nearly two years.

The Letters

Once the newspaper serial of *Cumulative Pollution* got rolling in the *Asahi* newspaper, letters poured in from readers across the archipelago. Housewives, in particular, were incensed at what they learned. One letter to the editor printed in the *Asahi* began with a seasonal greeting before commenting on the irony of giving toxic synthetic detergents as gifts. It begins, "The insect cries of June have commenced," and then continues:

> In dribs and drabs department stores and shopping districts will begin their "battle of Obon festival gifts." Ever since the synthetic detergent stockpiling in the autumn of 1973, synthetic detergents

have been delivered to our home as Obon festival and year-end gifts. Despite a vague sense that water was being polluted through the drainage of synthetic detergent even before I read *Cumulative Pollution* serialized in this newspaper, I continued to use them since they were given to us as gifts and were convenient. But each week, as I read more and more of the novel, I was seized by the awareness that using synthetic detergents was a crime, so I made the decision to switch to powdered soap at the beginning of last month. In the storage room of our small home, large sealed boxes of synthetic detergents lay dormant. While I mull over how to dispose of them, another summer of gift-giving season arrives. If it were close friends, I could explain the situation and ask them to stop sending the gifts, but most are not close so it's become a headache. I wish people would not gift synthetic detergents.[59]

Other letters were more detailed in their complaints toward fellow citizens using synthetic detergents. One housewife pleaded with readers to abandon their use:

The main component of latent ABS and LAS sticks to the hands and to the tableware, gets absorbed by the skin and causes liver damage, deformities, auxiliary carcinogenesis, bad blood pressure, synergistic effects with PCB, RHC, and mercury, and causes unbelievable pain. Detergents are copiously discharged from every household in Japan and daily pollute our tap water. . . . Housewives who should be sensitive to pollution habitually use them because they are convenient, so they themselves contribute daily to the pollution. In order not to encourage cancer and deformities in their children, housewives themselves should immediately boycott detergents and use solid and powder soaps of the past. There are plenty of housewives who complain that they can't get these [traditional] soaps so encourage your local grocer and supermarket to get them. [60]

Another housewife, thirty-year-old Kodera Junko, admitted her own environmental illiteracy. She, too, "like Ariyoshi," thought that cabbage was something healthy to put on the table, but has since realized that it is too contaminated with fertilizer.

Some letters depicted tragic consequences of household insecticides. One housewife reported the death of her niece from bug spray:

> My niece, who had never been ill in her life, died suddenly at
> the age of 26. The cause of her death was weakening of the heart
> caused by poisoning by insecticide. The area where she sprayed the
> commercially available insecticide was dark and the insects' holes
> were small so she put her face too close to them and inhaled a large
> amount of insecticide. That night, she lost consciousness, but it
> was after she had locked the house. Unfortunately, her husband
> was away on business and so no one knew there had been an acci-
> dent. While unconscious, she vomited. Then she developed a fever,
> dropsy, oxygen deficiency, and finally succumbed. With nuclear
> families as widespread as they are now, this is an incident that is
> likely to happen again.[61]

In addition to telling stories of illnesses and deaths caused by detergents and insecticides, housewives also began to question the degree to which government agencies had any interest in their families' health. Just as Ariyoshi's book suggests that, through the specter of cumulative pollution, political and cultural relations appear, housewives voiced concern that bureaucrats and politicians did not have the interests of the younger generation in mind, "illustrated by their lack of protocol and regulations for what we put in our mouths."[62] In a letter of March 4, 1975, forty-nine-year-old housewife Takahashi Kiyoko said that she had watched a television show in which critic Akiyama Chieko suggested that it is scary (*osoroshii*) that no rebuttals against *Cumulative Pollution* have been made by farmers, corporate workers, or academics. Another wrote: "I was a foolish housewife with faith in what society's elites were doing. My eyes have been opened. . . . How scary it is that I had been using synthetic detergents made by major Japanese industrial corporations without oversight. . . . Why do they sell a harmful detergent in such a beautiful box? Why does the Ministry of Health and Welfare allow kitchen detergents strong enough to kill cockroaches to be produced?"[63]

Farmers responded by pointing out what Ariyoshi herself had already implicitly suggested, that the domestic household is a microcosm for broader ecological health. One farmer wrote, "Who are the ones who detest malformed produce with bugs on it? Isn't it the consumers? Take some responsibility for yourselves and stop blaming us. Farmers are the victims here."[64] Another farmer asked whether Ariyoshi suggests that they go back to the days of raising crops without pesticides and fertilizers:

> Ms. Ariyoshi has stated that even a novice like me could clearly tell the difference between rice fields that use pesticides and rice fields that don't, but in thirty plus years . . . I can't tell the difference. I would like you to tell me how they differ at just a glance. . . . Herbicides have been invented, planting and harvest work has been mechanized. At last we have been freed from farming on all fours. Are you saying that we should return to the harsh farming practices of the old days? However much one claims that the land is "alive," isn't it obvious for us farmers, whose livelihood depends on it, to choose "dead" soil that yields the greater harvest?[65]

Another farmer talked about the problem of available labor when choosing how to fertilize: "It's well-known that to increase the fertility of soil, compost is superior to chemical fertilizers, but since eighty percent of farmers aim to finish farm work using the seasonal worker, they cannot afford to spend a whole winter slowly and carefully making compost as they did in the past."[66]

Readers' anger toward the lack of requirements and regulations is well-documented in the letters from both sexes: "Our collective sentiments are of endless resentment and heart-wrenching despair towards irresponsibility and dishonesty by bureaucrats who haven't responded with a single word of clarification or refutation vis-a-vis Ms. Ariyoshi's persuasive and pragmatic viewpoint. All things considered, it is worrisome that even today, let alone a year later, as we are surrounded by countless reasons for concern, they seem to want to tell us that we should be content regardless of the spread of pollution as long as food production continues to grow at an unprecedented rate."[67] Another male reader suggested that readers begin writing campaigns:

> Now that the novel has ended, I appeal to those readers who have read *Cumulative Pollution* to put into practice the following suggestions. Not only did we realize that we must take some kind of measure against the severity of cumulative pollution but we now know the administrative realities that produce it. For our own

healthy living and that of our children, and to revive the days of living with a peace of mind, . . . let us seek answers by writing to such
bureaus as the Ministry of Health and Welfare or the Department
of Forestry, or the corporations involved in activities you consider
unjust, or what was hard to swallow or what angered you from this
novel. Don't do this in the form of protest, but by asking politely
for an explanation as in, "I think such and such is unsound and
would kindly appreciate an explanation." If each of us throughout the country showers them with questions to create a highly
unstable public situation, the government will be forced to reflect
on the problem. I would like to create that opportunity. We cannot
afford to stand still and do nothing. That would only mean rushing to our demise. We have reached the point where we must take
some action. Also, if you are sending a letter, don't forget to enclose
a return stamp.[68]

Though the early hook was the portrait of a political candidate who con-
currently was enduring a heated political race, this plotline was dropped
to spotlight the subject of cumulative pollution. The novel has since influenced grassroots activism and civic movements to treat land and human
health as inextricably intertwined.[69] Scientists and scholars have cited the
text as monumental in awakening broader public understanding of toxins' effects on human health. A 2007 article in a Japanese pesticide science
journal cites *Cumulative Pollution, Silent Spring,* and *Our Stolen Future* as
essential texts in creating the first public understanding of chemical contaminants.[70] Another article suggests that these three texts had a far greater
impact on the understanding of endocrine disruptors among the general
population than the work of scientists.[71]

Res Nullius

Cumulative Pollution was cited in the wake of the TEPCO nuclear reactor meltdowns as a founding text for building the concept of uncertain
risk. Its concept of pollution as a product of multiple, cumulative factors
was an idea that was relatively new at the time.[72] This domestic turn in
toxic discourse, which links rural land and the rural home with the urban
home through the biotrope of cumulative pollution, encourages a perspective on environment as "agricultural, suburban, urban, as part of the

same territory—never totally ruined, never completely unnatural."[73] The biotrope of cumulative pollution emphasizes the material agencies of industrial technologies that have penetrated the world at every level: production, consumption, market, and home. It aids a new conceptualization of space in ecocritical writing that disrupts the rural–urban dichotomy and attends to the agency, invisibility, and ubiquity of chemical toxins. Steingraber describes how chemicals "at vanishingly small concentrations" can deeply disrupt our "most easily duped biological system," the endocrine system, while chemicals mixed in our bodies may have unanticipated results, including cancers. We have seen the impacts of these endocrine disruptors on all sorts of species, particularly frogs. As we understand more about how chemicals interact within bodies, not only do the paths of toxins become far less clear, but the scale and impact of these toxins also become more difficult to assess.[74] Cumulative pollution as a biotrope in the context of Ariyoshi's novel develops a critical imagination of this nonhuman agency.

Ariyoshi's novel shows how environmental pollution requires a new way of spatially articulating the agency of chemicals. The cumulative effects of industrial toxins will not be addressed if they are imagined as always particular to a singular site, but this introduces the problem of responsibility. As the continual, daily release of radiation from the TEPCO plant in Fukushima enters into a spatial no-man's land, it is rendered *res nullius*, property belonging to no one, which has made it difficult to prosecute those clearly responsible for emitting radiation into the environment. In August 2011, for example, a company operating a golf course in Nihonmatsu City in Fukushima prefecture applied for a provisional disposition in the Tokyo district court, demanding that TEPCO decontaminate the golf course, since high radiation levels after the accident had seriously impacted business. In response, TEPCO irresponsibly claimed that: "The radioactive material dispersed from the nuclear reactors does not belong to TEPCO. Therefore TEPCO has no responsibility for decontamination."[75] The Tokyo district court declined the application for provisional disposition. Radiation, in this context, is deemed *res nullius*, an accounting that works in the interests of industrial capitalists. This system requires an adjustment of ethics, Peter Singer argues in his discussion of atmospheric pollution: "Our value system evolved in circumstances in which the atmosphere, like the oceans, seemed an unlimited resource, and responsibilities and harms were generally clear and well defined. If someone hit someone else, it was clear who had done what. Now the twin problems of the ozone hole and of climate change have revealed bizarre new ways of killing people."[76] Making polluters responsible for cumulative exposure requires creating "multipollutant" toxicity reference values and efforts of transnational monitoring systems that have the will and the power to indict for damage to humans, animals, land, and water.

CHAPTER 4

Literature without Us

*She had read somewhere that watching kurage was beneficial to your
health because it reduces stress levels, only the problem was that a lot of
other housewives had read the same article, so it was always crowded in
front of the tank.*

—Ruth Ozeki, *A Tale for the Time Being*

Ecological Totalities

This book began with a comparison of how two authors responded so differently to seismic shifts on the northeastern seaboard of Japan. Murakami
Haruki invoked what I have called the biotrope of the cherry blossom.
He tied the pale flower to familiar ethnic national history in his speech
on Japan's ability to rebound from nuclear meltdown. This reference to
an intertextual tradition was meant to ease concern about how environmental refugees would fare. Recovery efforts would be successful and the
Japanese would prevail. In contrast, Ishimure Michiko spoke of heaving
tectonic plates that can and will change the planet in ways that civilizations and people cannot predict. For her, moving tectonic plates are not so
easily folded into cultural discourse.

An ecocritical perspective does not mirror culture or prove social constructivist claims as "correct" through reference to the material world.[1]
Rather, it attends to the materiality and semiotics of an entity. The present
book introduced the concept of the biotrope in part to address the ways
in which matter can often be eclipsed by cultural humanistic claims. The
concept of the biotrope, with its material and figurative senses, encourages us to consider the various literary and filmic representations of our
lively world in ways that do not simply replicate cultural constructs and
humanistic universals. Put differently, any hermeneutics dependent on
a priori cultural claims is necessarily questioned when we attend to the

agency of the material world. There are different kinds of biotropes. The material aspects of a biotrope can be put toward serving the interest of cultural humanistic meaning, but even in this case, the biotrope embodies the "always already ongoing historicity" of the thing itself. The new materialist perspective of Karen Barad describes the ways in which matter is not "little bits of nature" awaiting "the mark of an external force like culture or history for their completion." Each element has its own history and agency.[2]

In this chapter, I explore further how claims of cultural difference can impede ecocritical thinking. Specifically, I explore whether a "planetary" perspective is a productive angle from which to critique cultural humanism. Recently, the concept of the "Anthropocene" has dominated ecopolitical discourse in the humanities and geophysical sciences. The term has been used with increasing frequency by humanists and scientists to mark a geophysical shift in which humans are changing earth and atmospheric systems like never before. Nobel-laureate atmospheric chemist Paul Crutzen popularized the term "Anthropocene" from a concept coined by the late biologist Eugene Stoermer in the 1980s to mark the human capacity to fundamentally change earth and atmospheric systems in geologic epochal terms. Since then, the concept has rapidly spread. It stresses the unprecedented scale of anthropogenic change to earth systems including global warming, species extinction, decreased biodiversification, acidification of the oceans, and other globally systemic environmental problems.[3] This discourse of anthropogenic culpability describes environmental problems as a result of human activity. Environmental damage is not reduced to a site but is ascertained at the scale of the planet. The culprit is not identified as a specific polluter, such as a corporation or class or race. Rather, the culprit is identified at the level of species. Homo sapiens are the drivers of devastating environmental change in Anthropocene discourse. At its base, Anthropocene discourse summons an ecopolitics that frames ecological crisis at the unprecedented scale of a global commons.

The "Anthropocene" as a concept appeals to two kinds of environmentalists: those who believe in rationalism to solve the problem of radical change to earth systems and those who consider our future with a grim, existentialist humility.[4] Anthropocene discourse requires thinking at the level of species as declared in the name of the concept itself and, in that sense, is trapped by a tautology of human exceptionalism. For this reason, philosopher Frédéric Neyrat considers it a flawed site of environmental-ist critique because it summons forth a "constructivist euphoria" that identifies the human species as able to control geophysical changes to the planet at the same time that it invites apocalyptic thinking.[5] Homo sapi-ens can apparently think their way out of this current crisis, but only as long as they move quickly enough. Otherwise, homo sapiens (some with Neanderthal DNA) as individuals and as a species will be mortally sub-jected, along with so many other species, to terrestrial, oceanic, and cli-matological changes beyond human control. This latter apocalyptic vision differs from previous ways we have imagined the end of the world, which has been primarily through nuclear annihilation. For nuclear apocalypse, human agency is still required—somebody is needed to "push the but-ton." Somebody is needed to pour the radioactive material into the wrong flask or fly an airplane into a reactor. In the case of nuclear annihilation, human error or human enmity is what catapults us into Alan Weisman's "world without us."

In contrast, Anthropocene discourse emerges as a problem not of an in-dividual but of a species. Recently, the International Union of Geological Sciences determined that there is sufficient evidence to warrant changing the name of our geologic epoch from Holocene to Anthropocene, but where to put the start date of this new epoch? Options range from the start of agricultural labor, to the invention and common use of the steam engine in the eighteenth century, to when radiation was first introduced into the earth's stratigraphy and the use of chemicals and nitrogen fixation technologies soared. This book has focused on the impacts of mercury, cumulative pollution, and radioactivity since the start of the "great accel-eration" because, under any measure, chemical invention and fossil fuel emissions have soared in the post–World War II period.

The totalizing language of Anthropocene discourse needs the human species to operate as an intelligible entity for political action. For some, such a global commons is the only way to achieve ecopolitical change. This was the claim of comparative literature scholar Masao Miyoshi. At the end of his life, he became passionate about the need to develop a language of a global commons within the humanities, and he published essays in Japanese and English on the direction that he thought literary studies should take using the term "planetarianism." For him, ecopolitics requires an approach that sublimates difference at the level of culture, eth-nicity, gender, and so on in the name of a global commons:

For the first time in human history, one single commonality
involves all those living on the planet: environmental deterioration as a result of the human consumption of natural resources.
Whether rich or poor, in the East or the West, progressive or
conservative, religious or atheist, none of us can escape from
the all-involving process of air pollution, ozone layer depletion,
ocean contamination, toxic accumulation, and global warming. . . .
Literature and literary studies now have one basis and goal: to nur-
ture our common bonds to the planet—to replace the imaginaries
of exclusionist familialism, communitarianism, nationhood, ethnic
culture, regionalism, "globalization," or even humanism, with the
ideal of planetarianism.[6]

In Miyoshi's view, a global commons necessary for ecocritical practice begins with a critique of identity politics and the nation-state, an argument
he makes in a number of his essays, including "Japan is Not Interesting."[7]
In his interview with Yoshimoto Mitsuhiro, Miyoshi explained:

It all started with my rejection of identity politics. This means
rejecting alliances and dedication to one's own group beyond dif-
ferences in history and geography. And once one refuses alliances
to one's own group, where should one go from there? Clearly
one must reject the group of one's nation-state. One cannot be
satisfied with the nation-state. As an intellectual concept it is not
only bankrupt, but in reality in so many ways it has already been
abandoned. Creating a global political economy and the protection
of citizens are the only missions of the nation-state, but those are
hardly realized.[8]

Miyoshi considers his planetary perspective to merely describe the present situation under capitalism: the pursuit of capital has led the state to
work for profit beyond national boundaries, and in the process, it has
abandoned its citizens. Consequently, the nation-state no longer functions as the center for producing identities and cultural knowledge. For
evidence, he turns to artists who, he writes, work outside of the state frame
anyway. For instance, the music industry is in error in continuing to label
music as of a particular nation-state, as in "Japanese" or "Korean." Miyoshi

also explains how cultural and literary studies must recognize the state's fundamental lack of interest in citizens: "We must dismantle, to the degree possible, the nation-state as a cultural concept. The way to do this is through environmental conservationism."[9]

Miyoshi had long questioned the category of the nation as the dominant unit for identity formation. Additionally, as in "Japan is Not Interesting," Miyoshi critiqued ethnicity-based identity formations as dependent on a false sense of homogeneity: "All ethnic and social groups have internal minorities who need the support of the outside world. We cannot distort world affairs for the self-interest of totalizing and totalized tribes and families and ownerships. In fact, we need to recall that ethnic or cultural groups are not private properties or corporations. We cannot let any ethnic groups privatize or monopolize its identity."[10]

Miyoshi historicizes his critique of identity politics, saying that the logic of difference was liberating in the first half of the twentieth century when it was used to define experience against monocultural totalities. Now, however, comparative literature, gender, and ethnic studies have become spaces of atomization where incommensurable cultural or ethnically defined entities have no point of contact. This pursuit of gender and ethnic identity, he argues, is warmly embraced by a transnational corporatism that uses gender and ethnic identity for the production of markets, while such atomization works against necessary alliances of neighbors who share environmental predicaments:

> The disintegration of not just comparative literature, but literary studies as a whole, may be already under way. If our fractured groups are engrossed in their self-interests, outsiders have good reason to feel repulsed by them. The general public wants to understand its place in the "globalized" world, and there is a deep concern with the waste-based economy. And yet those who have traditionally intervened in such issues are preoccupied with their internecine struggles conducted in a language of their own. The public is excluded and unwanted as long as it refuses to learn the jargon of partisans and to become partisan.[11]

To blame the humanities for failing to be a cogent agent of criticism and intervention is overly reductive for critical theorist David Palumbo-Liu, who finds Miyoshi's critique of multiculturalism and identity politics "un-characteristically ill-informed and totally unsubstantiated."[12] Certainly, Miyoshi could have been more thorough in his discussion of the manipulation of cultural and ethnic constructions by global capital, or he could have illustrated precisely how public policy reductively manages ethnic identity. In ecocritical terms, if partisan language produces unequal access to the shared commons of the globe, just how this happens deserves further attention.

Tom Cohen, a cultural theorist and coeditor of a book series on climate change, takes the whole of humanistic discourse to task, making the bold claim that the humanities has been so interested in the human subject, including human culture and questions of human identity, that humanist scholarship itself is complicit in global warming:

> The mesmerizing fixation with cultural histories, the ethics of "others," the enhancement of subjectivities, "human rights" and institutions of power not only partook of this occlusion but "we theorists" have deferred addressing biospheric collapse, mass extinction events, or the implications of resource wars and "population" culling. It is our sense of justified propriety—our defense of cultures, affects, bodies and others—that allows us to remain secure in our homeland, unaware of all the ruses that maintain that spurious home.[13]

Our current state of environmental collapse, for Cohen, requires a humanities that goes beyond the human. Miyoshi goes even further when he remarks that "a new kind of environmental studies will need to decide whether human extinction is worth thinking about."[14]

The innovative aspects of such dystopian remarks lie in the urgent appeal to reconsider what we do in literary studies and the humanities. Miyoshi suggests that we respond to the end of the cold war, the start of the neoliberal global economy, and continued environmental deterioration by considering economic disparity with our shared environment as an impetus. His awkward term "planetarianism" treats global ecological thinking as an ideological agenda that projects a sense of urgency, in contrast to the term "Anthropocene" that is used to identify and describe the impact of one species on the planet. Unfortunately, Miyoshi introduced his concept of "planetarianism" later in life, so he did not have a chance to pursue the full possibilities of the concept and how he intended to employ it further.

Miyoshi was not alone in his desire to rethink the bounds of his own discipline at the level of planet. For example, in 2003, celebrated economist Hirofumi Uzawa released his book *Economic Theory and Global Warming,* in which he theorizes an economic system based on the ecological event of global warming. This system would account for the environmental disequilibrium that impairs economic advancement in developing countries and "lower[s] the welfare of all people in all future generations decisively."[15] Historian Dipesh Chakrabarty has suggested how his discipline might respond to challenges posed by climatological change by expanding the usual humanistic frame beyond the scale of the human subject.[16] In what historian Julia Adeney Thomas called his "version of the species pumped up for action on a global scale," Chakrabarty argues that narrow constructions of history, ones that minimize geological perspectives, cannot account for humanity's global force, which is a point briefly addressed in Miyoshi's *Site of Resistance.*[17] More recently, in the popular press, Naomi Klein has published *This Changes Everything: Capitalism and Climate Change* as her third volume in a sustained critique of contemporary global capitalism. She argues that a different kind of capitalism—one that considers anthropogenic impact on a planetary scale—is the only way for all species to survive the future, though she does not fundamentally question capitalism as the economic system that will sustain us. In any case, scholars from a range of disciplines have provided guidance about how to proceed.

At the turn of this century, comparative literature scholar Gayatri Spivak suggested an overhaul for comparative literary studies at the scale of the planet. Around the time that Miyoshi began to talk of "planetarianism," Spivak coined the term "planetarity" and explained how planetarity in postcolonial theory avoids the pitfalls of dogmatic and exclusionary storytelling that speak at the level of private authority, which is too parochial: "The old postcolonial model—very much 'India' plus the Sartrian 'Fanon'—will not serve now as the master model for transnational to global cultural studies on the way to planetarity. We are dealing with heterogeneity on a different scale and related to imperialisms on another model." Those "imperialisms on another model" are international compacts like the EU, GATT, NAFTA, and the financialization of the globe.

Spivak is not interested in jettisoning humanistic learning of cultures. Rather, she suggests the need to see diversity within a cultural formation. To make this point, she uses the biotrope of the earth: "One must not make history in a deliberate way. One must respect the earth's tone. One might be obliged to claim history from the violent perpetrator of it, in order to turn violation into the enablement of the individual, but that is another story. After the effacement of the trace, no project for restoring the origin."[18] The planetary scale of address is, for Spivak, an opportunity to "turn identitarian monuments into documents for reconstellation." This is all in keeping with a refusal of identity politics as they currently exist in the academy, which Spivak baldly states can be "neither smart nor good."[19] History that has placed "itself in the forces of nature and thus away from the specificity of nations" is preferable because it displaces cultural props and the authority of identity-based collectivities.[20] Spivak writes at the scale of the planetary not to posit a global commons that would erase difference, but rather in order to interrupt literary and area studies' export of national or ethnic ethos in reading. She stresses the need for a relation to the world that identity politics (and the current formation of comparative studies) stifles. Even in writing about "claiming history from the violent perpetrator of it," she does not suggest a return to an essentialist identity. There is "no project for restoring the origin."

Miyoshi and Spivak may both write at the scale of the planetary in order to interrupt literary and area studies' export of national or ethnic ethos, but there they part ways.[21] Miyoshi is deeply invested in producing a new totality for thought: shrinking coastlines, unequal access to water, ruined farmland, and other examples of shared climatological crisis require us, as humans, to jettison the logics of difference. As he sees it, "No one can escape from the environmental crisis, and no segment of life can be free from it (even though the rich will try to survive longer than the poor, of course)."[22] Miyoshi's planetary thinking articulates a commons born of fundamental conditions having to do with global warming, but without his parenthetical remark that the rich will try to buy their way through the first stages of the global climate change, he risks throwing the proverbial baby out with the bathwater. Anthropogenic impact will deeply affect many, but especially those already living in poverty. And since women more often live in poverty, this is a gendered issue. Meanwhile, Spivak mainly stresses the need for histories and cultural formations of the world that are more expansive but stifled under the current formation of comparative literature.

Discourses of the Anthropocene suggest that particularity means nothing without the totality. But historian Julia Adeney Thomas has argued that, in fact, the particulars can make all the difference in terms of whether we even find ourselves in danger in the first place. Microbiologists give us a radically different perspective on the human, and "not all of them [are] endangered by anthropogenic environmental change."[23] At the same time, Thomas makes the point that it is the historian's role to determine who the "we" of climate crisis is and by which measure we are in crisis and that this ethical work should take place at the scale of human history rather than planetary history. This perspective dovetails with that of comparative literature scholar Claire Colebrook, who writes that Anthropocene discourse may save us from behaving in parochial ways that are ultimately damaging to the planet, but the planetary scale is frequently unmanageable with all of its diverging forces and "timelines that exceed any manageable point of view."[24]

Concurrent to Miyoshi and Spivak's critique of comparative literature's parochialism, philosopher and ethicist Peter Singer was just publishing his own planetary treatise, *One World: The Ethics of Globalization,* which argues for an ethics that operates at a planetary scale.[25] He suggests the futility of thinking at the level of nation or through cultural practice, which "really serves the interests of only a small minority of the population." In the introduction of the present volume, I suggested that ideas of nature have been important to the development of nation as an imagined political and cultural community and that particular biotropes have driven a shared sensibility among citizens who likely never encounter most of the other members of the nation yet consider themselves as sharing similar values and participating in the same institutions. One of Singer's strategies for developing an ethics for environmental and human health is to question how we have defined "our own kind" and how we have decided when we have special obligations to "our own kind." Specifically addressing the power of national identity, he encourages a more profound investigation of who we imagine our own kind to be:

> [If] the modern idea of the nation rests on a community we imagine ourselves to be part of, rather than one that we really are part of, then it is also possible for us to imagine ourselves to be part of a different community. . . . We need to ask whether it will, in the long run, be better if we continue to live in the imagined communities we know as nation-states, or if we begin to consider ourselves as members of an imagined community of the world. . . . Our

problems are now too intertwined to be well resolved in a system
consisting of nation-states, in which citizens give their primary, and
near-exclusive, loyalty to their own nation-state rather than to the
larger global community, and such a system has not led to a great
enough will to meet the pressing needs of those living in extreme
poverty.[26]

In arguing for an ethics to address new underclasses under globalization,
Singer recognizes that we are not all in this together. In other words, his
approach accounts for one of the fundamental problems of planetary
thinking, which is the nation-state. The work of Ishimure illustrates time
and again that those who have labored for industry have had their environments destroyed right under their very noses by the interests of corporate
nationalism.

The scientific acknowledgment of anthropogenic culpability on a planetary scale is not new. It had been discussed openly as early as 1988, when
the director of NASA's Goddard Institute, James Hansen, stated in testimony at a Congressional hearing that science was 99 percent unequivocal
that the world was warming and that we needed to act collectively to reduce emissions or risk a host of unintended consequences.[27] Recognition
of the human species' capacity to fundamentally change earth systems
raises an alarm. Homo sapiens may destroy themselves and take the rest
of the world with them. Still, does the concept challenge the fundamental aspects of Enlightenment humanism that contributed to aspects of our
current predicament, especially the extinction of species? Are we able to
fundamentally challenge whom we consider to be "our own kind" through
this concept? The concept of the Anthropocene is useful for articulating
the culpability and survival of our species; a planetary perspective will
foreground other agencies and even dream of putting homo sapiens in the
shadows.

"Let's Burn Up the Twentieth Century"

Obligate storytelling and the cinema of slow violence contribute to a
broader view of who "our own kind" is. They feature more than the desires
and struggles of humans, and they may even explicitly critique humanistic
interests. When biotropes are interpreted for how they can act as more
than metaphors for human emotion and interests, the range of "our own

kind" gets greatly expanded. Ishimure recently wrote about a desire to metamorphose into a faint flicker of light. She then wished the same for all humans, that they would all be only faintly visible from the yawning darkness of space.[28] The wish to metamorphose into faint flame is a wish to disappear the self, just as in her obligate storytelling. But the biotrope of the dim flame also expresses a wish for humanity to do the same, and in wishing for humanity to lose its brightness and become as a dim flame, Ishimure rejects the self-congratulatory history of human progress and innovation.

Literary criticism stands to make itself more relevant if it can posit better methods for addressing the pressing ecopolitical issues of our time at a scale that does not replicate geopolitical and humanistic approaches to being. Literary theorist Timothy Clark offers a compelling approach for literary interpretation for these times. He begins by rightly pointing out that, despite our global reach, we continue to read, write, and engage in the hermeneutic endeavor on a parochial scale and that this is a problem:

> One scale forms a kind of norm for human beings, the usually
> taken-for-granted-scale of bodily, terrestrial existence and per-
> ception, its up and down, sense of distances and orientation: we
> experience phenomena at a mostly fairly stable and consistent
> speed—too slow and our perception would give us an almost static
> world in which nothing happened; too fast, and everything would
> blur into indistinctness. We inhabit distance, height and breadth in
> terms of the given dimensionality of our embodied, earthly exis-
> tence. This particular physical scale is inherent to the intelligibility
> of things around us, imbued with an obviousness and authority
> which it takes an effort to override.[29]

On the one hand, as a species, we have caused earthly change on a scale never before witnessed. On the other hand, these climatological changes are so vast that humans may not be able to control them.

These anthropogenic changes to the planet are often difficult to spot at the human scale. This situation is described by Rob Nixon as a problem of representation in his conceptual framing of "slow violence" as discussed in chapter 2. Clark's proposal to read at the hypothetical scale provides a new angle for how to read beyond human interest:

With climate change, however, we have a map, its scale includes
the whole earth but when it comes to relating the threat to daily
questions of politics, ethics or specific interpretations of history,
culture, literature, etc., the map is often almost mockingly useless.
Policies and concepts relating to climate change invariably seem
undermined or even derided by considerations of scale: a campaign for environmental reform in one country may be already
effectively negated by the lack of such measures on the other side
of the world.[30]

For Clark, considerations of scale show that we often make "deranged"
jumps in trying to account for global climate change, and this leads to
erroneous fantasies of agency. "Deranged jumps" in scale occur when a
choice like buying a car gets tied altogether too easily to planetary health.
In these jumps, human agency is strained "in a bewildering generalizing of
the political that can make even filling a kettle as public an act as voting."[31]
These jumps in scale wrongly lead to the conclusion that human agency,
above any other kind of agency, is the primary motivator of change at a
time when earth systems are more unpredictable than ever under global
warming and not at all beholden to human agency.[32] Reading at the hypothetical scale will impede such fearless belief in the human's capacity to
control environment in the context of anthropogenic change.

In Clark's conceptual scales for reading, the hypothetical scale is joined
by two others. First, literary analysis, he argues, has tended to occur at the
human scale. In this "cozy" interpretive scale, texts are read for how they
emerge through a human narrator's world. Criticism tends to orient the
text toward humanist values like loyalty, romance, tragedy, and treachery:
emotions and actions that keep us "recognizably human."[33] This is the first
scale. Another common humanist scale in literary criticism, especially in
area studies, emerges in reading for culture or a generation. This kind of
analysis works at the spatial scale "of a national culture and its inhabitants"
and the time frame of a historical period or human generation.[34] For literary criticism, this scale of interpretation means that we "think, interpret
and judge as if the territorial bounds of the nation state acted as a self-
evident principle of overall coherence and intelligibility within which a
history and culture can be understood, ignoring anything that does not
fit such a narrative. After all, literary criticism itself evolved primarily as
an institution of cultural self-definition at this scale."[35] This second scale

is most common in cultural criticism. It is precisely what Miyoshi and Spivak critique when they argue against reading a text for ethnicity, culture, or national identity or through a "methodological nationalism" that jettisons what does not fit in cultural models.[36] To put an ecocritical spin on the problem of this analytic scale, we could say that this type of literary analysis not only jettisons what does not fit in cultural models but also requires that we actively make things fit, such that we read *bios* for *ethnos*.

Clark's third way of reading, the "hypothetical" scale is different. It is a scale through which planetary meaning and relevance is addressed. The hypothetical scale offers a method for stimulating literary analysis in our current climatological context by intervening in the long-term conventions of area studies formulated in the cold war, replacing collective identities, thereby intervening also at a level of planet. This kind of reading, I suggest, would make room for more-than-human agencies and their time frames and scales, and it may provide a sense of how we could further develop literary criticism to account for animals and matter. Reading at the hypothetical scale stands to make literary criticism more capable of showing nonhuman agencies: "Viewed on very long time scales, human history and culture can take on unfamiliar shapes, as work in environmental history repeatedly demonstrates, altering conception of what makes something 'important' and what does not."[37] When we engage the hypothetical scale, the planet is no longer primarily the theatrical backdrop for human endeavor and human drama and biotropes are freed from being beholden to a geopolitical or humanist logic.[38] In other words, reading at the hypothetical scale becomes a way to account for biotropes beyond strictly geopolitical or cultural humanist relevance.

One need not choose a particular scale at which to read; stories can be read at multiple scales simultaneously. Recognized with literary awards in both Germany and Japan, Tawada Yōko's writing provides multiple opportunities to try out different scales of reading, as in her post-2011 collections of short stories. One prominent short story, "The Island of Eternal Life," invites analysis at both the human and hypothetical scale, though only the hypothetical scale produces an ecopolitical reading. In this story, a Japanese expat passes through the security check at a New York City airport on her way back to Germany just after a nuclear meltdown has occurred in Japan. Security workers are loath to hold her passport even though she has not been to Japan for decades, and she experiences a strange dreamlike hallucination that the chrysanthemum on her Japanese passport is misshapen as if having mutated after radiation exposure. As she travels through the airport, despite not having been to Japan for decades, she is treated by the airport agent as if she might be contaminated. The agent's hand reaches out to grab her passport, then seems to freeze in midair. After the traveler explains that she has not been to Japan for thirty years, she feels ashamed at denying her homeland. She feels an unfamiliar surge of nostalgia for her birthplace: "It seems strange even to me the way I hung on to my old passport just when having one had become such a bother."[39]

In the protagonist's mind, the chrysanthemum appears to have seventeen petals instead of sixteen. In a geopolitical reading, the chrysanthemum is symbolic of a failed empire, the chrysanthemum having signified the imperial family for countless generations. In the context of the story, since the meltdown, the emperor and prime minister have both been abducted, Japan is run by a little known underground entity, and children are dying while the aged live on. An interpretation at the hypothetical scale would interpret the mutation of the chrysanthemum as an opportunity to discuss the role of radiation, and the expansive time and potential illness that radiation introduces. The hypothetical reading, coupled with the counterpoint of the geopolitical scale, points to the absurdity of worrying about the failure of an empire under the disastrous consequences of high radiation levels for thousands of years to come, and suggests the irrelevance of ethnic identity for a nation whose children won't survive their grandparents. The radiated biotrope also reveals the absurdity of the idea that significant historical agency is the preserve of human beings alone.[40]

Wu Ming-yi's *The Man with the Compound Eyes* began with the survival of boy-hero Atile'i on an island of plastic caught in a Pacific gyre. It concludes with Atile'i in that same Pacific, this time steering his own handmade boat. Just as he sets out to cross the expanse of the Pacific to find his long-lost love, a "shooting star" of a nuclear bomb detonates just off the shore of tiny Wayo Wayo island and blows it to smithereens. In response, a fleet of sperm whales travels in rank and file through the Tropic of Capricorn and three typhoons and straight onto the shores of Valparaiso, Chile, where they beach themselves on the coastline of a town whose name evokes a paradise in the cleft of mountains. The novel's description of the deaths of these whales on Valparaiso's sandy shore is long and gruesome: "As if they wanted to force memory from their brains, they would hammer the sand with their heads, leaving huge pits on the beach and making a heavy, hopeless monotone that would pass clear on through to the other side of Chile's coastal mountains, giving the farmers working in the fields pain of the chest."[41] Experts gather and watch as the whales take days to die, decompose, and then explode from built-up gasses in their corpses. The conclusion of *Man with the Compound Eyes* may lack subtlety, but the whale multitude, described as the avatars of the second sons of Wayo Wayo, the southern Pacific island, die as a hoard of 365, one for every day of the year. Humans gather to shed buckets of tears, but the profuse quantities do not change the salinity of the oceans a bit. Mourning makes no difference.

Just as was done with the biotropes discussed in the introduction of this book, the animal tropes here are analyzed for their semiotic aspects, while their ongoing historicity as agential entities is acknowledged. In the case of the whale pack, the ecopolitical import of the scene is greatly reduced without acknowledgment of whale histories. In general, animal tropes may appear more lively than non-animal biotropes, given the myriad kinds of entanglements that animals have with each other and with humans. Particularly at stake when it comes to animal biotropes, as far as *Ecology without Culture* is concerned, is to increase the interpretive range for these biotropes so that they are not reduced to being a singular capacious sign for the "universality of nature," or "the animal," or an "always already supplement" to humanistic meaning.[42] Much of posthumanist philosophy depends upon such a concept of "the animal," which treats animals as philosophically interesting without being particularly concerned with the specifics regarding particular species and their histories and contexts (although there are notable exceptions, including Donna Haraway's writing about border collies and Shunkin's detailed analysis of the rendering of cows). The capacity to keep animal historicities in play alongside the semiotic richness of an animal biotrope opens up ecopolitical interpretive possibilities. We can see more clearly how animal biotropes are semiotic sentinels particularly suited for the expression of a planet in crisis, especially if they are read at Clark's hypothetical scale.

Man with the Compound Eyes, like Tawada's "Island of Eternal Life," first invites interpretation at the geopolitical scale with its references to the South Pacific islands. These islands are well-known as the site where the U.S. military ran countless atomic bomb tests as if the oceans were not populated by anything or anyone worth caring about. By the twenty-first century, the United States had performed around 1,054 nuclear weapons tests, with a substantial percentage of them run in the "Pacific Proving Ground." The ironically named Operation Greenhouse, for example, was detonated on the island of Enewetak Atoll. The scene of whales driven to beach themselves after the detonation of a bomb in the novel is an indictment of the U.S. military's utter disregard for the southern islands and their inhabitants.

At the same time, *Man with the Compound Eyes* is invested in more than a geopolitical indictment of the U.S. military. The novel delves under the surface to describe populations hidden from human eyes. When the bomb was detonated:

> Every creature in the entire ocean heard a deafening sound, like
> no sound that had ever been heard before, as if some mighty being
> were departing. A great gash opened up deep in the trench, and a
> shock wave was transmitted toward the two ends, raising a tsunami
> of unprecedented power. Of iron will, that wave pushed another
> piece of the Trash Vortex toward Wayo Wayo. In three minutes and
> thirty-two seconds, it would, like a gargantuan carpenter's plane,
> peel away everything on the island, the living and the nonliving,
> into the sea.[43]

At the geopolitical scale, the novel levies its ecopolitical critique at the U.S. military, as well as the indigenous and non-indigenous capitalists of Taiwan, but at the hypothetical scale, the ecopolitical critique of the novel is leveled at the human species. The sperm whales are mammalian sentinels whose 365 deaths explicitly link whale deaths to human culture through one of humanity's most central concepts: calendrical time. In this way, ecopolitical critique at the spatial scale of geopolitical history is eclipsed by ecological critique at the hypothetical scale of the survival of species. At this hypothetical scale, the cultural props that atomize humans no longer hold sway as primary ciphers for determining ecological health or identity. Rather, species difference is the foundation for ecological critique.

The eerie scene of 365 whales beating their heads against the sand on the shores of Valparaiso in *Man with the Compound Eyes* is created not only through the image of self-inflicted violence by mammals but also by the image of a hoard of similar non-human beings doing the same thing at the same time. There is an ecological basis for this kind of apocalyptic scene. It is becoming increasingly familiar to see stories of mass beachings of whales and fish on ocean shores. Chile's Valparaiso, in fact, has experienced mass fish die-offs on its shores that are likely related to toxic algal blooms. One hypothesis for the blooms is that extensive aquaculture, which adds too many nutrients to the water, has caused blooms of naturally occurring algae, which get "overfed" when aquaculture is not adequately monitored. Warming seas have also been cited as a reason for these blooms. Ocean monitoring groups like NOAA now track blooms so that coastal managers can prepare for their impact, since consumers can get sick from eating shellfish that have fed on these blooms. In *Man with the Compound Eyes,* the biotrope of the whale hoard signals damage at a scale that extends far beyond the time frame of a few human generations or centuries. Rather, the life patterns that have been common to the species for millennia are shown to have been disrupted. The animal biotrope, when it is analyzed at the hypothetical scale, offers a critical ecological perspective because it matters beyond human generational history.

The Last Wilderness

Tawada published an entire collection of short stories after the events of March 2011 that ends with an apocalyptic play called "Animals' Babel," in which six species of animals (bear, cat, dog, rabbit, squirrel, fox) speak to one another after a great flood. The play begins in a celebratory tone as the animals discuss what is for them the good news that the homo sapiens have gone extinct. The "perverse civilization" of factory farms, the cementing of river banks to make them smooth and firm, the mass use of plastics, and roadkill is over. Then a philosophical debate ensues in which Cat and Dog discuss whether they are really better off without humans. Dog says, "It's generally thought that life's better without the existence of homo sapiens. And it's true. They were like cancerous cells on the earth. But I still miss humans."[44] Cat replies, "But we're all relieved that the two-legged authority is over. Are you trying to aestheticize the past?"[45] The animals don't come to any sort of conclusion, but they agree that they are living at the precipice of a new world in which everything has changed because the species at the top of the food chain has gone, but the disappearance of humans is not the only difference. The animals describe how the ocean and mountains are coming together, how fish have risen from toxic seas to walk on land, and how "10,000 years feels like a minute." In the time it takes to read a few pages, humans, who proceeded in the course of a few millennia to engineer most every corner of the earth, have become extinct and geologic time has taken over. The epoch of the Holocene seems a mere minute in the broader scheme of things. The animals discuss whether they should build a shelter in this new world and, in a veiled reference to the 2011 tsunami, decide against it "because if it falls, there will be rubble everywhere."[46]

The short play takes a turn at its conclusion, however. Squirrel and Dog have just spotted humans beyond the proscenium. Surprised to see humans alive, they each ask a question of the audience:

> DOG: "Are you the last of the humans?"
> CAT: "As the miracle human survivor of this flood, what do you want to do from here on out?"
> SQUIRREL: "I can't believe there is a human survivor. But you look tired. If you could change the past, which part of world history would you change and how?"
> FOX: "I didn't used to think this, but when you look at humans they really have a human face. What's the reason for the extinction of humanity do you think?"
>
> . . . and so on.

The title of this play, with its reference to the Tower of Babel, appears to refer to human history, and the rising seas seem to symbolize the Biblical flood of Christian history. Or it could be the flood of the northeastern seaboard of Japan after the 2011 tsunami, since Tawada had written this book in response to the tsunami and nuclear meltdown. If we are armed with that knowledge, it is possible, as with "Island of Eternal Life," to read the short play parochially, as dystopian allegory for recent human experience. The mythical references, however, invite us to read at the hypothetical scale. In the myths of Babel, humanity's desire to extend its reach to everything resulted in cacophony and chaos. The animals speak for the world before the destroying hand of humanity, and these lines highlight animal interest. And these animals don't forgive. Instead, they do what real animals cannot. They shout out accusatory questions at the human audience whom they consider to be the lackluster inhabitants of a world they hope to survive.

An elegant example of dystopian writing that features animal survivors in a changed world is Ishimure's award-winning poem "My Dear
Weatherbeaten Skull." A few years ago, suffering from debilitating
Parkinson's disease, Ishimure endured a painful fall in the entryway of her
home. She lost consciousness and remained in a coma for three months.
Her dreams were the only things she remembered from those months despite frequent visitors. In that unconscious state, she dreamed of what she
later described as the next century's wilderness. That wilderness was of un-
plowed fields of skinny, non-descript flowers, blind moles tilling the soil,
and top-heavy insects wobbling across featureless grasses. In that dreamscape, she was a light, yellow butterfly of the kind found in Okinawa called
habira. Her body felt like a shell while her spirit floated up, gently flapping
like a butterfly with a quiet *hira hira hira*. She flapped to the strand of her
childhood:

> Where the continent meets the sea meets the river, where the pure
> water and deep tidal water mix, where those going and those com-
> ing meet in returning to their world. The history of living things
> can't be a singular one but formed through mingling with each
> other. . . . There is another landscape, where the sea winds blow
> across the treetops of ancient mountains. When the wind blew, I
> who had become a butterfly, stopped on a branch near the sea in
> an ancient wood where akou trees reside. Akou trees are the ones
> that grow along the strand and absorb the ocean tide. Called feel-
> ing roots, their roots grow at the tips of the branches. At the sea's
> shore, they grow in the tides of the strand. Amakusa has many large
> trees, and their branches face the sea.[47]

In this primordial place, fluttering through the humid air, the butterfly
Ishimure lit upon the various grasses that covered the new wilderness.

In her coma-induced dream state, she looked out at this new wilderness from the eyeholes of her own post-mortem skull. When she finally
awoke from her prolonged slumber, Ishimure wrote the following poem
and named it "My Dear Weatherbeaten Skull":

> Under the cliff, weatherbeaten
> is my
> dear long-lost

skull
with two holes for eyes
and evidence of a hole for the mouth

Flowers in the air
among the sound of mixers
give off a faint fragrance

The sky is filled with the sound of cars
and the sound of bulldozers
The smell of suspended iron claws
suffocate me
I couldn't catch the last remaining voice
of the countless heads
Because the heads were blown to smithereens

The bellybutton ties of babes
flutter in the indecipherable wind

In the expansive silence under heavens
The Kalavinka bird's throat is parched
Isn't there something to drink?

There they are There they are
I see them
Beyond my empty eye sockets
There
The tunnel-digging mole at the head
works away   And the mole crickets
If you put them in your palm
they move their four arms and legs like fish fins.
And like festival floats
pull themselves to the shore beyond the mud
They look like grasshoppers

The field that
those legless worms have planted
grows vast

Near the small spring
purple dayflowers grow
and fill with dew
at dawn

The throat of the Kalavinka bird
who sings more of tranquility for hell than of heaven
will be moistened[48]

The first-person voice of this award-winning poem haunts.[49] It ema-
nates from the drafty interior of a bony skull, a last ghostly whisper among
piles of severed heads, remnants of humans apparently destroyed by their
own mechanical devices. From the nose holes of the skull, the beloved self
of the poem can still smell the stench of human industry in a bulldozer's
rusted metal. The pungent odor lingers in the air as a memory of industrial
times past. The fragrance emitted from the flowers cannot conceal the mil-
dew rust, but no longer in use, the bulldozer's claw hangs listlessly in the
air. Instead of machines turning the earth, the mole and the worm turn the
soil with little fanfare as they search for food. The mole may till to eat the
worm. The worm tills as it gorges itself on organic matter and soil. Humans
do not exist at the exceptional level of productivity, fecundity, and growth.
Instead they are relics without bodies or flesh. Even the speaker thinks of
her own bony skull as a beloved object of an earlier epoch. But the poem
is not about the desire for a luddite return to an agrarian state symbolized
in the furry and slimy bodies of earth tillers, because it concludes with a
prophetic lament depicted in the otherworldly body of a half-humanoid
and half-winged mythical bird. The Kalavinka mourns humanity's disappearance with a dry throat. It no longer sings of the heavens, but only to
calm a hell that lingers in the stench of iron and humanity's bony nostrils.

This is the only poem featured in a book that Ishimure published three
months after the tremendous 9.0 earthquake that rocked fragile nuclear
generators built so close to shore that they shorted in the rising sea-
water and caused the meltdown of three reactors in Fukushima. Ishimure's
depiction of a world without humans in this poem in *Toward a Paradise
of Flowers* (2014) was not necessarily prompted by the nuclear reactor
meltdowns, although she has written about the problem of radiation and
nuclear power in the same volume.[50] Rather, the poem is indicative of
Ishimure's broader oeuvre in how it addresses a broad span of historical

and geological time to tell the tale of industrial modernity the world over. In a few short stanzas, it develops three worlds, one perspective, and two time scales. One scale is a human scale of time and perspective: the world as it appears from a human eye socket of a being that lives a life's span. But that human world is of the past.

The second time scale is an epochal one and includes the world as it was before humans and as it will be after them. Ishimure describes this world in *Toward a Paradise of Flowers* as "a world of grasses who were our parents." The eternal future without humans is embodied in the mythical Kalavinka bird who assuages this new future with a parched throat. The poem presents worlds beyond human scale and interest and in doing so addresses our very moment—the wink of an eye in geological time—in which humanity has made itself such a geophysical force on the planet that it stands to snuff itself out. Even before icecap melt was in evidence, Ishimure's writing was not aimed at reproducing desires of a humanistic world. She writes for a different conception of earthly time.

Were we to read Ishimure's poem within Clark's second scale of methodological nationalism or within the frame of national *ethnos*, we might contextualize it within industrial modernity of Japan's postwar age of high economic growth and bubble era consumer culture and interpret it as a powerful critique of the damage that industrial modernity has writ on the Japanese landscape. We might also develop her use of the Kalavinka bird imagery to argue for her work as specifically drawing on East Asian religious thought in order to stake a claim for her work as exemplary of a "non-Western" critique of industrial modernity. Finally, we might place Ishimure's work specifically within a national literary canon and hold tight to her as a "Japanese author" whose work is relevant inasmuch as she lives on the archipelago. We would treat her work primarily with regard to its relevance within the modern nation-state. The problem is that Ishimure's work itself is explicitly critical of depending on the entity of Japan as a useful frame for knowing or creating an image of the world. Japan, in her work, is always a site criticized for its reproduction of the logic of consumerism among other things.

After the release of radiation from nuclear meltdown, Ishimure wrote the poem "Praying to a Flower" for the strength of a single bloom. She wrote this in response to nuclear reactor meltdown as the only thing she felt she could contribute, and its aesthetic embrace of the biological world over ethnic national interest is fundamental to her broader rejection of industrial modernity. The hypothetical scale resists familiar coordinates of race, class, and gender and the habits of area studies. The laboring animal or insect need not labor in the name of allegorical significance. In the poem "My Dear Weatherbeaten Skull," the talking skull, peering out through her eyeholes, watches the tiny mammals and insects plow the fecund field. The scene is absurd when read at the humanist scale. The image of the weatherbeaten skull looking out from her own extinction to the planet living on without us makes no sense if all we are looking for are humanist values. But read at the hypothetical or epochal scale, the poem generates a perspective that imagines, with a feeling of sincere gratitude, a world without humans.

In conversation with photographer Fujiwara Shin'ya, Ishimure was frank about her contemplation of a world without us: "The thing to contemplate for the modern human is that we breathe the sea and the land. And with us, plants, animals, and the hundreds of thousands of living things breathe. That breath is on the verge of being extinguished. And only humans can do that. The question is, will we destroy ourselves together?"[51] The aesthetics of her poem seem to suggest that we will. But the earnest mole and small insects ambling their way across fields compose a humble picture of a world without us. It is not the stuff of apocalyptic fiction. Rather, it develops a picture of another epoch that will grow out of our self-destruction. In "My Dear Weatherbeaten Skull," the human resembles a displaced object, like an abandoned toy. Despite witnessing the new wilderness, the human voice has nothing to do with that new world. Written from the point of view of the speaker as bodiless observer, the poem even suggests that the witness has little significance beyond expressing gratitude. The figure of the extinct human species, now powerless to produce any change on the earth, is replaced with moles and worms. The human voice that narrates the world without eyes is an empty, observing skull with no capacity to act, no body or mind to control. The skull can only witness the movements of other species who remain on earth. The time for human agency has passed. Taking up the space left by the disappearance of homo sapiens are creatures who exhibit their own kind of agency, perhaps minimal, but as befitting a mole or a worm. These figures enact their own stories through their miniature worlds. They go about their business with little regard for the loss of human life that seems to haunt the skull and the Kalavinka. The apocalyptic vision in this poem is quiet in its attention to small creatures. It is certainly not the stuff of so much speculative fiction nowadays that is dominated by disaster narratives and a perceptual scale that is usually profoundly humanistic as it describes the planet hovering over a precipice driven by global warming and collapsing earth systems. By narrating this new wilderness from the perspective of a skull rotting on the ground, Ishimure provides a witness, but not any kind of witness that reality produces.

In epochal time spans (and not apocryphal ones), difference is expressed in terms of species difference. The talking skull of a homo sapien, looking through her eyeholes, watching the activities of a mole introduces a sense of absurdity. The weatherbeaten skull, "dear to herself," looks out from her own extinction to the planet marching on without its 7,000,000 human bodies peopling its every nook and cranny, and only sighs. A sigh of relief, perhaps? In reading the animal biotropes outside the bounds of humanist logic, there is no need to sustain the fiction that significant historical agency is the preserve of human beings alone.[52]

With this hypothetical reading we begin to see why the *figure* is so important to Spivak in her discussion of the planetary (though she uses the term "planetarity") when she says that metaphors are necessary because there is no formulaic access to the world beyond known identities: "All around us is the clamor for the rational destruction of the figure, the demand for not clarity but immediate comprehensibility by the ideological average. This destroys the force of literature as a cultural good."[53] Metaphors allow a way out of "methodological nationalism," but they only do so as long as we read for that which is not identical to our cultural props and humanistic universals. This planetary is not of data modeling and large-scale thinking that suppresses detail, but a worm's eye view of a human trauma. Planetarity is the detour we make when we read animal biotropes beyond allegory and at a scale beyond that of the cartographic. It is a critical perspective that eschews social agency or the authority of experience as the bedrock of theorizing.[54]

In the history of literature, there are few who have dedicated as much writing to the agonies caused by the excesses of industrial modernity as Ishimure. For more than half a century, she has described how lives have been changed in the wake of industry and rapid economic development. Whether in *Paradise in the Sea of Sorrow*, in her collection of essays on corporate capital and labor, *Migrants of the Capital*, or in her recent *Toward a Paradise of Flowers* published in the wake of nuclear meltdown, Ishimure deftly expresses how economic development has indentured its human

and natural resources. But very infrequently has she depended on a formulaic, rational access to human experience to express environmental
injustice.

Ishimure's revitalization of a centuries-old form of Noh theater proves
another example of her imaginative critique of industrial capitalism.
Shiranui, as translator Bruce Allen writes, is a haunting requiem for the
many victims of mercury poisoning through an apocalyptic vision. This
genre is a form that traditionally crosses into a mythopoetic space of reality and dreams where the past, present, and future are developed through
transhistorical intertextuality and genre form. In Ishimure's reworking
of the form (because she refuses to employ traditional forms when the
landscape is so changed under industrial modernity), the Noh aesthetic
takes on an explicit apocalyptic perspective through animated landscape
and animal biotropes. The chorus sings of the Shiranui Sea, which is also
where the play was performed in the dark evening with large plates of
thick flames lighting the entrance to the stage. The site where it was performed was on the reclamation land where millions of living organisms
were buried alive when the Chisso corporation was forced by the government to clean the mercury-poisoned sea by burying the muck of the bay
in huge metal barrels. The chorus intones: "Sooner or later, an ominous
change will come upon the world of living beings. The coming of such a
fate, in which the pulse of life will perish, is unavoidable. Human beings,
especially, do not realize that they are nothing but hollow, unknowing
corpses—even when their spirit has been extracted from their bodies and
just their mortal remains linger on." The chorus goes on to describe that
the humans have gone too far and poisoned the sea: "The situation is utterly beyond redemption." The play features the Shiranui Sea, who herself
speaks, wondering when it was that the scales of the fishy messengers of
spring lost their "crystal colors." A Boddhisatva in the garb of an old man
recalls the sea when that was all there was: "At one time the bottom of the
sea was . . . where all the young lives of all living beings were first born.
Later those young lives would travel up to the land and turn themselves
into plants and insects and human beings." The antagonists are without
physical representation in this play, invoked only in the voice of a regretful
and frenzied Shiranui who is on the verge of death.

This play ends with the sea and the mountain, brother and sister, together. Their health is not secure, yet they take their remaining energy and
try to reanimate the nearly dead world. Musical chanting begins through

the figure of "Ki," the source and origin of all music and apparition of rocks and trees. Ki begs the cats to return. He invites those first biological sentinels of the Shiranui Sea's poisoning to return. The cats in this play symbolize the tragic illness for all beings in Minamata, but they also represent their own historicity at the spatial scale: the terrible history of the many cats who died from mercury poisoning or were killed in the medical experiments as physicians and researchers tried to learn what was poisoning all denizens who ate from the sea. At the planetary or hypothetical scale, cats are all life forms as they first emerged from the brine of our original ocean. The deeply sonorous chanting and drumbeats urge these creatures to appear once again, not as the mourned dead, but as if from that original place of life: "You, O lovely and beloved cats who died such miserable deaths on this beach, come forward, before all the other beings, come out to dance. If you find the sounds of the striking of stones beautiful, then come out as sacred cats and dance, dance wildly. Become butterflies, and dance, dance! Tonight the air is filled with the fragrance of tangerines."[55] The cats are invited first.

The human imagination, for better or for worse, is a powerful thing. Representational worlds can allow us to forget our deep dependence on the material world. Conversely, they can imagine, like *Shiranui*, the apocalypse. But they can also imagine a world without us in order to imagine a world anew with us.

Acknowledgments

The tidal moon glows with an uncertain hue of yellowish gold
illuminating a deceptively strong surf that plays at caressing the shore
A short-legged dog keeps a quick pace along the beach, neither
    walking nor running
tempting waves that seem new though they must be old
Amid these either ors and neither nors
There are
some things I'm sure of.

I HAVE BEFORE ME the overwhelming task of thanking colleagues, students, and friends who generously helped me in myriad ways as I wrote this book. I am filled with gratitude for those who spoke to me freely about their love of the natural world and shared their uninhibited expressions of sorrow at compromised environments and strained animal lives. Those stories encouraged me to continue to plumb the relationship of culture to environment.

Conversations with colleagues over the years helped me clarify what was at stake for me in writing this book. My first thanks is to Livia Monnet, whose brilliance and friendship I deeply value. I'm grateful for her translation skill that brought Ishimure Michiko's tour de force to the Anglophone world. For years, I've benefited deeply from discussions with my colleagues at the University of Minnesota at workshops on campus and a microbrewery or two in the Twin Cities. Jason McGrath has been an essential friend and colleague. I thank him for introducing me to the novel *Man with the Compound Eyes*. Travis Workman was always willing to talk about various facets of humanism and cultural production; my Aldrich Avenue comrade Hiromi Mizuno pushed me to provide more examples; Paul Rouzer's great sympathy helped me through difficult times; Maki Isaka's careful scholarship has always been a model for me in writing; and Joe Allen kept my mailbox stuffed with articles in animal studies. I thank Thomas Lamarre for his critical insights and for his path-breaking work on animals in representation. Miyawaki Toshifumi kindly sponsored me during a five-month research sojourn generously funded by the Japan Foundation. During that trip, I met the talented Kaneko Ai, whose moving performances in Minamata and support of nuclear refugees have inspired me to read a much broader range of poetry by contemporary writer-activists. I thank her for introducing me to performer and interlocutor for Ishimure's plays and poetry, Kasai Ken'ichi, who probably doesn't know the impact his approach to environmentalism and art has had on me. Accompanying both of them to meet Ishimure Michiko will always be remembered as a highlight of my life. I thank Masami Yuki and Bruce Allen for their continued research and translation of Ishimure's writing and for including me in their ecocriticism projects. While I am a skeptic of sorts when it comes to area studies, I think it is essential to expand the field of ecocriticism through the study of theory and texts from around the globe. Those who bring non-Anglophone texts into larger comparative conversations about environment, theory, and representation are forging new ground for ecocriticism. I thank Yuki Fumiko for introducing me to the wonderful group of people at Kichijōji. Jim Fujii has been an anchor for me always. If only we could all be as compassionate a friend and human being as he is. I thank my UW twin, Davinder Bhowmik, for her everlasting encouragement and for introducing the beauty of Okinawa to me and Lorenz. Julia Adeney Thomas is a voracious reader and generous colleague with compelling ecocritical perspectives. Ian Miller's comments on a draft proved very helpful. Simona Sawhney has always been my rudder. Rebeka Ndosi's wisdom knows no bounds and I feel lucky that our sons' friendship brought us together. Joseph Larsen and Hannah Taube are two students who have helped me with technical difficulties and reminded me how much our younger generations are invested in environmental health. Emily Durham selflessly came in at the last hour with fresh eyes. Matt Bockley helped take care of things that inevitably emerge in daily life with a child.

Others I'd like to thank for their encouragement and wisdom are Jonathan Abel, Brett de Bary, Michael Bourdaghs, Tony Brown, Su Chen, Yao Chen, Steve Chung, Kevin Doak, Elise Domenach, Fujiwara Toshi, Aaron Gerow, Melvin Giles, Jonathan Mark Hall, Marilyn Ivy, Reginald Jackson, John Namjun Kim, Motoo Kobayashi, Yasuko Makino, Anne McKnight, Tim Murray, Nakagawa Shigemi, Markus Nornes, Gregory Pflugfelder, Suvadip Sinha, Douglas Slaymaker, Suga Keijiro, Akiko

Takenaka, Christophe Thouny, John Treat, Hisaake Wake, Ann Waltner, anonymous readers for the University of Minnesota Press, and the Boss writing camp. I couldn't have had sequestered away time for research and writing without the funding of the Institute for Advanced Study at the University of Minnesota, the Japan Foundation, and the Society for the Humanities at Cornell University. Time with brilliant cohorts at the University of Minnesota and Cornell was invaluable. I'd especially like to thank the University of Minnesota Press editor Jason Weidemann for his guidance and Mike Stoffel and Ana Bichanich for their brave editing and patience. I alone am responsible for any flaws.

Those who know me won't be surprised that I've also got to thank Eugene, whose company means the world to me. This short book took a while for me to write, and during that time Eugene, with his four legs, and I, with my two, took many walks. We walked through four or more spring seasons and on those spring walks, I marveled at the way the Minnesota landscape renews itself from the ground up in such a brief span of time. For those not familiar with Minnesota, it's a curiously dramatic place, meteorologically speaking. Winters are so frigid that hardly anything seems to survive above ground during the cold months. Sure, the red twig dogwood offers up pretty scarlet branches against the white snow, dark berries cling to a few hardy bushes, and pin oaks hold on to their marcescent leaves. But all in all, winter proves to be a mostly modern landscape of simple lines and a monochromatic palette. Come spring, though, the air warms, rain falls, and almost overnight new leaves unfurl and the grass has grown a foot high. The renewal is dramatic and profound. It's a renewal that I wish for many species of the world, whether polar bears up north or raccoons trying to survive in the city Pom Poko–style. That spring renewal may never come for many. But I can be grateful for the landscapes and species that manage, sometimes against all odds, to regenerate themselves from year to year.

My final expression of gratitude goes to my parents, and to two people who have made all the difference in how Lorenz and I have experienced the world—my brother Keith and his husband, my brother-in-law, David. This is just to say, thanks.

Notes

Introduction

Japanese and Chinese names are given with the surname first when the author has written in Japanese or Chinese. The names of all authors of English-language texts are given with personal names first and surnames last.

1. Wu Ming-yi, *Man with the Compound Eyes,* trans. Darryle Sterk (London: Vintage Books, 2014), 39.

2. Ibid., 40.

3. Ibid., 18.

4. Ibid.

5. Ibid., 17.

6. Timothy Morton, *Ecology without Nature* (Cambridge, Mass.: Harvard University Press, 2007), 1.

7. Ibid., 19.

8. Tina Hesman Saey, "Body's Bacteria Don't Outnumber Human Cells So Much After All," *Science News* 189, no. 3 (February 6, 2016): 6, https://www.sciencenews.org/article/body%E2%80%99s-bacteria-don%E2%80%99t-outnumber-human-cells-so-much-after-all.

9. Timothy Clark, *The Cambridge Introduction to Literature and the Environment* (Cambridge: Cambridge University Press, 2011), 89.

10. Ibid., 93.

11. Ibid.

12. Kim writes, "An ethics of avowal is ultimately about constructing a reimagined 'we' in resistance to the neoliberal elites waging war against racialized groups, animals, nature, and others" (Claire Kean Kim, *Dangerous Crossings* [New York: Cambridge University Press, 2015], 19).

13. Ibid., 21.

14. Stacy Alaimo, *Bodily Natures* (Bloomington: Indiana University Press, 2010).

15. Edward Said, *Culture and Imperialism* (New York: Vintage Books, 1993), xiv.

16. Serenella Iovino and Serpil Oppermann, *Material Ecocriticism* (Bloomington: Indiana University Press, 2015).

17. An extreme example of ethnic nationalist biotropes is found in the comments of haiku poet Kuroda Momoko, who writes: "Seasonal words are our national treasures. They are like jewels, polished and made more precious by time. Some seasonal words have been in use since the Edo period. When we pick up one of these jewels and use it in a haiku, it is rich with history. They are the shared consciousness of our people. They capture the essence of Japanese life" (Momoko Kurado, *Introducing Haiku Poets and Topics, A Project of the World Kigo Databse,* March 14, 2010, http://wkdhaikutopics.blogspot.com/2008/03/kuroda -momoko.html).

18. Nicole Shukin has referred to the use of animals in representation as productive for culture and capital because the animal sign has a "mimetic capaciousness" that allows it to represent both the literal and the figurative. Its potency, which she calls its "fetishistic potency," lies in this capacity "to appear to speak from the universal and disinterested place of nature," when in fact the animal is not a neutral signifier (*Animal Capital: Rendering Life in Biopolitical Times* [Minneapolis: University of Minnesota Press, 2009]).

19. Donna Haraway, *How Like a Leaf: An Interview with Thyrza Nichols Goodeve* (New York: Routledge, 2000), 137.

20. Lawrence Buell, *Writing for an Endangered World* (Cambridge, Mass.: Belknap Press, 2003), 10.

21. In this speech, Murakami asserted: "Whether or not that spiritual perspective has been influenced by those natural catastrophes of Japan is beyond my understanding. Nevertheless, we have overcome wave upon wave of natural disasters in Japan and we have come to accept them as 'unavoidable things' (*shikata ga nai mono*). We have overcome those catastrophes as a group and it is clear we have carried on in our lives. Perhaps those experiences have influenced our aesthetic sensibility" ("Speaking as an Unrealistic Dreamer: Speech by Murakami Haruki on the Occasion of Receiving the International Catalunya Prize," trans. Emanuel Pastreich, *The Asia-Pacific Journal* 9, no. 29.27 [July 19, 2011], http://apjjf .org/2011/9/29/Murakami-Haruki/3571/article.html).

22. Ibid. I have changed Pastreich's translation of "national mindset" to "ethnic mentality" to better reflect the original.

23. In *Traditional Japanese Literature,* ed. Haruo Shirane (New York: Columbia University Press, 2012), 95.

24. Clark, *Introduction to Literature and the Environment,* 78.

25. The Japanese term for this was "minzoku-teki mentariti-."

26. Fukushima photographer Fujiwara Shin'ya called Murakami's claim that all citizens are responsible for the meltdown because of their shared silence on nuclear power "the quick and easy claim of a spectator" in Ishimure Michiko and Fujiwara Shin'ya, *Namida furuhana* (Tokyo: Kawade Shobō Shinsha, 2012), 147.

27. "Murakami Haruki-san: Tandoku interview: 'Kozetsu' koe, Risō shugi e,"

Mainichi Shinbun, November 3, 2014, http://mainichi.jp/shimen/news/20141103ddm010040055000c.html.

28. Elizabeth Grosz, *Time Travels* (Durham, N.C.: Duke University Press, 2005), 43.

29. Ibid.

30. Ibid., 44.

31. Ibid.

32. Ibid., 47.

33. Shiga Shigetaka, *Nihon Fūkeiron,* ed. Kondo Nobuyuki (Tokyo: Iwanami Shoten, 1995; originally Tokyo: Seikyōsha, 1894).

34. The seven special features of Japan according to Shiga are: the persistent change of the climate; profuse steam; the beauty of trees and plants; steep terrain; volcanic phenomena; distinctive shoreline and islands; and abundant vegetation.

35. Richard Okada, "'Landscape' and the Nation State: A Reading of *Nihon Fūkeiron,*" in *New Directions in the Study of Meiji Japan,* ed. Helen Hardacre and Adam Lewis Kern (Leiden: Brill, 1993), 97.

36. Christine Marran, *Poison Woman: Figuring Female Transgression in Modern Japanese Culture* (Minneapolis: University of Minnesota Press, 2007), 40, 45.

37. Nobuko Toyosawa, "An Imperial Vision: *Nihon Fūkeiron (On the Landscape of Japan,* 1894) and Naturalized Nature," *Studies on Asia,* 4th ser., 3, no. 1 (March 2013), 30.

38. Morton, *Ecology without Nature,* 156.

39. Ibid., 141.

40. Shirane's discussion specifically focuses on ever-expanding detailed glossaries that provide guidelines for invoking seasonal flora and fauna in Japanese-language poetry. Called *saijiki,* these glossaries have fed a literary tradition that depends upon the use of conventional forms including the use of seasonal words, determined syllabic rhythm of 5–7, and transhistorical intertextuality, aided by poetry glossaries that provide guidelines for the use of these biotropes (Haruo Shirane, *Japan and the Culture of the Four Seasons* [New York: Columbia University Press, 2012]).

41. A later story by Murakami is instructive in how nature still holds the place of the transcendental in even the most postmodern of writers. Years before the wave claimed thousands of lives on the northeastern seaboard, Murakami had written a short story about a fictional tsunami, "The Seventh Man" (in *Blind Willow, Sleeping Woman,* trans. Jay Rubin [New York: Vintage, 2007]). In this story, an enormous wave takes the life of the seventh man's childhood friend. The seventh man feels that the tragedy stole forty years from his life: "It just barely missed me, but in my place it swallowed everything that mattered most to me and swept it off to another world. I took years to find it again and to recover from the experience—precious years that can never be replaced" (163). The biotrope

of the tsunami is heavy with existentialist meaning for the seventh man, who even remarks on the utter interchangeability of the wave with some other existentialist force. The wave symbolized that thing to which he surrendered himself: "In my case, it was a wave," he said. "There's no way for me to tell, of course, what it will be for each of you. But in my case it just happened to take the form of a gigantic wave. It presented itself to me all of a sudden one day, without warning, in the shape of a giant wave. And it was devastating" (164). Nature performs the humanist existentialism in this portrait of an anomalous ocean event. The materiality of the wave matters little to this narrative. It is a portrait of a suburban town of neither wild nor fully developed land, a modern wasteland. But the ocean waves continued to lap the shore "like before" and people walked along the surf "like before" in a transcendental biotrope of the sea.

42. Okada, "'Landscape' and the Nation State," 94.

43. Ibid., 105.

44. Tsurumi Kazuko, *The Adventure of Ideas* (Tokyo: Japanime, 2012). Tsurumi's collected works have been published in Japanese by Fujiwara Shoten in eight volumes as *Tsurumi Kazuko Mandala*.

45. Ibid., 118–19.

46. Naoki Sakai, "Theory and Asian Humanity: On the Question of Humanitas and Anthropos," *Postcolonial Studies* 13, no. 4 (2010): 443.

47. *Contested Natures*, ed. Phil Macnaghten and John Urry (London: Sage Publications, 1998), 234.

48. http://www.sciencedaily.com/releases/2011/06/110608153538.htm.

49. This kind of ethnic environmental narrative of loss is rife in the work of Umehara Takeshi and Yasuda Yoshinori and is described by Margaret Sleeboom as one that appeals to an ethnic nationalist tradition of regional spirituality and morality (*Academic Nations in China and Japan* [London: RoutledgeCurzon, 2004]).

50. In conversation with Ishimure, Tsurumi Kazuko finds Japanese classical poetry useful to lament Japan's eroded environment (*Kotoba hatsuru tokoro* [Tokyo: Fujiwara Shoten, 2002]). This is another way in which traditional biotropes are praised by Tsurumi to express an ethnic nationalist culture.

51. Marilyn Ivy, *Discourses of the Vanishing* (Chicago: University of Chicago Press, 1995), 8.

52. Ibid.

53. Yasuda Yoshinori, "Animism Renaissance," *Nichibunken Newsletter* no. 5 (January 1990), 2–4. Yasuda, a scholar at the Nichibunken, has edited a number of volumes with Umehara Takeshi, who also engages in ethnic environmentalist discourse on ancient environmental history.

54. Ibid.

55. Responses were submitted by Miyamoto Masao and Ian Reader in *Nichibunken Newsletter* no. 6 (May 1990).

56. Julia Adeney Thomas, *Reconfiguring Modernity* (Berkeley: University of California Press, 2001), 169 (italics mine).

57. Ironically, this stance is taken as Japanese industry has expanded wildly overseas and antipollution groups were effectively silenced. Environmental activist and scholar Ui Jun writes, "However, with the advance of Japan's imperial armies into China, followed by general mobilization for Second World War production, military-related industries continued to discharge pollutants into natural environments and all the efforts at pollution control that were seen in the 1920s were forgotten. All antipollution citizens' movements were totally suppressed, with the exception of the Osarusawa Mining and Ishikari River Kokusaku Pulp situations, where industrial discharge and environmental pollution problems were intense. After Japan's defeat in the war, industries were closed down and this gave nature a little breathing space to recuperate from the pollutional ravages of the war years. Then, as Japan began to rebuild its industrial structure, environmental destruction began once again to rear its ugly head, and local movements against this destruction began to appear, though the majority of the population had little or no time for such issues" (*Industrial Pollution in Japan* [Tokyo: United Nations University Press, 1992], at http://archive.unu.edu/unupress/unupbooks/uu35ie/uu35ie02 .htm). For an analysis of the technological, colonial, and literary, see Gregory Golley's powerful book *When Our Eyes No Longer See: Realism, Science, and Ecology in Japanese Literary Modernism* (Cambridge, Mass.: Harvard University Press, 2008).

58. Jane I. Dawson, *Eco-Nationalism: Anti-nuclear Activism and National Identity in Russia, Lithuania, and Ukraine* (Durham, N.C.: Duke University Press, 2012), 97.

59. Stuart Hall, "The West and the Rest: Discourse and Power," in *The Formations of Modernity: Understanding Modern Societies; an Introduction, Book 1*, ed. Bram Gieben and Stuart Hall (Cambridge: Polity Press, 1993), 185–227.

60. Eduardo Viveiros de Castro, *Cannibal Metaphysics*, ed. and trans. by Peter Skafish (Minneapolis: Univocal, 2014), 40–43.

61. Nandita Sharma, "Strategic Anti-Essentialism: Decolonizing Decolonization," in *Sylvia Wynter: On Being Human as Praxis*, ed. by Katherine McKittrick (Durham, N.C.: Duke University Press, 2015), 166. Read also Sylvia Wynters, "1492: A New World View," in *Race, Discourse, and the Origin of the Americas: A New World View (Symposium Held at the Smithsonian Institution, 1991)*, ed. Vera Lawrence Hyatt and Rex Nettleford (Washington, D.C.: Smithsonian Institution Press, 1995).

62. Sharma, "Strategic Anti-Essentialism," 170.

63. George Hutchison and Dick Wallace, *Grassy Narrows* (Toronto: Van Nostrand Reinhold, 1977).

64. See "Planetary Dashboard Shows 'Great Acceleration' in Human Activity

Since 1950," *The International Geosphere-Biosphere Programme,* http://www
.igbp.net/news/pressreleases/pressreleases/planetarydashboardshowsgreat
accelerationinhumanactivitysince1950.5.950c2fa1495db7081eb42.html.

65. See James A. Foley, "Seven Nations Contributed to 60 Percent of Global
Warming: Study," *Nature World News,* http://www.natureworldnews.com/
articles/5664/20140116/seven-nations-contributed-60-percent-global-warming
-study.htm, and Concordia University, "Global Warming's Biggest Offenders,"
http://www.concordia.ca/news/stories/cunews/main/stories/2014/01/15/
global-warming-sbiggestoffenders.html?utm_source=slide1&utm_medium=cqc
-banner-global-warming-sbiggestoffenders&utm_campaign=homepagebanner.

66. A term from Naoki Sakai's "Asian Theory and European Humanity—On
the Question of *Anthropological Difference,*" July 2014, draft, http://studylib.net/
doc/6690111/asian-theory-and-european-humanity, a revision of an original publication in *Postcolonial Studies* 14, no. 4 (2010): 441–64. As Sakai indicates elsewhere ("Translation and the Schematism of Bordering," http://www.translating
-society.de/conference/papers/2/), the "Dislocation of the West" is his own
name for an ongoing project in his work and is taken from his earlier "Dislocation of the West," *Traces: A Multilingual Journal of Culture Theory and Translation* 1
(2001): 71–94.

67. Frédéric Neyrat, "The Western Relation: The Politics of Humanism," trans.
Flannery Wilson, Maxime Blanchard, and John Namjum Kim, in *The Politics of
Culture,* ed. Richard Calichman and John Namjun Kim (New York: Routledge,
2010).

68. Ursula Heise, *Sense of Place and Sense of Planet* (Oxford: Oxford University
Press, 2008).

69. See Brett Walker, *Toxic Archipelago: A History of Industrial Disease in
Japan* (Seattle: University of Washington Press, 2010), for a discussion of
(1) the fetishization of white skin in Japan as contributing to cadmium disease
and (2) Confucianist paternalism as discouraging laborers from complaining
about environmental abuses, both examined in attempt to assess, as part of an
hybridinal approach, why some of the archipelago's people have become ill from
industrial toxins.

70. Karen Thornber, *Ecoambiguity: Environmental Crises and East Asian Literatures* (Ann Arbor: University of Michigan, 2012), 16.

71. Rob Nixon, *Slow Violence: Environmentalism of the Poor* (Cambridge,
Mass.: Harvard University Press, 2013), 233.

72. Ibid.

73. Ibid., 237.

74. Verena Andermatt Conley, *Ecopolitics: The Environment in Poststructuralist Thought* (London: Routledge, 1997); Ian Jared Miller, *The Nature of the
Beasts: Empire and Exhibition at the Tokyo Imperial Zoo* (Berkeley: University of

California Press, 2014); and Fabio Rambelli, "Buddhist Environmentalism: Limits and Possibilities, *Poetica* 80 (2013): 21–50.

1. Obligate Storytelling

1. See Vinciane Despret and Michel Meuret, "Cosmoecological Sheep and the Arts of Living on a Damaged Planet," *Environmental Humanities* 8, no. 1 (2016): 26.

2. Tsuchimoto Noriaki, "Ishimure Michiko-san nakariseba, eiga wa?" in *Ishimure Michiko zenshū, Geppō*, no. 24 (Tokyo: Fujiwara Shoten, 2004), insert.

3. Ishimure Michiko, *Paradise in the Sea of Sorrow (Kugai Jōdo)*, trans. Livia Monnet, Michigan Classics in Japanese Studies 25 (Ann Arbor: University of Michigan Press, 2003). The translator has chosen to translate the title of Ishimure's work with the term "sorrow" to capture the essence of the Sino-Japanese character 苦, which also connotes "suffering" or "pain." I refer to Monnet's translation throughout this book. Other translations of Japanese texts are mine unless otherwise noted.

4. Tsuchimoto, "Ishimure Michiko-san nakariseba, eiga wa?" insert.

5. Jody Porter, "Mercury levels still rising near Grassy Narrows First Nation," *CBC News*, June 15, 2015, http://www.cbc.ca/news/canada/thunder-bay/mercury-levels-still-rising-near-grassy-narrows-first-nation-report-says-1.3109261.

6. Thomas W. Clarkson, "The Three Modern Faces of Mercury," in "Reviews in Environmental Health," supplement, *Environmental Health Perspectives* 110, no. S1 (2002): 11: "In the late 1950s and early 1960s serious outbreaks of alkyl mercury poisoning erupted in several developing countries. The largest, most recent outbreak occurred in rural Iraq in the winter of 1971–1972. Some 6,000 cases were admitted to hospitals. An epidemiologic follow-up suggested that as many as 40,000 individuals may have been poisoned. These outbreaks were caused by preparing homemade bread directly from the treated seed grain. Several factors contributed to these mass health disasters. The warning labels were not written in the local language. Well-known symbols for poisons in the Western world, such as the skull and crossbones, have no meaning to rural Arabs. . . . Typically, a red dye is added to the treated grain to indicate the presence of a fungicide. This was counterproductive, as the victims washed away the dye, thinking they had also removed the poison."

7. John Berger, "Uses of Photography," in *About Looking* (New York: Vintage Books, 1991), 62.

8. Vincianne Despret, "Ethology between Empathy, Standpoint and Perspectivism: the Case of the Arabian Babblers," http://www.vincianedespret.be/2010/04/ethology-between-empathy-standpoint-and-perspectivism-the-case-of-the-arabian-babblers/.

9. John Berger, "Millet and the Peasant," in *About Looking*, 83.

10. Ibid., 84.

11. Ibid.

12. Ishimure Michiko and Tsurumi Kazuko, *Kotoba hatsuru tokoro* (Tokyo: Fujiwara Shoten, 2003), 116.

13. Rachel Carson's *Silent Spring* (1962) founded the United States' environmental movement, but Ishimure's bestselling *Paradise in the Sea of Suffering* brought pollution damage caused by industry to readers of Japanese like no other work. Five years later, Ariyoshi Sawako's *Cumulative Pollution* (1974), discussed in chapter 3 of this volume, would create an ecopolitical firestorm.

14. Kitagawa Fukiko, "'Utsukushii kokyō' no egaki-kata," in *Kankyō to iu shiza: Nihon bungaku to ekokuriteishizumu*, ed. Watanabe Kenji et al. (Tokyo: Bensei Shuppan, 2011), 108–15.

15. In writing the poem, the empress was following the imperial tradition of writing sympathy poems for imperial subjects who experienced tragedy. The Japanese version of the poem is: 帰り来るを／立ちて待てるに／季（とき）のなく／岸といふ文字を／歳時記に見ず.

16. Timothy Morton, *Ecology without Nature: Rethinking Environmental Aesthetics* (Cambridge, Mass.: Harvard University Press, 2007), 141.

17. Philippe Descola, *The Ecology of Others*, trans. Genevieve Godbout and Benjamin Luley (Chicago: Prickly Paradigm Press, 2013), 61.

18. Philippe Descola, *Beyond Nature and Culture*, trans. Janet Lloyd (Chicago: University of Chicago Press, 2013), 77.

19. Ibid., xv.

20. Ishimure and Tsurumi, *Kotoba hatsuru tokoro*, 85.

21. Ibid., 117.

22. Akio Mishima, *Bitter Sea*, trans. Richard L. Gage and Susan B. Murata (Tokyo: Kosei, 1992), 95.

23. See Masami Yuki, "Toward a Language of Life: Ecological Identity in the Work of Kazue Morisaki," in *East Asian Ecocriticisms*, ed. Simon Estok and Won-chung Kim (New York: Palgrave MacMillan, 2013), 17–34.

24. From a 1973 dialogue with Ueno Eishin, "*Kugai jōdo* kishikata yukusue," in *Ishimure Michiko zenshū*, vol. 3 (Tokyo: Fujiwara Shoten, 2004), 512. In this dialogue, Ishimure and Ueno consider the final words at death to be literature (*bungaku*).

25. Ueno described his efforts to write the experience of miners in southern Kyushu as an attempt to brand in writing the curse of the dead stolen by the dark earth's depths (Ueno Eishin, *Nihon kanbotsu ki* [Tokyo: Miraisha, 1961], 83). My removal of standard punctuation in translating the coal miners' last testaments here is to signal how they had communicated their messages without punctuation

and in syllabary usually reserved for foreign words and science texts. This sylla-bary was likely used because angular lines could be more easily etched in iron and stone with nails and other hard implements.

26. Ishimure Michiko, "Ningen ga yadotta shizen," in *Ishimure Michiko zenshū,* vol. 7 (Tokyo: Fujiwara Shoten, 2005), 270.

27. When Ishimure berated Japan's founding national literary establishment for its utter lack of interest in the environmental health of the archipelago, she referred to their anemic response to Japan's first modern environmental disas-ter from industry, the Ashio copper mine disaster at the turn of the century, at which time the literary establishment was pursuing the problem of how to repre-sent the interiority of a modern subject in Japanese literature (Ishimure, *Kotoba hatsuru tokoro,* 121). In a recent conversation with Fukushima photographer Fu-jiwara Shin'ya, Ishimure told him of her early dissatisfaction with tanka aesthet-ics (Ishimure Michiko and Fujiwara Shin'ya, *Namida furuhana* [Tokyo: Kawade Shobō Shinsha, 2012], 47).

28. Ruth Ozeki, "Thoughts in Language," http://www.ruthozeki.com/thoughts-in-language.

29. Ishimure, *Paradise in the Sea of Sorrow,* 306–7.

30. Ishimure, "Nami to ki no kataru koto," *Gendai Shisō* 26, no. 6 (May 1998), 30–9.

31. Ishimure, *Paradise in the Sea of Sorrow,* 320.

32. Those dependent on their environment for work and food were particu-larly vulnerable to the toxins produced by industrial modernity, even if the im-pact of mercury on the body depended on the species, age, and gender of the victim. This difference made it often impossible for those whose symptoms did not exactly fit the five required manifestations of the disease to be certified to qualify for compensation. In other words, the variation of symptoms caused by methyl mercury from person to person provided an excuse for the medical certification board to deny certification and, therefore, compensation. As the number of victims grew, medical certification boards increasingly demanded consistent manifestations of all five officially recognized symptoms across the board. But bodies do not so easily mirror each other. The consistency that the certification board sought was often absent, with only some symptoms being ex-hibited visibly. Their misplaced desire for consistent evidence of the manifesta-tion of the disease illustrates that kind of "misplaced concreteness" that Donna Haraway identifies as a biological determinism that is not of this world, not for anyone ("Anthropocene, Capitalocene, Chthulucene," [lecture presented on May 9, 2014, at the "Anthropocene: Arts of Living on a Damaged Planet" conference, University of California, Santa Cruz, May 8–10, 2014], http://opentranscripts .org/transcript/anthropocene-capitalocene-chthulucene/). Obligate storytelling

animates the necessary relations of beings and matter—the ways in which beings and matter are obligated to each other—but for each body, not for an abstract collectivity.

33. Ishimure noted an exception. The patient's medical chart in some cases did exhibit a sense of obligation by accounting for the diseased. The medical chart of twenty-year-old "M," prepared by a young doctor on November 24, 1970, contrasted sharply with that depicted in *Paradise in the Sea of Sorrow*. She called him one who avoided the "cruelty of terminology" to remark upon the subjectivity of the bedridden child wracked with congenital mercury disease ("Shisha-tachi wa hazukashimerareru: Minamata-byō kokuhatsu no genten," in *Ishimure Michiko zenshū*, vol. 5 [Tokyo: Fujiwara Shoten, 2004], 409).

34. Ishimure Michiko, *Hana no okudo e* (Tokyo: Fujiwara Shoten, 2014), 186.

35. Ishimure, "Shisha-tachi wa hazukashimerareru," 408.

36. Ibid. The original for "countless existences" is *senman muryō no sonzai*.

37. Ishimure had explicitly criticized the imperial state's oppressive policies in the essay "Kiku to Nagasaki" (Chrysanthemums and Nagasaki). She recalls that during wartime, Okinawans were forced to speak in standard Japanese and forego their local idiom, and those who used the latter were forced to wear a red letter as punishment. Okinawans struggled to use the dominant national language, but when they were among themselves, they returned to dialect "like ocean seaweed opening up like a flower" ("Kugai jōdo no sekai," in *Ishimure Michiko zenshū*, vol.14 [Tokyo: Fujiwara Shoten, 2008], 486). For her, one problem with standard Japanese of the postwar period was that it was so tightly wound up with imperial militarism of the early twentieth century.

38. See the introduction of Ishimure, *Paradise in the Sea of Sorrow*.

39. Kawamura Minato, "Kaze o yomu, Mizu ni kaku," *Gunzō* 52, no. 6 (June 1997): 384–404.

40. Isabelle Stengers, "Wondering About Materialism," in *The Speculative Turn: Continental Materialism and Realism*, ed. Levi Bryant, Nick Srnicek, and Graham Harman (Melbourne: Re.Press, 2011), 375. Stengers also writes that "with the knowledge economy, we may have scientists at work everywhere, producing facts with the speed that new sophisticated instruments make possible, but that the way those facts are interpreted will now mostly follow the landscape of settled interests," 377.

41. Ishimure, "Ishi no omoi," in *Ishimure Michiko zenshū*, 7:425.

42. Ishimure Michiko, *Rumin no miyako* (Tokyo: Daiwa Shobō, 1973), 18–19.

43. Ishimure, "Ningen ni yadotta shizen," in *Ishimure Michiko zenshū*, 7:269.

44. Ibid., 269–70.

45. Ryoko Sekiguchi, *Heliotropes*, trans. Sarah O'Brien (Montreal: La Presse, 2008), 42.

46. Ibid., 15.

47. Ibid., 23.

48. Ibid., 38.

49. Ibid., 29.

50. Ibid., 42.

51. Ibid., 53.

52. Ibid., 75.

53. Jane Bennett, "Powers of the Hoard: Artistry and Agency in a World of Vibrant Matter," presented as the introductory lecture of the Vera List Center's 2011–2013 focus theme "Thingness," September 13, 2011, The New School, New York, Vimeo video, 1:14:44, https://vimeo.com/29535247. See also Bennett, "Systems and Things: A Response to Graham Harman and Timothy Morton," *New Literary History* 43, no. 2 (Spring 2012).

54. See Bennett, "Powers of the Hoard."

55. Steven Shaviro, "Consequences of Panpsychism," in *The Nonhuman Turn,* ed. Richard Grusin (Minneapolis: University of Minnesota Press, 2015), 24.

56. Diana Coole and Samantha Frost, *New Materialisms* (Durham, N.C.: Duke University Press, 2010), 4.

57. Shaviro, "Consequences of Panpsychism," 22.

58. Fish with increased fatty tissue that live high up the trophic tier and in less strong currents tend to carry greater toxins. For example, the tilefish, in general, is more apt to carry mercury in its body, because of the amount of fatty tissue and its habitat, than the bluepoint oyster. In the Shiranui Sea, the trophic tiers—from plankton to anchovy, then to other, larger fish, and then to cat or bird or human—meant that the methyl mercury released by the Chisso corporation into the Shiranui Sea poisoned the biomass, then plankton, and then smaller creatures, becoming accumulated and magnified as it traveled through bodies up the trophic tiers. Through the process of biomagnification, those toxins became increasingly noxious up the tiers.

59. Stacy Alaimo, *Bodily Natures: Science, Environment, and the Material Self* (Bloomington: Indiana University Press, 2010), 2.

60. Ishimure, *Paradise in the Sea of Sorrow,* 263.

61. Ibid., 149.

62. Ishimure Michiko, *Lake of Heaven,* trans. Bruce Allen (Lanham, Md.: Lexington Books, 2008), 323, 325–26.

63. Ibid., 115–16.

64. Ibid., 111.

65. Gilles Deleuze and Felix Guattari, *A Thousand Plateaus: Capitalism and Schizophrenia,* trans. Brian Massumi (Minneapolis: University of Minnesota Press, 1987), 272–75.

66. Lori Brown, "Becoming-Animal in the Flesh: Expanding the Ethical Reach of Deleuze and Guattari's Tenth Plateau," *PhaenEx* 2, no. 2 (Fall/Winter 2007): 272.

67. Ibid., 263.

68. Deleuze and Guattari, *A Thousand Plateaus,* 240.

69. Steve Baker, "What Does Becoming-Animal Look Like?" *Representing Animals,* ed. Nigel Rothfels (Bloomington: Indiana University Press, 2002), 67.

70. Ibid., 16.

71. Paraphrase of Gregory Bateson, *Steps to an Ecology of Mind* (New York: Ballantine, 1972), quote by Felix Guattari in *The Three Ecologies,* trans. Paul Sutton (London: Continuum, 2005), 93n56.

72. Ishimure Michiko and Nishijima Takeo, "Kankyō hakai," *Ronza* 58, no. 2 (February 2000): 106.

73. Iwaoka Nakamasa, *Roman-shugi kara Ishimure Michiko e* (Tokyo: Atenesha, 2007).

74. Ishimure Michiko, "Mizuumi no ue no fuji," in *Ishimure Michiko zenshū,* vol. 12 (Tokyo: Fujiwara Shoten, 2004), 324.

75. Philippe Descola, *Beyond Nature and Culture* (Chicago: University of Chicago Press, 2013), 129.

76. Ishimure, *Lake of Heaven,* 8.

77. Ibid., 9.

78. Ibid., 16.

79. Ibid., 290.

80. For this notion, see Ursula K. Le Guin's May 8 keynote lecture of the "Anthropocene: Arts of Living on a Damaged Planet" conference, University of California, Santa Cruz, May 8–10, 2014, Vimeo video, 24:04, vimeo.com/97364872.

81. See Mary Jacobus, *Romantic Things: A Tree, A Rock, A Cloud* (Chicago: University of Chicago Press, 2012), 5: "An inanimate world is not a dead world; it may indeed be what matters most when it comes to the long-term survival of human life. Things give meaning to the world; they are not merely given meaning by the uses we make of them or by the symbolic significance we attach to them in our systems of exchange."

82. Ibid., 78.

83. Ibid., 5.

84. Ishimure Michiko, "Tamashi no igon ni mukiau," *Asahi Shinbun,* June 17, 2011, http://www.asahi.com/jinmyakuki/TKY201106170317.html.

85. On March 8, 2011, mere days before the triple nuclear meltdown, Minamata victims received a final compensation order. They had been fighting Chisso since November of 1959 in sit-ins in Minamata, Kumamoto City, and Tokyo; they engaged in four court cases over a half a century. Fifteen thousand have applied as victims, although some estimates put the number of exposed humans at two-hundred thousand.

86. See Daniel O'Gorman, "'Planetarity' and Pakistani Post 9/11 Fiction," *Alluvium* 1, no. 7 (2012), http://dx.doi.org/10.7766/alluvium.v1.7.02.

87. Livia Monnet, "Another World in this World: Slow Violence, Environmental Time, and the Decolonial Imagination in Ishimure Michiko's *Villages of the*

Gods," in *Ishimure Michiko's Writing in Ecocritical Perspective,* ed. Bruce Allen and Masami Yuki (Lanham, Md.: Lexington Books, 2016), 143.

88. Haraway, "Anthropocene, Capitalocene, Cthulucene."

89. See Gayatri Chakravorty Spivak, "Terror: A Speech After 9-11," *Boundary 2* 31, no. 2 (Summer 2004): 81–111.

90. Tawada Yōko, public lecture at the University of Minnesota, March 29, 2010.

91. Jacques Derrida, *The Animal That Therefore I Am,* ed. Marie-Louise Mallet, trans. David Wills (New York, NY: Fordham University Press, 2008).

92. Wu Ming-yi, *Man with the Compound Eyes,* trans. Darryle Sterk (London: Vintage Books, 2014), 302.

93. Ishimure, *Hana no okudo e,* 187.

94. Ibid.

2. Slow Violence in Films

1. Kido Tamiko, "Fairyland," in *Reverberations from Fukushima: 50 Japanese Poets Speak Out,* ed. Leah Stenson and Asao Sarukawa Aroldi (Portland, Ore.: Inkwater Press, 2014), Kindle loc. 1860.

2. Tsuchimoto Noriaki, *Minamatä Kanja-san to sono sekai* (1971; Tokyo: Shiguro, 2006), DVD.

3. Martin Lefebvre, "Between Setting and Landscape," in *Landscape and Film,* ed. Martin Lefebvre (Hoboken, N.J.: Routledge, 2006), 23. See also Adrian Ivakhiv, *Ecologies of the Moving Image* (Waterloo, Ont.: Wilfred Laurier University Press, 2013), Kindle loc. 1970.

4. Martin Lefebvre, "On Landscape in Narrative Cinema," *Canadian Journal of Film Studies* 20, no. 1 (Spring 2011): 62.

5. Ivakhiv, *Ecologies,* Kindle loc. 1648.

6. Gilberto Perez, *The Material Ghost: Films and Their Medium* (Baltimore, Md.: Johns Hopkins University Press, 2000), 23–24. See also Ivakhiv, Kindle loc. 1809.

7. Lefebvre, "On Landscape," 63 (quoting a question posed by geographer John Whylie). The answer, for Lefebvre, is essentially both, but narrative must also play a fundamental role. It must be determined whether narrative is that which conceals landscape or can be interpreted as revealing it (ibid. 76).

8. In his 2013 dissertation at the University of Minnesota, "Beyond the Niche: Ecological Cultural Production in the Iberian Peninsula," ecocriticism scholar John Trevathan argues that, for landscape painting, the production of space through the mode of spectatorship gets in the way of ecological art production because "spectatorship" compresses and simplifies a wide range of complex phenomena to one perceptive mode: the eye.

9. Sakamoto Naomitsu was recently awarded the Kumamoto Daily's Cultural

Prize for his first collection of poetry *Hikari umi* (Tokyo: Fujiwara Shoten, 2014), in which he dedicates this poem to Tsuchimoto and the frail bodies of those he filmed (121–22; translation mine).

10. Rob Nixon, *Slow Violence and the Environmentalism of the Poor* (Cambridge, Mass.: Harvard University Press, 2011), 2.

11. Ibid., 3.

12. Ibid., 6.

13. Fujiwara Toshi, *Mujin chitai* (Tokyo: Trigon Film, 2012), DVD.

14. Rob Nixon, "Interview with Allison Carruth and Robert Marzec," *Public Culture* 26, no. 2 (Spring 2014): 292.

15. Nixon, *Slow Violence*, 15.

16. Hayashi Kyoko, "From Trinity to Trinity," trans. Kyoko Selden, *The Asia-Pacific Journal* 3 (May 2008), http://www.japanfocus.org/-Hayashi-Kyoko/2758/article.html.

17. See Nixon on ecologies of the gaze in Njabulo Ndebele's writing (*Slow Violence*, 183–86).

18. Frederick Buell, *From Apocalypse to Way of Life* (New York: Routledge, 2004), xii.

19. Ibid., x.

20. The slow pans and long takes of some filmmakers' work, including Jia Zhangke, have been analyzed through the theoretical framework of "slow cinema," for which the passage of time is a dominant concern, but the formal emphasis on long takes and relative lack of narrative has little in common with Tsuchimoto's film style, and slow cinema as a concept has no explicit ecocritical aspect in its theorization yet. See: Song Hwee Lim, *Tsai Ming Liang and a Cinema of Slowness* (Honolulu: University of Hawaii Press, 2014); *Slow Cinema*, ed. Taigo de Luca and Nuno Barradas (Edinburgh: Edinburgh University Press, 2016); and Ira Jaffe, *Slow Movies: Countering the Cinema of Action* (New York: Columbia University Press, 2014).

21. See Kamanaka Hitomi and Norma Field, "Complicity and Victimization: Director Kamanaka Hitomi's Nuclear Warnings," *The Asia-Pacific Journal* 9, issue 18, no. 4 (May 2011): 3 for discussion of *Hibakusha—Sekai no Owari ni*.

22. Linda Nash, *Inescapable Ecologies: A History of Environment, Disease and Knowledge* (Berkeley: University of California Press, 2007), 1.

23. Quoted in Stacy Alaimo, *Bodily Natures* (Bloomington: Indiana University Press, 2010), 11.

24. For a rich discussion of Tsuchimoto's medical films, see Justin Jesty, "Making Mercury Visible: The Minamata Documentaries of Tsuchimoto Noriaki," in *Mercury Pollution: A Transdisciplinary Treatment*, ed. Sharon L. Zuber and Michael C. Newman (Boca Raton, Fla.: CRC Press, 2012). The Japanese title of the trilogy is *Igaku toshite no Minamata-byō: San-busaku*.

25. Akira Mizuta-Lippit, *Electric Animal: Toward a Rhetoric of Wildlife* (Minneapolis: University of Minnesota Press, 2000), 23–24.

26. Ibid., 185.

27. John Ott, "Iron Horses: Leland Stanford, Eadward Muybridge, and the Industrialised Eye," *Oxford Art Journal* 28, no. 3 (October 2005): 413–14.

28. Ibid., 415–16.

29. Ibid., 421.

30. Siegfried Kracauer, *Theory of Film* (Princeton, N.J.: Princeton University Press, 1997), 5.

31. Lisa Cartwright, "Science and the Cinema," in *The Visual Culture Reader,* ed. Nicholas Mirzoeff (New York: Routledge, 1998), 201–2. See also Cartwright, *Screening the Body: Tracing Medicine's Visual Culture* (Minneapolis: University of Minnesota Press, 1995), 4.

32. Giorgio Agamben, "Notes on Gesture," in *Means Without End,* trans. Cesare Casarino and Vincenzo Binnetti (Minneapolis: University of Minnesota Press, 2000), 49–59, at 54. Agamben refers here to Deleuze's "movement image": "Every image, in fact, is animated by an antinomic polarity: on the one hand, images are the reification and obliteration of a gesture (it is the imago as death mask or as symbol); on the other they preserve the *dynamis* intact (as in Muybridge's snapshots or in any sports photograph). The former corresponds to the recollection seized by voluntary memory, while the latter corresponds to the image flashing in the epiphany of involuntary memory. And while the former lives in magical isolation, the latter always refers beyond itself to a whole of which it is a part." He speaks further here of the need to break a "spell" by which images are connected to a long history of a movement or gesture: "Cinema leads images back to the homeland of gesture" (ibid.). Cinema, also, we could say, leads images back to the spectacle of locomotion.

33. See Harada Masazumi in the television documentary *Minamata to mukiau—Kiroku eiga sakka Tsuchimoto Noriaki no 43 nen,* part 2, Youtube video, 10:32, https://www.youtube.com/watch?feature=player_embedded&v=eb94z32DCA8#!. See Fujiwara Toshi, *Eiga wa ikimono no kiroku de aru: Tsuchimoto Noriaki no shigoto* (2007).

34. Tsuchimoto Noriaki, "Eiga de nasu beki wa nani ka," in *Tsuchimoto Noriaki: Wa ga eiga hakken no tabi* (Tokyo: Nihon Tosho Senta, 2004), 260.

35. The legal resolution, the continued dumping of effluent into the bay even after scientists had proven organic mercury to be the cause of neurological damage, the "fair and balanced" approach of the media, and the town's reliance on the factory all contributed toward the attempted erasure of the culpability of the corporation. In his book titled after his famous dictum "eiga wa ikimono de aru," Tsuchimoto included two essays on the question of invisibility, not in reference to toxins, but in reference to the way that victims were afraid to reveal their disease.

36. Hidaka Rokurō, "Hitotsu no shiso-teki jiken: Eiga Igaku toshite no Minamata-byō to Shiranuikai," in Tsuchimoto Noriaki, *Gyakkyō no naka no kiroku* (Miraisha, 2004), 353.

37. Physicians who appear to objectify the victims aggressively while making these films were not heartless. They sought to discover the symptomology of this unknown disease in order to solve the riddle of why patients were experiencing these symptoms, and some had long-term relationships with their patients. Tsuchimoto made these films available to a wide range of people, including denizens living in and around the Shiranui Sea, because he hoped that, by seeing the symptoms, others could recognize their own and apply for compensation. He was highly appreciative of the doctors' medical films as compact "objective resources, even as they gave witness," as he put it, "to the murder of Minamata disease" ("Lecture transcript 5," October 18, 1986, Tsuchimoto Noriaki's home page, http://brskn.web.fc2.com/; citations of Tsuchimoto's writing that do not contain page numbers were retrieved from his website, which was created and is maintained by his wife Tsuchimoto Motoko).

38. Ivakhiv, *Ecologies*, Kindle loc. 796. He takes the term "ecology of images" from Andrew Ross.

39. Ibid., Kindle loc. 796.

40. Ibid.

41. Ibid., Kindle loc. 817.

42. Ibid., Kindle loc. 838.

43. Ibid., Kindle loc. 968.

44. Ibid., Kindle loc. 859.

45. Ibid., Kindle loc. 903.

46. Ivakhiv's goal in elaborating on ecologies of images is to formulate "criteria by which filmmaking can be judged as contributing to better or worse socioecological relations," (ibid., Kindle loc. 903).

47. In 1968 and 1969, the General Assembly determined the conference's principal purpose to be "to serve as a practical means to encourage, and to provide guidelines . . . to protect and improve the human environment and to remedy and prevent its impairment." At this meeting, Indira Gandhi spoke of the importance of eliminating poverty for environmental protection measures. The twenty-six principles are:

1. Human rights must be asserted and apartheid and colonialism condemned.
2. Natural resources must be safeguarded.
3. The Earth's capacity to produce renewable resources must be maintained.
4. Wildlife must be safeguarded.

5. Nonrenewable resources must be shared and not exhausted.

6. Pollution must not exceed the environment's capacity to clean itself.

7. Damaging oceanic pollution must be prevented.

8. Development is needed to improve the environment.

9. Developing countries therefore need assistance.

10. Developing countries need reasonable prices for exports to carry out environmental management.

11. Environment policy must not hamper development.

12. Developing countries need money to develop environmental safeguards.

13. Integrated development planning is needed.

14. Rational planning should resolve conflicts between environment and development.

15. Human settlements must be planned to eliminate environmental problems.

16. Governments should plan their own appropriate population policies.

17. National institutions must plan development of states' natural resources.

18. Science and technology must be used to improve the environment.

19. Environmental education is essential.

20. Environmental research must be promoted, particularly in developing countries.

21. States may exploit their resources as they wish but must not endanger others.

22. Compensation is due to states thus endangered.

23. Each nation must establish its own standards.

24. There must be cooperation on international issues.

25. International organizations should help to improve the environment.

26. Weapons of mass destruction must be eliminated.

48. Tsuchimoto Noriaki, *Gyakkyō no naka no kiroku* (Tokyo: Miraisha, 2004), 110.

49. The sites of the film screenings were called 巡海映画上映地.

50. Denizens of these areas were often not enthusiastic about being diagnosed for fear it would impact marriage prospects for family members.

51. The idea of unrepresentability is discussed eloquently in William Haver's chapter on Ota Yōko's literature and Hiroshima in his book *The Body of This Death* (Redwood City, Calif.: Stanford University Press, 1997).

52. Tsuchimoto Noriaki, "Shiranuikai junkai eiga wa," *Katsudō keikakusho noto,* 1977 (from the Tsuchimoto Motoko archive, http://brskn.web.fc2.com/).

53. A sum of 360,000 yen was initially donated by four donors, and Irokawa

Daikichi loaned his VW van. The films that were screened varied and could include: films related to Minamata, three films in the Iwanami Film documentary
series on "The Living Sea," Tsuchimoto's 1963 film on the building of the national
railway, *Aru kikan joshi,* and various animation.

54. Kyo Maclear, *Beclouded Visions: Hiroshima-Nagasaki and the Art of Witness*
(Albany, N.Y.: SUNY Press, 1998), 7.

55. The U.S. military held at least four nuclear tests of bombs in the spring of
1954 at Rongelap Atoll and contaminated 856 Japanese fishing boats with radioactive materials, causing thirteen deaths by cancer and other illnesses and causing
tuna to be irradiated according to fishermen, who called them "genshi maguro,"
or "atom tuna" (Yuki Tanaka, "Godzilla and the Bravo Shot: Who Created and
Killed the Monster," *The Asia-Pacific Journal* 3 [June 2005], http://japanfocus
.org/-Yuki-TANAKA/1652/article.html).

56. Mclear, *Beclouded Visions,* 7.

57. See the flyer released at the opening of *Genpatsu kirinukichō,* "Shinbun no
beta-kiji ni kuro-zu-appu shi-nagara genpatsu taikoku-ka e no purosesu o tadoru"
(from the Tsuchimoto Motoko archive, http://brskn.web.fc2.com/).

58. Martin Lefebvre, "The Art of Pointing: On Peirce, Indexicality, and Photographic Images," in *Photography Theory,* ed. James Elkins (London: Routledge,
2007), 222.

59. 放射能 or 放射線 are the highlighted terms.

60. "*Genpatsu kirinukichō* ni tsuite," from the 4th Yufuin Cultural Documentary Film Festival (from the Tsuchimoto Motoko archive, http://brskn.web.fc2
.com/).

61. John Whittier Treat, "Lisbon to Sendai, New Haven to Fukushima:
Thoughts on 3/11," *Yale Review* 100 (April 2012): 14–15. This project began in
Arco, Idaho on December 20, 1951, when an appropriately named Experimental
Breeder Reactor (EBR-I) illuminated four light bulbs using 5 MW. A mere three
years later, former prime minister Nakasone Yasuhiro proposed a bill in the Japanese Diet to "study" the feasibility of domestic nuclear power in 1954, the year
after U.S. forces had left Japan. American reactors were sold to Japan, and now
437 nuclear power plant units are installed in thirty-one countries, with sixty-
eight plants in fifteen countries under construction. As of the end of 2011, the total
electricity production since 1951 amounted to 69,760 billion kWh. At the end of
2012, the cumulative operating experience amounted to 15,080 years. See "Nuclear
power plants, world-wide," *European Nuclear Society,* https://www.euronuclear
.org/info/encyclopedia/n/nuclear-power-plant-world-wide.htm.

62. The nuclear testing proliferation that began in a southwestern corner of the
United States and continued around the globe until 1953, with tests in seven countries (over half by the United States), also reflects a project of mimesis.

63. The term "ecosystem people" comes from Ramachandra Guha and Juan

Martinez-Alier, *Varieties of Environmentalism: Essays North and South* (New York: Routledge, 1997), 12–13, and refers to the fact that the urban poor experience a different ecological impact than the rural subsistence communities. The important point is "not to suggest that ecosystems people possess some romantic, timeless, organic bond to the pulse of nature, but rather to acknowledge that their often precarious conditions of survival depend on different combinations of temporal awareness" (Nixon, *Slow Violence,* 61–62).

64. Tsuchimoto Noriaki, *Minamata no zu, monogatari* (1981) (Tokyo: Shiguro, 2006), DVD.

65. Jesty, "Making Mercury Visible," 146.

3. *Nes Rullius*

1. The Japanese term used is 帰還困難区域.

2. In 1960, when Endō turned seventeen, Fukushima prefecture's governor at the time, Satō Zen'ichirō, announced that Futaba would be the site for implementing Japan's new nuclear power policy. In 1964, TEPCO began buying land for construction of the plants, and Endō's father sold his land (Ueda Toshihide, ed., "Shijita hatten: Fukushima no kanashimi," *Asahi Shinbun* 24 [March 2015]).

3. Laura Beans relates that drilling of seven major shale basins in the United States has provided critical cash flows for farmers who are near insolvency. For instance, County Commissioner Robert Wirkner said of Carroll County in eastern Ohio: "The inflow of cash came at a critical time for the region's agriculture-based economy"; farmers were "one step away from insolvency. . . . When the oil people came, the signing bonuses helped get them back on their feet" ("Study Finds More Costs Than Benefits From Fracking," *Eco Watch,* July 9, 2014, http://ecowatch.com/2014/07/09/more-costs-than-benefits-from-fracking/).

4. Christopher Mathias, "New York Towns Threaten Secession Over Gov. Cuomo's Ban on Fracking," *The Huffington Post,* February 20, 2015, http://www.huffingtonpost.com/2015/02/20/new-york-fracking-secession-southern-tier-cuomo_n_6722296.html.

5. See Ibid.

6. Kainuma Hiroshi, *On "Fukushima": Genshiryoku-mura wa naze umareta no ka* (Tokyo: Seidosha, 2011), 40.

7. Quoted in Akio Mishima, *Bitter Sea: The Human Cost of Minamata Disease,* trans. Richard L. Gage and Susan B. Murata (Tokyo: Kosei Publishing Company, 1992), 27. See also Ishimure Michiko, *Rumin no miyako* (Tokyo: Daiwa Shobō, 1973), 11.

8. The lyrics went, "The light shining on Yajiro Mountain / Reflected in the Shiranui Sea / The roofs of the factory / The smoke stifles / The sky of the town," (Ishimure, *Rumin no miyako,* 11).

9. Kamanaka Hitomi and Norma Field, "Complicity and Victimization: Director Kamanaka Hitomi's Nuclear Warnings," *The Asia-Pacific Journal* 9, no. 4 (May 2011), http://apjjf.org/2011/9/18/Norma-Field/3524/article.html.

10. Ibid.

11. Kamanaka Hitomi, "Rokkasho, Minamata, and Japan's Future: Capturing Humanity on Film," trans. Ann Saphir, *The Asia-Pacific Journal* 5, no. 12 (Dec. 2007).

12. Originally published in 1972 and now available in Kusano Hisao, *Mura no onna wa nemurenai: Kusano Hisao tokushū* (Tokyo: Nashinokisha, 2004), 32–24.

13. Satō Shigeko, *Genpatsu nanmin no shi* (Tokyo: Asahi Shinbun Publishing, 2012), 56–57.

14. Between 1960 and 1980, eighteen million people migrated to the cities. During the surrounding span of 1950–1985, the farmer population in the workforce decreased from 50 percent to 14.3 percent (Kainuma, *On "Fukushima,"* 289).

15. Raymond Williams, *The Country and the City* (New York: Oxford University Press, 1973).

16. Rachel Carson, *Silent Spring* (New York: Mariner Books, 1962), 1.

17. Ibid., 2.

18. Ibid., 32.

19. Ibid., 173.

20. Ibid., 192.

21. Ariyoshi Sawako, "Norinshō o chinmoku saseta: Shōsetsu *Fukugō osen* no bukimi-na api-ru," *Shūkan Shinchō*, May 22, 1975, 43.

22. Carson, *Silent Spring*, 15. Like Ariyoshi, Carson garnered early massive attention in print media: "When *The New Yorker* published parts of *Silent Spring* during June and July, a gentle author was transformed into a controversial one. The response to Rachel Carson's book shows clearly that one man's pesticide is another man's poison. Hundreds of letters—99 percent of them favorable—poured into *The New Yorker*. Newspapers throughout the country published editorial comment. Two Senators and three Representatives read selections into the Congressional Record. Houghton Mifflin ordered 100,000 copies of the book printed" (Lorus Milnes and Margery Milne, "There's Poison All Around Us Now," *New York Times*, September 23, 1962, https://www.nytimes.com/books/97/10/05/reviews/carson-spring.html).

23. Carson, *Silent Spring*, 22

24. See chapter 1 of Jack Doyle, *Trespass Against Us: Dow Chemical and the Toxic Century* (Monroe, Me.: Common Courage Press, 2004).

25. Carson, *Silent Spring*, 15.

26. Vandana Shiva, *Staying Alive: Women, Ecology, and Development* (Berkeley, Calif.: North Atlantic Books, 2016), xiii.

27. Michael Marder and Anaïs Tondeur, *The Chernobyl Herbarium* (London: Open Humanities Press, 2016), 16.

28. Ariyoshi Sawako, *Fukugō osen sono go* (Tōkyō: Ushio Shuppansha, 1977). This is a further work done subsequent to the publication of the novel. As the title differs from that of the novel only slightly, it will not be shortened when cited after this in order to keep the two works distinct. The original novel will always be cited as *Fukugō osen* (Tokyo: Shinchō Bunko, 1975).

29. But where Ishimure very specifically used the term "poison" or "to poison" (*doku* or *doku-suru*), Ariyoshi employed the term *osen*, which is not as powerful an image but still signifies "contamination."

30. Often called the "four pollution events," they were: the "Ouch-Ouch" (*itai-itai*) disease in Toyama prefecture, which was caused by lead mining upstream on the Jinzū River by the Mitsui Mining and Smelting's Kamioka Mining Station; Yokkaichi asthma, which occurred in the city of Yokkaichi in Mie prefecture between 1960 and 1972 when severe smog caused by sulfur oxide released with the burning of petroleum and crude oil by pyrotechnical processing facilities and refineries built in the area between 1957 and 1973 caused a range of pulmonary illnesses such as emphysema, asthma, and bronchitis; Minamata disease, for which symptoms caused by industry began to emerge in 1956, with fishermen petitioning the government for compensation for their unsaleable fish in 1960, saying that the Ise Bay fish had bad flavor and were not selling; and the Niigata Minamata disease, for which a class action court case was brought against Showa Yokkaichi Oil and initially adjudicated in September 1970, with an initial ruling for 544 individuals.

31. Okada Yoneo, "Kankyō wa watashi de aru," *Shisō no kagaku* 5, no. 125 (December 1971): 12 (italics mine). Okada headed a "safe agriculture" movement.

32. Ibid., 19.

33. Serialized from October 14, 1974, to August 31, 1975.

34. "On average the *Asahi* newspaper receives 200 letters from readers per month and author Ariyoshi gets mountains of letters at her home" (Ariyoshi, "Norinshō o chinmoku saseta," 42).

35. *Fukugō osen sono go* (*After Cumulative Poison*) included essays by historical novelist Shiba Ryōtarō, economist Miyamoto Ken'ichi, and writer Nosaka Akiyuki, among others.

36. The rebuttal to Ariyoshi's novel was titled *Shōsetsu* Fukugō osen *e no hanshō,* ed. Yusa Katsuhiko (Tokyo: Kokusai Shōgyō Shuppan, 1975) and contained contributions from Iwamoto Tsunemaru, Nishikawa Setsuko, Hayashi Toshio, Misato Tomomasa, Yamaguchi Seiya, Yamane Ichirō, and Yusa Katsuhiko.

37. The novel begins with the preparations for a political race that actually took place in 1974, in which the famed Ichikawa Fusae had been called upon to run for office at the age of 81. Ichikawa had initially been elected to the Diet in 1952 as representative of Tokyo. Her election in 1974 was her fourth term in office, and she was later reelected to the House of Councilors in 1980 with the highest number of votes from the national constituency. The year the novel began serialization,

1974, Ichikawa had been awarded the Ramon Magsaysay Award for Community Leadership for her efforts in support of social equality (Ishimure accepted this award for her publication of *Paradise in the Sea of Sorrow,* though she had refused other literary awards offered to her by the Japanese literary establishment). Ariyoshi was not only not selected for a literary award for *Cumulative Pollution,* but was instead criticized by many in the national literary establishment for writing such "popular" problem novels. In short, her readers were far more interested in her book than the national literary establishment.

38. Photographs from 1974 depict Ariyoshi supporting Ichikawa's candidacy, and *Cumulative Pollution* depicts the narrator traveling with the political candidate.

39. The 1975 annual "White Paper" by Japan's Ministry of Defense reported that 21,990 people were certified victims of mercury, cadmium, and arsenic, and the 1978 White Paper recorded that 65,880 people in Japan were certified victims of the same toxins. By 1978, Tokyo and Osaka had higher degrees of sulfur dioxide, which has significant impact on health, than New York City. It might also be noted that Japan had tripled its energy consumption in urban areas, multiplied the GNP six-fold, and increased automobile ownership ten-fold in the previous decade. Greater production led to higher numbers of certified victims of chemical compounds.

40. Ariyoshi, *Fukugō osen,* 41.

41. Ishimure Michiko and Tsurumi Kazuko, *Kotoba hatsuru tokoro* (Tokyo: Fujiwara Shoten 2007), 116.

42. Ibid., 120.

43. Ariyoshi, *Fukugō osen,* 613.

44. Ariyoshi, *Fukugō osen,* 82.

45. Ariyoshi addressed this in ibid., 130. See also Yusa, *Shōsetsu* Fukugō osen *e no kyokō,* 9.

46. Ariyoshi also said that her experience reading Ishimure's *Paradise in the Sea of Sorrow* was critical to understanding that pollution could not be captured in conventional fiction.

47. Ariyoshi, *Fukugō osen,* 297.

48. Ibid., 121.

49. *My Year of Meats* by American writer Ruth Ozeki, for example, is narrated by "Jane Takagi-Little," a Japanese American "DES daughter" who produces a television show, *My American Wife!,* that is sponsored by an American meat-export lobby to increase its sales in Japan. She gradually comes to learn how DES and other hormones used to increase food production affect human health: "DES changed the face of meat in America. Using DES and other drugs, like antibiotics, farmers could process animals on an assembly line like cars or computer chips. Open-field grazing for cattle became inefficient and soon gave way to confinement feedlot operations or factory farms, where thousands upon thousands of penned cattle could be fattened at troughs. This was an economy of scale. It was

happening everywhere, the wave of the future, the marriage of science and big business" (*My Year of Meats* [New York: Penguin, 1999], 125). Narratives of how industrially produced foods impact female bodies are often told through first-person narratives. For example, Sandra Steingraber writes autobiographical narratives of "discovery" about gender and contaminants.

50. Ursula Heise, *Sense of Place, Sense of Planet: The Environmental Imagination of the Global* (Oxford: Oxford University Press, 2008), 62.

51. Ibid., 6.

52. Stacy Alaimo, *Bodily Natures: Science, Environment, and the Material Self* (Bloomington: Indiana University Press, 2010), 103.

53. Ibid.

54. Ariyoshi, *Fukugō osen*, 402.

55. Ibid., 74.

56. Takahashi Tetsuya, "What March 11 Means to Me: Nuclear Power and the Sacrificial System," *The Asia-Pacific Journal* 12, no. 1 (May 2014), http://www.japanfocus.org/site/make_pdf/4114.

57. Carson's *Silent Spring* mentions Japan in the context of people dying from the use of Parathion. She states that, in 1954, the average yearly rate of deaths from Parathion was 100 in India, 67 in Syria, and about 336 in Japan.

58. Hara Tsuyoshi, *"Chimmoku no haru" no sekai* (Tokyo: Kamogawa Shuppan, 1998), 92.

59. "Thirty-six-year-old housewife," letter to the editor, *Asahi Shinbun*, June 8, 1975.

60. Letter to the editor, *Asahi Shinbun*, November 10, 1974.

61. Letter to the editor, *Asahi Shinbun*, October 18, 1974.

62. Letter to the editor, *Asahi Shinbun*, February 28, 1975.

63. Letter to the editor, *Asahi Shinbun*, June 17, 1975.

64. Ariyoshi, "Norinshō o chinmoku saseta," 44.

65. "Fifty-five-year-old male farmer," letter to the editor, *Asahi Shinbun*, February 28, 1975.

66. "Forty-year-old male agricultural cooperative worker," letter to the editor, *Asahi Shinbun*, February 22, 1975.

67. "Retired sixty-five-year-old male," letter to the editor, *Asahi Shinbun*, June 4, 1975.

68. "Thirty-five-year-old public officer," letter to the editor, *Asahi Shinbun*, July 6, 1975.

69. For example, the group "Daichi wo Mamoru Kai."

70. Yoneyama Katsuyoshi, "Nōyaku no tsurezure," *Nihon Nōyaku gakkaishi* 32, no. 4 (2007): 23.

71. Murase Masatoshi, "Denjiha no seitai he no eikyō : horumon sayō kasetsu no teishō," *Bussei Kenkyū* 82, no. 1 (April 2004):182.

72. Hayashi Kōichirō, "Sekyuriti tantōsha wa genpatsu jiko kara nani o manabu

beki ka—tōsei kankyō to gabanansu no shiten kara," *Jōhō Sekyuriti Sōgō Kagaku* no. 3 (November 2011): 16.

73. In "The Trouble with Wilderness; or, Getting Back to the Wrong Nature," environmental historian William Cronon makes the point that "wilderness" and "nature" are not something "out there," but something we create culturally and that we should not conceptualize "nature" as outside the human (in *Uncommon Ground: Rethinking the Human Place in Nature,* ed. William Cronon [New York: W. W. Norton, 1995], 69–90). Here, I draw attention to how Ariyoshi's and Carson's texts powerfully articulate the links between rural environments and the home.

74. I would like to thank my enterprising student Miyauchi Hajime for his thorough research of materials published in the *Asahi* newspaper during the serialization of *Cumulative Pollution.*

75. Takahashi, "What March 11 Means to Me,"

76. Peter Singer, *One World* (New Haven, Conn.: Yale University Press, 2002), 19.

4. Literature without Us

1. Karen Barad's "agential realism" makes a similar point: "The human is reconfigured away from the central place of explanation, interpretation, intelligibility, and objectivity to make room for the epistemic importance of other material agents." See Chris Calvert Minor, *Human Studies* 37, no. 1 (June 2014): 123–37.

2. Barad's exact phrase is "always already an ongoing historicity," Tim Ingold, *Making: Anthropology, Archaeology, Art and Architecture* (London: Routledge, 2013), 31. See Karen Barad, *Meeting the Universe Halfway: Quantum Physics and the Entanglement of Matter and Meaning* (Durham, N.C.: Duke University Press, 2007).

3. In "Planetary Boundaries: Exploring the Safe Operating Space for Humanity" (*Ecology and Society* 14, no. 2 [2009], https://www.ecologyandsociety.org/vol14/iss2/art32/), Johan Rockström and his colleagues have developed nine critical planetary boundaries or thresholds that should not be crossed, pertaining to (1) climate change, (2) ocean acidification, (3) stratospheric ozone depletion, (4) the biochemical flow in nitrogen and phosphorus cycles, (5) freshwater over-usage, (6) expanded and intensified land use, (7) biodiversity loss, (8) atmospheric aerosol loading, and (9) chemical pollution (cited in Julia Adeney Thomas, "History and Biology in the Anthropocene: Problems of Scale, Problems of Value," *American Historical Review* 119, no. 5 [2014]: 1588).

4. For a brief history of the use of the term "Anthropocene," see Elizabeth Kolbert, "The Anthropocene Debate: Marking Humanity's Impact," *Environment 360*, May 17, 2010, http://e360.yale.edu/feature/the_anthropocene_debate_marking_humanitys_impact_/2274/. The choice to date the change to climate by anthropogenic factors at post-1945 is based on radiation stratigraphy and the

rapid rise of atmospheric CO_2 concentration, which has risen from 310 to 380 parts-per-million since 1950. Additionally, in this period, nitrogen fixation by humans exceeds that by plants, causing damage to water systems and land. Other factors such as desertification, ocean acidification, and biodiversity loss are also cited.

5. Frédéric Neyrat and Elizabeth Johnson, "The Political Unconscious of the Anthropocene: A Conversation with Frédéric Neyrat," *Society and Space*, 2014, https://societyandspace.com/material/interviews/neyrat-by-johnson.

6. Masao Miyoshi, "Turn to the Planet: Literature, Diversity, and Totality," *Comparative Literature* 53, no. 4 (Fall 2001): 295.

7. More recently, Tom Cohen and Claire Colebrook have begun editing a new series for Open Humanities Press called "Critical Climate Change" that is to include "experimental monographs that redefine the boundaries of disciplinary fields" in response to the symptoms of anthropogenic change.

8. Masao Miyoshi and Yoshimoto Mitsushiro, *Teikô no ba e—arayuru kyôkai o koeru tame* (Tokyo: Rakuhoku Shuppan, 2007), 314.

9. Ibid., 317.

10. Masao Miyoshi, *Trespasses: Selected Writings*, ed. Eric Cazdyn (Durham, N.C.: Duke University Press, 2010), 204.

11. Ibid., 259–60.

12. David Palumbo-Liu, "Crossing the Lines: Masao Miyoshi's *Trespasses*," *Criticism* 54, no. 2 (2012): 343–51, at 345.

13. Tom Cohen, "Introduction: Murmurations—'Climate Change' and the Defacement of Theory," in *Theory in the Era of Climate Change*, vol. 1, *Telemorphosis*, ed. Tom Cohen (Ann Arbor, Mich.: Open Humanities Press, 2012), 15.

14. Miyoshi, *Trespasses*, xxxi.

15. Hirofumi Uzawa, *Economic Theory and Global Warming* (Cambridge: Cambridge University Press, 2003), ix.

16. See Dipesh Chakrabarty, "The Climate of History: Four Theses," *Critical Inquiry* 35 (Winter 2009): 197–222.

17. Thomas, "History and Biology in the Anthropocene," 1590. Miyoshi said about history that "we should end with thinking that history begins with human civilization" and that we should theorize "what physicists mean when they say that we sense space and time in the 11th dimension" (*Teikô no ba e*, 316).

18. Gayatri Chakravorty Spivak, *Death of a Discipline* (New York: Columbia University Press, 2003), 88–89.

19. Ibid., 92.

20. Ibid., 94. Wai Chee Dimock's discussion of planetary literature for American literary studies argues that literature escapes the confines of state power to be constitutive of the planetary literary order because, in literature, "the inscriptional power of the state is not complete" and "the jurisdictional power is not absolute" ("Literature for the Planet," *PMLA* 116, no.1 [January 2001]: 173).

Dimock has also written that: "literary studies requires the largest possible scale, that its appropriate context or unit of analysis is nothing less than the full length and width of our human history and habitat. . . . It is a prefabricated box. Any literature crammed into it is bound to appear more standardized than it is: smaller, tamer, duller, conforming rather than surprising" ("Planetary Time and Global Translation: 'Context' in Literary Studies," *Common Knowledge* 9, no. 3 [2003]: 489). One of Donald Pease's compelling critiques of this idea is that literature (and literary theory) easily exports national ethos and, consequently, that "Dimock's account of the operations of planetary literature would appear to engender an equivalence between the globalization of American literary studies and the Americanization of the planet" ("The Extraterritoriality of the Literature for Our Planet," *ESQ: A Journal of the American Renaissance* 50 [2004]: 15).

21. Pease, "The Extraterritoriality of the Literature," 15.

22. Miyoshi, *Trespasses*, 14.

23. Thomas, "History and Biology in the Anthropocene," 1588.

24. Claire Colebrook, *Essays on Extinction*, vol. 1, *Death of the Posthuman* (Ann Arbor, Mich.: Open Humanities Press, 2014), 11.

25. Peter Singer, *One World: The Ethics of Globalization* (New Haven, Conn.: Yale University Press, 2004).

26. Ibid., 171.

27. See Rob Nixon, "Naomi Klein's 'This Changes Everything,'" *New York Times*, November 6, 2014, https://www.nytimes.com/2014/11/09/books/review/naomi-klein-this-changes-everything-review.html.

28. She expressed this about the galaxy in the director Kin Tai's 2013 documentary film about her writing, *Hana no okudo e (Towards the Paradise of Flowers)*. To exist as faint, humble light was her hope for humanity. Her planetary thinking addresses two scales at once: the scale of geophysical history and the scale of a flame.

29. Timothy Clark, "What on World is the Earth: The Anthropocene and Fictions of the World," *Oxford Literary Review* 35, no. 1 (2013): 5–24, at 9.

30. Timothy Clark, "Scale," in Cohen, *Telemorphosis*, 137.

31. Ibid., 151.

32. Ibid., 152.

33. Ibid., 158.

34. Ibid.

35. Ibid., 159–60.

36. For a discussion of methodological nationalism, see Andreas Wimmer and Nina Glick Schiller, "Methodological Nationalism and Beyond: Nation-State Building, Migration, and the Social Sciences," *Global Networks* 2, no. 4 (2002): 301–34.

37. Clark, "Scale," 159.

38. Ibid., 161.

39. Tawada Yōko, "The Island of Eternal Life," trans. Margaret Mitsutani, in *March Was Made of Yarn: Reflections on the Japanese Earthquake, Tsunami, and Nuclear Meltdown,* ed. David Karashima and Elmer Luke (New York: Vintage Books, 2012), 3–12. The Japanese-language original ("Fushi no shima") can be found in *Sore demo san-gatsu wa, mata,* ed. Shuntarō Tanikawa et al. (Tokyo: Kōdansha, 2012).

40. Clark, "Scale," 162.

41. Wu Ming-yi, *Man with the Compound Eyes,* trans. Darryle Sterk (London: Vintage Books, 2014), 300.

42. For example, Akira Mizuta-Lippit writes of "the animal" treated as supplements in criticism when he refers to their literary likenesses as beings who have no compelling ontology, despite "sustain[ing] the existence of every category of being as essential supplements" (*Electric Animal: Toward a Rhetoric of Wildlife* [Minneapolis: University of Minnesota Press], 184).

43. Wu, *Man with the Compound Eyes,* 298.

44. Tawada Yōko, *Kentōshi,* (Tokyo: Kōdansha, 2014), 223.

45. Ibid.

46. The reference of rubble takes us directly to a reading of the spatial scale because, when this collection came out, "rubble" was the term most used to describe the wasteland created by the tsunami of March 2011. The story creates that sense of geological time through its animal characters.

47. Ishimure Michiko, *Hana no okudo e* (Tokyo: Fujiwara Shoten, 2014), 33–34.

48. Ibid., 42–47.

49. The collection won the 32nd annual Hanatsubaki Award for Contemporary Poetry. This poem is featured in the January/February 2015 issue of *Hanatsubaki.*

50. The hopeful title *Toward a Paradise of Flowers* is followed by a shadowy blurb describing its contents as "the 'hope' that precedes despair." This poem is also featured in a film of the same title directed by Kin Tai and translated by Bruce Allen.

51. Ishimure Michiko and Fujiwara Shin'ya, *Namida furuhana* (Tokyo: Kawade Shobō Shinsha, 2012), 149.

52. Ibid., 161.

53. Spivak, *Death of a Discipline,* 71.

54. Ibid., 73.

55. Ishimure Michiko, *Shiranui: A Contemporary Noh Drama,* trans. Bruce Allen and Yuki Aihara, in *Ishimure Michiko's Writing in Ecocritical Perspective: Between Sea and Sky,* ed. Bruce Allen and Masami Yuki (Lanham, Md.: Lexington Books, 2016), 189–98, at 197.

Index

aesthetic imperialism, 10
aesthetic ontology, 27–28, 34, 39, 46, 48
Agamben, Giorgio, 67, 161n32
agential realism, 170n1
Alaimo, Stacy, 5, 44, 106–7
Allen, Bruce, 141
Amagusa, 79, 135
Anderson, Benedict: *Imagined Communities*, 10
animal biotrope(s), 131–33, 140–41; non-animal biotropes, 131
animal locomotion, 63–67
animals: agency and, 23; allegorical significance and, 139; animal interest in narrative and, 134; "Animal's Babel," 133; animism and, 48; anthropocentrism and, 15; becoming and, 46–47; bodies as material and semiotic subjects and, 28; historicities and, 131; humanism and, 53; hypothetical scale and, 129; in *Minamata Mural*, 88; in motion, 63, 65; movement, 67; populations, visibility, and, 11; in representation, 148n18; "the animal," 131, 173n42; sign, 148n18; toxins and, 5, 7, 105; tropes and, 131; violence to, 58; vulnerabilities and, 4
animism, 16, 48–49; renaissance, 15–16

Anthropocene, 18, 20, 22, 52, 118–26, 160n4, 170n4
anthropogenic change, 61, 118, 123–28, 170n4, 171n7
anthropogenic culpability, 118
anthropomorphization, 49
anthropos, 6, 11, 21, 23, 89
apocalypse, 119, 142
apocalyptic, 119, 132–33, 141; cinema, 82; fiction, 60, 139; thinking, 119; vision, 72, 75, 119, 139, 141
Ariyoshi Sawako, 99, 101–3, 112, 167n29, 168n37; biotropes and, 100, 105, 108, 114; and China, 102; and conventional fiction, 104; cumulative pollution and, 98–99, 102, 111; *Cumulative Pollution* and, 92, 98–105, 107, 109–13, 152n13; domestic turn and, 104–8; *Silent Spring* and, 104; *The Twilight Years* and, 102–3
Asahi Journal (Asahi Ja-na-ru), 38
Asahi Newspaper (Asahi Shinbun), 102–3, 109

Barad, Karen, 118
Bates, Katherine, 6–7, 11, 12
becoming-animal, 46–47
Beller, Jonathan, 75
Bennett, Jane, 41–42
Berger, John, 30–31
bibun (beautiful writing), 32

bioaccumulation, 43–45, 66, 100, 108
biological diversity, 8; biodiversity, 9–12
biological sentinels, 30, 67, 142
biomagnification, 43, 108, 157n58
bioregional writing, 105
bios, 8, 11, 21, 129
biotrope(s), 6–12, 55, 117–18, 125–26, 129, 149–50n41; amber waves of grain as, 6–7; as bioregional, 106; cherry blossom as, 7, 11, 33, 51, 117; chrysanthemum as, 129–30, 156n37; classical literature and, 10–11, 31–33, 52, 150n50; as cosmopolitan, 106; cultural power of, 11, 125; cumulative pollution as, 98–99, 105, 113–14; *Cumulative Pollution* and, 100; earth as, 123; ecologocentrism and, 11; ethnic nationalism and, 148n17; imperial nationalism and, 10; Ishimure Michiko and, 33, 127; materiality and, 6, 12, 117, 126; in *On the Japanese Landscape*, 9–10; semiotics and, 6, 117–18; silent spring as, 96–98, 100, 104, 109; whale hoard as, 133. *See also* animal biotrope(s)
Brown, Lori, 46
brutality of jargon (*yōgo no zangyakusei*), 37
Buell, Frederick, 60
Buell, Lawrence, 103

cannibalistic civilization (*hitogui bunmei*), 3
capital, the. *See* Tokyo
Carson, Rachel, 60, 108, 166n22, 170n73; biotrope and, 96–100, 104, 109; cumulative pollution and, 98, 100; *Silent Spring* and, 98, 104, 108, 113, 154n13, 169n57

Cartwright, Lisa, 66
cat(s), 29, 43; as biological sentinels, 30, 142; experiments on, 62; in medical film, 62, 67, 88; in *Minamata Mural*, 88
Chakrabarty, Dipesh, 123
Chikuho coal mines, 34, 39
Chisso corporation, 29, 36, 57, 66–69, 77, 80, 157n58; culpability and, 73, 78, 88, 109; obligate storytelling and, 37; reclamation and, 87, 141
Chisso factory, 66, 78, 93
Clark, Timothy, 4, 23, 127–29, 131, 138
classical poetics, 7; critique of, 31–32
Coetzee, J. M., 28
Cohen, Tom, 122, 171
Colebrook, Claire, 125, 171
Conley, Verena Andermatt, 22
corporate nationalism, 126
Cronon, William, 170n73
Crutzen, Paul, 118
cultural claims, 4–6; exceptionalism and, 18; materiality and, 117–18
cultural exceptionalism, 52
cultural humanism, 5, 24, 28; material world and, 4, 10, 21; obligate storytelling and, 39; planetary perspective and, 118; scale and, 25. *See also* humanism
culture(s), 5, 6, 11, 15, 21–22, 24, 25, 34; animism and, 49; Karen Barad and, 118; Timothy Clark and, 128–29; Tom Cohen and, 122; constitutive exclusivity and, 16; decolonial imagination and, 52; ecocriticism and, 117; ecological forms of, 3–4; Elizabeth Grosz and, 8–9; Ursula Heise and, 106; landscape and, 89; Masao Miyoshi and, 119–20; nature and, 10, 18, 22, 33–34, 46,

48, 106; to nonhumans, 48; non-Western, 15; obligate storytelling and, 49; Nicole Shukin and, 148; Gayatri Spivak and, 123; whales and, 132

cumulative pollution, 98–99, 104, 111–13, 119; Ariyoshi Sawako and, 101–2; as biotrope, 99, 105, 114; Rachel Carson and, 100; ill health and, 103; *Silent Spring* and, 100; spatiality and, 109

Cumulative Pollution (Fukugō osen), 92, 98, 100–105, 108–13, 154n13, 168nn37–38; classical Japanese literature and, 104. *See also* Ariyoshi Sawako

data visualization, 60, 62, 78–79
Davis, Mark, 14
DDT, 96, 100, 104–5, 109
decolonial imagination, 52
Deleuze, Gilles: becoming-animal and, 46; minor literature and, 35; movement image and, 161n32
DES, 168n49
Descola, Philippe, 33, 48
Despret, Vinciane, 30
Disch, Thomas, 60
distributed agency, 56
domestic turn, 100, 105–6, 109, 113
dystopic sublime, 57

ecocosmopolitan imagination, 105–6
ecocriticism, 4, 6, 12, 18, 20, 22, 92
ecological imaginary, 2–6, 100
ecologocentrism, 10, 33
ecology of images, 75–76, 162
Ecology without Nature (Morton), 3
Empress Michiko, 32–33
endogenous technology, 12, 14

Enlightenment humanism, 19, 42, 46, 126
Enlightenment modernity, 4, 9, 18
environmental history, 45, 101, 129, 150n53
environmental refugees, 7–8, 33, 91, 97, 108, 117
ethnic environmentalism, 12–17, 28, 150n49, 150n53
ethnic nationalism, 8, 28, 33, 150n49
ethnocentricity, 33
ethnos, 6, 8, 11–14, 21, 23, 30, 89, 129, 138
eutrophication, 58, 101

fetal methylmercury intoxication, 43
Field, Norma, 61, 93–94
figure(s), 45; of the animal, 63; ephemeral, 51; human, 50, 56; Maruki Toshi and, 87–89; Gayatri Spivak and, 140
fracking, 92, 95
Fromm, Harold, 61
Fujiwara Shin'ya, 8, 139, 148n26, 155n27
Fujiwara Toshi, 57–59; *Cinema Is about Documenting Lives*, 68; *No Man's Zone*, 57–59
Fukushima Daiichi Nuclear Power Plant, 15
Fukushima Daiichi nuclear reactors, 15, 91
Fukushima Prefecture, 55, 59, 92, 101, 107, 108, 114, 137, 164n61, 165n2

geomorphing, 56
Ginza, 51
global warming, 23, 58, 60, 118–24, 128, 140
Grassy Narrows First Nation, 19, 29
great acceleration: age of the, 19–24, 119

Great Pacific Garbage Patch, 1
Grosz, Elizabeth, 8–9
Guattari, Félix, 35, 46, 75

Hamamoto Tsuginori, 76
Hansen, James, 126
Harada Masazumi, 72, 73, 76, 80
Hara Tsuyoshi, 109
Haraway, Donna, 6, 52, 131
Hayashi Kyōko, 59; "From Trinity to
    Trinity," 59
Haynes, Todd, 60; *Safe*, 60
Heise, Ursula, 21, 105, 106
Hidaka Rokurō, 72
Hiroshima, 87
honkadori, 32
horses in motion, 65
humanism, 19, 52, 53, 56, 120; Enlight-
    enment and, 19, 42, 46, 126; West-
    ern, 17. *See also* cultural humanism
human subjectivity, 51

Ichikawa Fusae, 103, 167, 168
image author *(eizō sakka)*, 79
imagined communities, 125
indigenous, 132; communities and, 82,
    86; populations and, 2, 61
industrial capitalism, 52, 65, 141
industrial film, 66–67
industrial gaze, 65
industrial landscape, 63
industrial modernity, 3, 15–23, 33, 40,
    138–40; affinities and, 24; biological
    sentinels and, 67; as cannibalistic
    civilization, 3; cinema and, 63; cri-
    tique of, 56; cumulative pollution
    and, 92, 101; dialectical imagina-
    tion of space and, 96–97; domestic
    household and, 101; domestic turn
    and, 109; impacts of, 30–33, 58, 61;
    Ishimure Michiko and, 140; *Lake*

of Heaven and, 45; *Paradise in the
Sea of Sorrow* and, 37; pollution
events and, 101; toxins and, 5, 23–
24, 68, 92, 155; Raymond Williams
and, 96
industrial pollution, 42, 69; locomo-
    tion and, 67, 69; Tsuchimoto
    Noriaki and, 74. *See also kōgai*
industrial toxins, 42, 61, 152n69; cumu-
    lative effects and, 114
intentional landscape, 56
Iovino, Serenella, 6
Irokawa Daikichi, 78, 163
Ishimure Michiko, 3, 28, 35–39, 47, 50–
    51, 87, 93, 97, 117, 168n37; Ariyoshi
    Sawako and, 104; biotropes and, 33;
    Chisso and, 94; corporate national-
    ism and, 126; corporate state and,
    35, 126; critique of conventional
    poesis and, 31–34, 104, 150n50,
    155n27; decolonial imagination
    and, 52; economic development
    and, 140; industrial modernity and,
    140; interiority and, 155n27; *Lake
    of Heaven* and, 45–52; language
    and, 35, 38, 156n33, 156n37; mercury
    poisoning and, 43; metamorpho-
    sis and, 44–48, 127; *Migrants of
    the Capital* and, 140; "My Dear
    Weatherbeaten Skull" and, 135–40;
    narrative and, 109; Noh theater
    and, 141; obligate storytelling and,
    30, 33–40, 44–53; *Paradise in the
    Sea of Sorrow* and, 29–30, 37–38,
    44, 57, 66, 104, 108, 140; rural areas
    and, 97; scale and, 138–39; *Shiranui*
    and, 141–42; Shiranui Sea and, 40;
    Toward a Paradise of Flowers and,
    137–40; *Villages of the Gods* and, 52;
    witnessing and, 140; world without
    us and, 137

Itō Hasumi, 72
Ivakhiv, Adrian, 56, 75–76
Ivy, Marilyn, 15
Iwaoka Nakamasa, 47

Jacobus, Mary, 51
Jesty, Justin, 62, 88

Kagoshima, 68, 79
Kainuma Hiroshi, 92–93
Kamanaka Hitomi: *Hibakusha* and,
    60–61; nuclear power and, 61, 93–
    94; radiation and, 93–94
Kawai, Masao, 15
Kawamura Minato, 38
Kido, Tamiko, 55
Kim, Claire Jean, 4, 15, 147n12
Kitagawa Fukiko, 32
Klein, Naomi, 123
kōgai, 101–2. *See also* industrial
    pollution
kōgai byōki (industrial disease), 69
Kracauer, Siegfried, 66
Kusano Hisao, 91, 94, 96

LaDuke, Winona, 19
Lake of Heaven (Tenko), 45–52. *See also*
    Ishimure Michiko
landscape, 2–3, 9, 11, 21, 50, 135; aes-
    theticism and, 32; biodiversity and,
    10; cinema and, 56–57; classical
    Japanese poetics and, 33, 52, 104,
    141; imperial interest and, 12; indus-
    trial modernity and, 63, 138; Maruki
    Iri and, 87; mise-en-scène and, 89;
    national interest and, 10; obligate
    storytelling and, 33; painting and,
    31–32, 88; transhistorical continu-
    ity and, 9, 14; Tsuchimoto Noriaki
    and, 61
Lefebvre, Martin, 56, 159n7

Le Guin, Ursula K., 27, 51
linguistic mutiny, 38
locomotion, 71, 161n32. *See also* animal
    locomotion
Lumière, August, 66

Maclear, Kyo, 82
Man with the Compound Eyes, 1–3, 130–
    33. *See also* Wu Ming-yi
Marshall Islands, 82
Maruki Iri, 86–88
Maruki Toshi, 86–88
Masami, Yuki, 34
material ecologies, 75
materiality, 6, 8, 9, 117, 150; biotropes
    and, 12, 117; mise-en-scène and, 56
medical gaze, 73–74, 81
mercury poisoning: victims of, 29–30,
    38–43, 55–58, 66–68, 73–74, 79–81,
    141–42, 153n6
metamorphosis, 36, 44–51, 127
metaphor(s), 4, 6, 25, 30, 60, 104, 126,
    140
methodological nationalism, 129, 138,
    140, 172n36
methyl mercury, 29–30, 43, 45, 66, 77,
    155n32, 157n58
metropole: and peripheries, 99. *See
    also* Tokyo
Miike coal mines, 34–35
Miller, Ian Jared, 22
Millet, Jean-François, 31
mimetic capaciousness, 11, 148n18
mimeticism, 45, 83–84, 86
Minamata, 19, 29–30, 43, 47, 53, 57–58,
    66, 72–80, 87, 142
Minamata, 30, 55, 57, 63, 73, 88, 97. *See
    also* Tsuchimoto Noriaki
Minamata Bay, 43
Minamata Convention on Mercury,
    76

Minamata Disease, 36–38, 69, 72–77, 88

Minamata Disease Research Center, 72

Minamata Medical Film (Igaku toshite no Minamata-byō), 62. *See also* Tsuchimoto Noriaki

Minamata Mural (Minamata no zu monogatari), 88. *See also* Tsuchimoto Noriaki

minor language, 35, 50

minor literature, 35, 50

mise-en-scène, 56, 60–62, 66, 87–89

Miyoshi, Masao, 119–25, 129; environmental studies and, 123–24; identity politics and, 121–24; planetarianism and, 119–24

Mizuta Lippit, Akira, 62, 173n42

Monnet, Livia, 38; decolonial imagination and, 52

montage, 61, 79

Morisaki Kazue, 34, 50; minor language and, 35–36

Morton, Timothy, 3; aesthetics as causality and, 49; ecologocentrism, 10; *Ecology without Nature*, 3–4; "the mesh" and, 56; nature-nations and, 11, 25

mujō, 7

Murakami Haruki, 7–8, 15, 33, 51, 117, 148n21

mushroom cloud, 59, 81–84

Muybridge, Eadweard James, 63, 65–66; *Animals in Motion* and, 63; *Human Figure in Motion* and, 63

"My Dear Weatherbeaten Skull" *(Watakushisama no sharekōbe)*, 135–40. *See also* Ishimure Michiko

Narcissus, 50; Bob Dylan and, 50

Nash, Linda, 61

native species, 14; nonnative species and, 14

nature, 3, 9, 10, 11; imperial identity and, 9–12; national identity and, 7–12

nature-nations, 11, 25

new materialism, 5–6, 41–44

New Mexico, 60

new wilderness, 135, 139–40

New York, 92

Neyrat, Frédéric, 119

Ndeble, Njabulo, 60

Nixon, Rob, 22, 58, 75, 127; *Slow Violence* and, 22, 58

North Pacific Subtropical Gyre, 1

nuclear power, 8, 84; contamination and, 7; fallout and, 97; meltdown and, 140; radiation and, 8; risk and, 92; Ukraine and, 17

nuclear power plants, 61, 84, 92–95, 108, 164n61. *See also* Fukushima Daiichi Nuclear Power Plant

Nuclear Scrapbook (Genpatsu kirinukichō), 82–86. *See also* Tsuchimoto Noriaki

nuclear villages, 93

obligate storytelling, 27–53, 126–27, 155n32

Ogata Masato, 74

Okada, Richard Hideki, 12

Okada Yoneo, 102

On the Japanese Landscape (Nihon Fūkei ron), 9–10, 12. *See also* Shiga Shigetaka

Oppermann, Serpil, 6

optics of ambulation, 62, 66–71

Orlowski, Jeff, 60; *Chasing Ice* and, 60

Ōtsu Kōshirō, 55

Ott, John, 63, 65
Our Stolen Future (Colborn, Dumanoski, Myers), 113
Ozawa Shōichi, 83–84, 86
Ozeki, Ruth, 28, 36, 105, 117, 168n49

Pacific Ocean, 1, 23, 55, 86, 130
Pacific trash vortex, 1, 53
palimpsest, 36, 45
Palumbo-Liu, David, 121
Pangcah, 2
Paradise in the Sea of Sorrow (Kugai jōdo), 29–30, 37–38, 44, 57, 66, 104, 108, 140. *See also* Ishimure Michiko
Perez, Gilberto, 56
planetarianism, 119–23
planetarity, 123, 140
planetary, 19, 126, 140; consciousness and, 106, 118; health and, 128; history and, 125; literature and, 171n20; Masao Miyoshi and, 120, 124; scale and, 123–26, 142; Gayatri Spivak and, 123–25; vocabulary and, 38
pollution sadism *(kōgai sadizumu)*, 72
polychlorinated biphenyls, 100; and *Cumulative Pollution*, 105, 107, 110

radiation, 81–84, 86, 114, 130
radioactive waste, 83
radioactivity, 58, 83, 86
Rambelli, Fabio, 22
res nullius, 114
romanticism: European, 3; Japanese romantics, 16–17
rubble, 59, 173n46
rural, 32, 92, 96–98; and urban, 101–2

sacrificial zones, 101
saijiki, 32, 149n40
Sakai, Naoki, 13

Sakamoto Fujie, 76
Sakamoto Naomitsu, 57; "Requiem for a Documentary Filmmaker," 57
Sakamoto Shinobu, 76
Satō Shigeko, 96
scale(s), 25, 58, 61, 118, 127–28, 138; economy of, 168n49; geopolitical, 127–32; human(ist), 127–28, 138–40; hypothetical, 127–34, 139–42; interpretive, 128; planetary, 123, 142
secondary nature, 11
secularization of space, 12
Sekiguchi, Ryoko, 40–41; *Heliotropes*, 40–41
self-colonization, 93
semiosis, 6; semiotics of an entity, 117
Sharma, Nandita, 19
Shaviro, Steven, 42
Shiga Shigetaka, 9, 11, 12; *On the Japanese Landscape,* 9–10, 12
Shirane, Haruo, 11, 149n40
Shiranui Sea, 29, 40, 43, 57, 62, 66, 71, 74, 77–78, 80, 87, 88, 141, 157n58
Shiva, Vandana, 92, 100
Silent Spring, 104
Singer, Peter, 114, 125–26
Sleeboom, Margaret, 15
slow cinema, 160n20
slow violence, 58, 87, 127; in moving images, 59, 60–61, 75–76, 82, 86–89, 126; Tsuchimoto Noriaki's films and, 61, 71, 74, 78–79, 81–88, 126–27; writing and, 59
social ecology, 75–76, 79–81
South Pacific islands, 82–83, 131
speculative fiction, 140
sperm whales, 130–32
Spivak, Gayatri, 123–25, 129, 140
Stanford, Leland, 63
Steingraber, Sandra, 105–7, 114

Stengers, Isabelle, 27, 39
Stoemer, Eugene, 118

Taiwan, 2
Takahashi Tetsuya, 108
Takeuchi Tadao, 80
Tawada Yōko, 53, 129, 131, 133, 134
Thomas, Julia Adeney, 17, 123–25
Thornber, Karen, 21
Three-Mile Island, 83–84, 101
tilefish, 157n58
Tokuomi Haruhiko, 37
Tokyo, 29, 32, 51, 57, 104; as capital, 92, 97; as metropole, 93, 95, 98; as metropolitan region, 108
Tokyo Electric Power Company (TEPCO), 92, 113, 114
Tourette, George Gilles de la, 67
Toward a Paradise of Flowers (Hana no okudo e), 137–40. *See also* Ishimure Michiko
toxins, 61
Toyosawa Nobuko, 10
transcendental ideas: of nature, 3, 22, 149n41
transcorporeality, 5, 44
transhistorical intertextuality, 31, 35, 141
Treat, John Whittier, 84
Tsuchimoto Noriaki, 29, 55–58, 61, 62, 66–72, 76–78, 81, 84, 88; and Ishimure Michiko, 57; medical films, 67, 72–74, 76, 78–80; *Minamata,* 30, 55, 57, 63, 73, 88, 97; *Minamata Medical Film: A Trilogy,* 62; *Minamata Medical Film: Clinical Practice and Epidemiology,* 81; *Mina-*

mata Medical Film: Pathology and Symptoms, 69–70; *Minamata Medical Film: Progress of Research,* 71; *Minamata Mural,* 86–88; *Nuclear Scrapbook,* 82–86
Tsurumi Kazuko, 12–14, 32, 104

Ueno Eishin, 35–36
Ui Jun, 151n57
Umehara Takeshi, 150n53
United Nations, 30, 76; Human Environment Convention, 76
urban, 92, 97; *Cumulative Pollution* and, 104; elites, 92; rural and, 101, 114
Uzawa, Hirofumi, 123

Van Gogh, Vincent, 31–32, 36
Viveiros de Castro, Eduardo, 18

waka, 33
Weisman, Alan, 119
West, the, 13, 15, 18–20, 22; and the Rest, 22
White Dog First Nation, 19, 29
Williams, Alan, 66
Williams, Raymond, 92, 96
Wu Ming-yi, 1, 28; *Man with the Compound Eyes* and, 130–33
Wynter, Sylvia, 19

Yamashita, Karen Tei, 28
Yasuda Yoshinori, 15–16
Yoshimoto Mitsuhiro, 120

zoopraxiscope, 63

CHRISTINE L. MARRAN is professor in the Department of Asian Languages and Literatures at the University of Minnesota. She has published on ecocriticism, Japanese literature and cinema, film theory, and gender.

?ormation can be obtained
Gtesting.com
\ USA
211218

9 781517 901592